ON HOSTILE SHORES

True, mostly bloodless, tales by a Junior Officer whose outfit made five big D-day invasions of World War II.

By

Sam Pershing Daugherty

ISBN: 1-4033-5167-8 (e-book)
ISBN: 1-4033-5168-6 (Paperback)
ISBN: 1-4033-5246-1 (Dustjacket)

This book is printed on acid free paper.

1stBooks – rev. 01/30/03

DEDICATION

To <u>John J. "Jack" McGrann</u>, fellow Ohio State Buckeye, my Superior Officer, and my good buddy from the time of our first assignment to Brigade Headquarters in London through the landings in North Africa, Sicily, Italy, Normandy, and Okinawa.

AND

To <u>James R "Shug"(for Sugar) Jordan</u> whom I assisted in walking off of UTAH Beach on D-day morning in Normandy when he was wounded and in mild shock, and with whom I, among many other "joint ventures", dug and shared a deluxe foxhole on Okinawa, so that we could finally "enjoy" the nightly "Kamikaze" activity. After the war, Shug went on to achieve such fame as to have an 85,000 seat football stadium and a main road dedicated to him at his Alma Mater, Auburn University.

Both "Shug" and Jack have been gone for several years now; may they rest in peace.

INTRODUCTION

This is being written because I believe that some of my experiences in WWII were unique, very interesting and often humorous. These experiences were unique because:

1. We were the only unit in the U.S. Army involved in D-day type assault on **their** soil against all **four** nations we fought in WWII. (Few readers can name all four).
2. Of the 28 officers who comprised our headquarters unit when it went overseas in August 1942, five remained until the A-bomb was dropped on Nagasaki in 1945 ending the war. Officers came and went; none were killed; but two were wounded. I believe that I am now the only survivor of the "final five". The others have passed on from natural causes.
3. We were definitely not Green Beret type heroes; although we were frequently "in the thick of things", and managed to spend a lot of time around the First Ranger Battalion in Algeria early in the war. I never even had occasion to fire my weapon after the landing in Sicily ('43). We were just a "bunch of poor dumb engineers" trying to do our job. (Besides if you fire your weapon, you are sooner or later responsible for cleaning it).

My experiences were interesting because I was frequently being sent on weird missions without any written orders or transportation. I hitched a lot of rides; on jeeps, trucks, landing craft and airplanes. (Never on a tank or a submarine). This story tells only **true**, largely bloodless, mostly documentable (see Appendices), anecdotes from a staff officer's point of view. It's all factual, except where I benignly misled you about the **reasons** (but not the destinations) for a few of my side trips or the true names of some of the **participants.**

To begin with, I was among the first half-dozen Army Officers formally committed by the War Department in May, 1942 to the **seizure of Europe**, assigning **me**, a Second Lieutenant with six weeks active duty, to the Engineer Amphibian Command at Camp Edwards, Massachusetts. I, a Buckeye from Ohio, who had hardly ever seen an ocean beach before, was rushed by Pan American Clipper to England in August, 1942. Then and there, I began my contributions to the demise of Benito Mussolini, and Adolf Hitler, as a member of Hq. First Engineer Amphibian Brigade, whose job it was to **expedite landings "on hostile shores."** When we finally closed our last European beach in Normandy in December 1944, with V-E day only five months ahead, we "pulled up stakes" and, after a brief rest period, flew to the Philippines. There, on the Island of Leyte, we staged to land as usual on "D-day" on an Island which many historians refer to as "Bloody Okinawa". There I made my usual (two cents worth) contribution to the demise of Japan's Emperor Hirohito.

During the course of the activities skimmed in the preceding paragraph, First Engineer Brigade troops suffered over 750 fatalities due to enemy action, which for a 5,000 man unit was probably a higher percentage than that of the average "combat" outfit. Most of our casualties were hidden from the media for "security reasons". In similar fashion, the suicide of the U.S.Navy Admiral, with Chain of Command (ONLY) responsibility for this calamity, was not made public for many years. This fact was kept quiet, even though down through the ages, the tradition, "The Captain Goes Down With His Ship" had become well established, and was how we, who knew the facts almost from the start, understood and forgave him. May he and the 739 others rest in peace.

Along the way we learned quite a bit about the inter-service, Army vs. Navy infighting, the Civil War, the comforting effects of a good stiff drink, and other jewels of information, which were of marginal value to us when we returned to the lark of earning a living as civilians.

Army vs. Navy?   We were in the middle of it.
The Civil War?   Half our guys were Clemson or Auburn Grads.
Stiff Drinks?   See the book.

I am indebted to my long time friend and Comrade-at-Arms, Dave Moore, for his first hand account of one of the major tragedies of WWII, "Exercise TIGER", which is included in the Appendix; to another old friend, Monsignor Ambrose A. McAvoy, Brigade Chaplain, for use of his account, "Priest Remembers D-Day" (also in the appendix); to Wes Taylor, of the Hilton Head Island Computer

Club, for his many, many hours of voluntary assistance in continually keeping my manuscript from getting forever lost in the "innards" of my computer, and for his enthusiasm in reading my work; and to Robin Seaver of that club for her wizardry in scanning the authenticating documents into the appendices; to the three Hogan sisters who taught me the wonders of the Internet during their Memorial Day visits; to GOOGLE the Internet search engine for providing me with some precise facts and dates; to Jim Rice, a long time Pan American Airways employee, who gave me the picture of the flying boat shown in Appendix A; to my beloved wife, Peggy for her patience in putting up with an octogenarian trying to learn to type and write a book at the same time; and to my son, Greg Daugherty, and his wife Dr. Sheila Smith for their support and encouragement.

There were a lot of good men in Headquarters, First Engineer Special Brigade who are not mentioned in these anecdotes. That only means that our paths didn't cross in a way that I can remember after all these years.

There was Sergeant Albert Sheldon-Dobson Clough III, a Syracuse blue blood, whose sardonic wit entertained us from London ('42) through Okinawa ('45). There was Sgt. Ed Kane, Clough's buddy from Algonac, Michigan an equally witty Democrat politician who had drafted himself after a family squabble. He finally got bored with sleeping on the ground after our first three invasions and then "came clean" with the army medics; confessed to being blind in one eye, and was rotated home from Naples at age 40 plus. Also to be remembered were Cpl. Babcock, our frustrated bugler and T/5 Petrosini, who worked magic with our GI haircuts using only a three inch paintbrush and a hand-driven clipper. I cannot leave out Abby Stern whose mail I over-censored one day to liven it up a bit, thus getting my butt into a jam. Nor can I overlook Cpl. Jack Arlinsky, whose appearance in a snapshot with some of his Arzew acquaintances "brought down the house". Sergeants DeVanney, MacGuinn, Karlsruher, Long Soo Hoo, and Applebaum are not to be forgotten. The names of Sgt. (Later Lieutenant) Valentine, Sergeants McMahon, Erickson, Stewart, Pfc. Bohannon, Cpl. Singer, and Pfc. "Red" Miller figure in certain episodes in the book..

To summarize our mission: Our Advance Headquarters would land with some of our 531st Shore Engineers, the Assault Infantry and other specialized units at or near H-hour on D-day. Our 531st Engineers would help clear the beach obstacles, breach the sea walls and prepare exits from the beach to tie in to the existing road net so that the assault division could get its tanks and tracked artillery ashore and across the beach. Meanwhile as the Infantry moved on, our Brigade's Advanced Headquarters would establish a command post, receive additional troops and prepare to take command responsibility for all beach and supply dump operations on about D + 3 days and until our advancing forces captured and cleared a seaport adequate for their needs.

To all of my former School Teachers of English Grammar, I offer my **most sincere** apologies for all of the dangling participles, split infinitives, bad abbreviations and capitalizations, poorly compounded sentences, etc., I wish that I had listened to you some seventy years ago. Now, at eighty-five I find that editing is a tougher job than ever I imagined..

Sam P. Daugherty
Hilton Head Island, SC
sambodot@aol.com

TABLE OF CONTENTS

CHAPTER I

BELVOIR—WASHINGTON, D.C.—EDWARDS

I had only been on active duty for about a month when Jim Mueller came to the Fort Belvoir, Virginia Engineer Replacement Training Center (ERTC) on a "head hunting" mission. Jim was an ROTC classmate of mine from Ohio State University, College of Engineering, Department of Ceramic Engineering.   Jim was a Captain, I was a lowly Second Lieutenant. It was now about five months after the disastrous sneak attack on our forces at Pearl Harbor. To be accepted as a volunteer I had needed to resign my job as a foreman in the melting department at Homestead Steelworks . It was not that easy to get into "this man's army" if you worked in a steel mill. I was a Reserve Officer working for a man I really admired who had been gassed, machine gunned and wounded by shrapnel in the "first war".   My boss, Bob Fatzinger, had ended up, in 1918, commanding an Infantry Battalion in the 28th Division and it seemed to me as though I just had to go. We talked it over and though he said he needed me in the mill, his only declarative statement was, "Sam, this will be the biggest show of your lifetime, and you'll always feel bad if you don't go". I wrote a letter to the War Department telling the army that I was an unemployed second lieutenant. Then I waited ……and waited …and waited. After almost four months of this, (I was actually still working in the mill) I took the bull by the horns and drove to the Army Corps Area headquarters in Baltimore and helped some bureaucratic Lt. Col. find my letter at the bottom of a pile of papers in his in-basket. I drove back to Pittsburgh that night with my orders to active duty in the inside pocket of my coat.

Back to Jim Mueller; Jim told me this story: he was currently working as Aide de Camp to Colonel Daniel Noce, a very senior West Pointer in the Corps of Engineers and a WWI veteran. Colonel Noce had received orders from the War Dept. to form an Engineer Amphibian Command to prepare means and train troops to perform the engineering and logistical functions needed to land our armed forces "on hostile shores". These orders gave Colonel Noce the potential to become a Major General which, among other, more important things, entitled him to two junior officer "gophers" or

1

Aides de Camp. Jim and Colonel Noce and several other officers, already recruited, were all looking for officer acquaintances to recruit for Col. Noce's new Command. He needed several thousand officers for the troops for the amphibious landings in both theaters of war. Jim, as the designated first Aide, wanted me to be the potential other Aide de Camp to the potential Major General Noce. It must have taken me about five seconds to accept; not for the specific job of Aide to a General, but for the opportunity to escape from the ERTC at Fort Belvoir. There were three big ERTC's in the country and each had scads of shavetail 2nd Lt. Platoon Leaders like me.

Jim had enough of what we now call "clout" to get me moved from nearby Belvoir into Washington, D.C. the next day. There I went to work in the "New State Dept. Building" which was temporarily occupied by War Dept offices pending completion of the Pentagon, then abuilding across the Potomac River.

It was May, 1942 and Washington was already bursting at the seams. We had the entire Engineer Amphibian Command in two office rooms in that "New State Dept. Building" when I was sent there. Jim had recruited two other Ohio State engineering graduates: Jim Willis and Jack McGrann. Willis had experience in army personnel, while McGrann had army experience with supply matters. McGrann is one of the stalwarts of this book, Willis is not to be found—although we were good friends, our paths never crossed again until several years after the war.

On my first day of work in the "New State Dept. Bldg." I met Jim Mueller at the entrance as planned and he took me to where the fledgling Engineer Amphibian Command was in the process of being formed. As I recall, there were some twelve officers and zero enlisted men working at desks in a very large room (bull pen). There were other men and women working at other desks doing *what* I never did find out. Colonel Noce was not there, nor were any officers above the rank held by Captain Mueller. Jim wasn't there again after that day. He transferred himself to Camp Edwards, Massachusetts, and I only saw him a few more times after that. He did show me a small three-desk, one-window, office next to the "bull pen" and told me that this is where I would work. It was not as confusing as it now sounds, considering what *we* were trying to do. We (now I was part of it) were trying to invent army organizations that were new to warfare.

2

Since the days of the Roman Legions (at least) war-making units had evolved into well-stereotyped organizations. Hitler had been demonstrating that fact since the invasion of Poland, starting September 1, 1939. However, *nobody* knew how to put a very large force together, without adequate logistical support, to conquer a huge, experienced, well-trained, well-equipped army like the German Army of 1942. All of the European land mass was in German hands and that meant that all of the seaports were strictly unavailable to the attacking force.

The officers in the bullpen were mostly engaged in matters of Personnel or Supply such as locating Army units that were not part of a high priority plan for something else, brainstorming to decide what special skills or tools were needed, finding individuals with those skills, etc. (This was long before such things as computers). They were also working to prepare for a large troop influx at Camp Edwards and all of the logistical problems that went along with *that.*

Colonel Noce and some of his cronies had worked up the initial Tables of Organization for the Engineer Amphibian Command and also the Tables of Organization for an Engineer Amphibian Brigade (EAB). The initial plans called for eight EABs just to take care of the contemplated invasion beaches of Europe. Tables of Organization showed in detail how many men of each grade or rank were to be assigned to each basic unit of the organization, and then, by assembling the basic units, how many men were to be assigned at full strength, to any sized unit: company, battalion, regiment etc. Then the T/O was also extended to show the weapons count: one rifle per private, one carbine per technician or corporal, one pistol per sergeant or officer, etc.. Actually, as I learned much later, in combat one carried whatever weapons he had to carry. However, I believe that in most units the guys tended to carry whatever was assigned to them by the T/O. I was given the job of cross-footing all of the data in the T/O's by Jim Mueller.

After about a week of working alone in the three desk office, I arrived one morning to find I had an office mate. He was Colonel Noce's executive officer, a West Pointer, Lieutenant Colonel named Arthur G. Trudeau. Now, in those days, the best and brightest graduating from West Point, nearly always went to the Corps of Engineers. Why this was the situation, I never knew for sure, but

3

Arthur G. Trudeau was, for my money, one of the smartest, sharpest people I ever met. He was probably about 40 when I first met him, and the last I heard of him armywise was as a Lieutenant General in command of all the ground forces in Korea, during *that* war. General Trudeau, after retiring from the army, held a very important position in one of the giant companies with headquarters in Pittsburgh.

Two days after Lt. Col. Trudeau arrived, another West Pointer showed up. He was Maj. Richard R. Arnold, Corps of Engineers, Class of '36. Major Arnold had been posing as a military attache to the Court of St. James, under the British Crown. Actually Dick Arnold had been serving as a liaison officer between the British and U.S. Armies and, according to him, had just returned from England by air for the eighth time since the war started in Europe. Dick was, in my opinion, one prince of a guy—besides being tall, dark and handsome. He was engaged to be married to a British woman. He became my unofficial supervisor, replacing Jim Mueller, although no one told me so, just as no one had told me that Jim was my boss, either.

I worked very hard on those T/Os for a few weeks getting all of the numbers to check out, then getting each blessed by the Office of the Chief of Naval Operations. Then one day in mid-July, Major Arnold asked me if I'd like to fly to England with him. We, and a few other people then at Camp Edwards, would form the advance section of the Engineer Amphibian Command. We didn't discuss what we'd be doing in England but it is a pretty safe bet, considering the job of the Engineer Amphibian Command, and the state of completion of that job, that our existence was only being used to stall off Russian demands for a second front. The raid on the port of Dieppe by the Canadians later that summer, which was a costly failure, to say the least, put thoughts of an invasion of the continent in 1942 out of the picture for everybody but the Russians; I am confident.

For Major Arnold and I, those last two weeks in July became a mad blur...get shots for all the contagious diseases known to mankind, make a will (Ha!), draw a pistol, a gas mask, field boots, watch, etc.,etc., sell my car, get dog tags to hang around my neck...Surprise! Surprise!, I even got promoted to First Lieutenant in all of the confusion. We had to prepare to travel as civilians because we would be traveling by way of a neutral country (Ireland). This made it a matter for the State Department; so I had to get a passport, passport photos, and an Irish Visa. I could not wear my uniform in a neutral country so at least had to make a pretense at dressing like a civilian. I bought a Mickey Mouse tee shirt at a Walgreen's store to wear over my shirt through Irish customs when the time came. We were warned by Pan American Airlines to maintain very strict secrecy about our flight timing, and were told to call Pan Am daily around noon to find out if we were to depart that night. As directed, I was staying at the Astor hotel in Manhattan those last few days.

After a couple of days of doing nothing but wait to call Pan Am at noon as ordered, I was overjoyed to be rewarded with the statement, "Report to the Passenger Terminal at La Guardia Seaplane Basin at ten this evening with all your papers and gear". That I did via a New York Taxi; this worried me a little bit, suppose the taxi driver was a spy? I soon turned that worrying from my mind over to Pan Am, as absurd on my part. Checking in at the passenger terminal in a one story shed, I got weighed along with all of my luggage, and was issued a one-way ticket to Foynes, Ireland along with a certificate for my overweight luggage. No money changed hands in this deal, it was all taken care of by my orders from the War Department. (I still have those two little documents and just to satisfy your curiosity I'll tell you, to get my body to London by flying boat cost the U.S. Gov't. $625.00 on August 3, 1942.- (See Appendix)

CHAPTER II

PAN AM TO ENGLAND

What with weighing our bodies and our luggage, checking our papers several times and the normal waiting around, we managed to kill about an hour and a half. Next we boarded what, in 1942, was a luxury air liner. There were 26 passengers and sleeping arrangements for all. I don't know how large a crew the flying boat required but I presume we had Pilot, Co-pilot, Engineer/Navigator, and at least two or three stewards. The crew was warming up the four engines as we went aboard through a door under the wing. We quickly found seats, fastened our seat belts and sat there waiting. Soon the Captain (Pilot) addressed us. He told us that we would first traverse the waters of the entire take-off area to determine if there were any hazards (telephone poles, etc) floating there. It was a beautiful night, but the only illumination available was from the headlights on the plane. We taxied around for quite a while. You could see the metropolitan New York skyline on the horizon when it was on the proper side of the plane and total blackness when we were headed in the other direction.

Finally the pilot decided there were no hazards to be seen and that we might just as well take off. So we did. He raced each of those four big engines up to a scary pitch and then backed it off to a mere whine; then he gave all of them full throttle simultaneously. I, who had only been airborne one time in my life, was impressed. I will be the first to admit that I lifted that big seaplane out of the water by lifting on the arms of my seat. We climbed slowly and more steeply as the surface tension of the water and the gravity of mother earth surrendered to the thrust of those four giant Pratt & Whitney engines. There was nothing further I could do now to help so I went to sleep.

When I awakened from my nap after a couple of hours we were, I would guess, cruising along beautifully at about ten or twelve thousand feet altitude and the faithful sun was just beginning to peek over the horizon. Now I've taken "the red-eye" from San Francisco to New York many times over the post war years and, as hardened as one becomes to that flight, it's *still* an awesome thing to witness; when your plane is bathed in sunshine and the folks in the cities below are still in the dark of night. According to a passenger seated

6

nearby, the small strip of land we were able to see was either the last of the Maine coast or the first of the Canadian. Before the morning was too far gone, the pilot began our first landing or whatever you called it when you brought a sea plane down into contact with the surface of the water and stopped its forward motion. From now on we'll call it "landing". We pulled up beside a floating pier and walked to a small diner-like structure nearby where we were served a hearty breakfast of pancakes, sausage, coffee and etc., while the crew attended to refueling the plane. Someone asked one of the kitchen staff where we were, and the reply was "Shidiac, New Brunswick". Our world travels were getting underway—but we didn't realize it as yet.

At this juncture we were all awake and moving around and we started to get acquainted. Arnold was seated forward of me, I was next to a window and beside me was a young soldier in uniform who wore a paratroopers wings. We talked quite a bit, but both were so impressed with secrecy requirements that we hardly exchanged first names. Next to the paratrooper, was a middle aged Major Host, who had graduated last in his class at *Annapolis*, had washed out of the Navy, and had been able to get a direct commission in the *army* as a Major after Pearl Harbor. He had a connection with Colonel Noce, but I never understood *what*. We saw him occasionally in London, and could almost understand why he was last in his class.

One of the most fascinating of the passengers was a man who never uttered a sound; he had a briefcase chained to his wrist, which fact this country boy found fascinating. I even watched him out of the corner of my eye one time when I happened to see him approaching the men's "John". Arnold told me that he was probably a diplomatic courier and would surrender his briefcase only to a State Department Official at the end of his journey or to death when it overtook him. Sounded real to me. There was one lady among the passengers, a well dressed woman of about 50 years. Major Arnold guessed that she was a female Director of Pan American Airways traveling on company matters.

Another interesting passenger, was an army Major, named Williamson. He had been, (he claimed) a fighter pilot in WWI, who had talked his way back into the WWII army to see the action and to help the cause. He was a likable guy, a member of our Advanced

7

Section Engineer Amphibian Command. Like Major Host, mentioned earlier, no one seemed to understand his assignment or what he could do. He loved to tell about shooting down German artillery observation balloons from his fighter plane in WWI. He always wore so much weaponry on his body that we all knew him as "Hardware Williamson".

We took off again and flew over the open waters of the North Atlantic for several hours. Our destination, I learned, was a place called Botwood, New Foundland where we landed without incident. I did manage to see what appeared to be an honest-to-john Newfoundland Dog. We refueled our bodies and our plane at Botwood and then the most dramatic event of the entire flight took place. While we were sitting in the longboat, en route to get back aboard the Clipper we stopped short of the plane and the Pilot strode out on the wing with a bullhorn in hand and wearing his leather puttees, riding pants, airman's slouched cap, and goggles, addressed us, the assembled passengers about as follows: "I am required by United States laws to make this announcement: We are about to take off on the longest leg of our trip . We will be flying in darkness most of the time and we will be exposed to hostile action some of the time. We are approximately 19,000 pounds over the allowable weight limit for this plane" (20 second pause) "If any of you would prefer to discontinue this flight at this time please feel free to do so." (10 second pause) "However, let me tell you that I have made this flight and this speech 27 times over recent months and we have always been overweight"... ...a ripple of self-conscious laughter spread across the crowd in the longboat as we all filed into our waiting flying boat.

Our takeoff was uneventful, as usual, and before too long the flight attendants, all males by the way, began to scurry around getting ready for our evening meal. We had a wide choice of aperitifs, I had only college drinking experience to fall back on, so I suppose that I had a beer, (perish the thought in such a sophisticated environment) and then we had a truly delicious meal of filet mignon, baked potato, green beans, salad and a choice of desserts. By this time the attendants had started to assemble the sleeping paraphernalia and we had to go to bed, like it or not. Most everybody slept in their clothes as I remember it, although it was theoretically OK to change to PJs in the men's room.

I was always a good sleeper, and being in the air over the north Atlantic did not seem to change that fact. One of the stewards finally wakened me with the words, "Sir, we are going to be at Foynes in one half an hour, and you had better get up". That kind of talk presents no problem if the only thing really required is to put on your shoes and tie the laces; splashing face, combing hair, brushing teeth were all niceties for which the thoughtful steward had allowed ample margin.

Our tickets had only been to Foynes in what was then, I guess, called Eire by good Irishmen. We Yankees, except for teachers of geography and the likes, probably thought of it as being in "Southern Ireland" or "Free Ireland". To the American of today, Foynes turns out to be a town on the River Shannon estuary, where the river is wide enough to "land" a huge seaplane. Hundreds of thousands of Americans today have flown to Shannon Airport from various cities in the USA via land based jet aircraft.

We again came down on the water and taxied to a floating dock without incident. We ate a plain, dull meal, (we were without doubt spoiled last night by the Pan Am dinner), and went through a trivial sort of admittance procedure. You couldn't fault the Irish for this performance. They were a neutral country, still in the strangle hold of the depression, going through a scandalously "hokey" admittance game with a bunch of middle-aged men, dressed mostly in military uniforms, thinly disguised to hide the warlike nature of their calling.

I had donned my Mickey Mouse tee shirt over my uniform shirt when I got up in the morning and, had already covered the letters "US" on my pistol holster, field glasses, and musette bag with adhesive tape. I was neutral! A uniformed official quickly stamped my passport and I entered a large waiting room where we were assembling to continue to England. There was a large number of men in the waiting room, most of them in the uniform of some country allied to the same cause as ours.

Sam Daugherty

It was explained to us via the public address system, that we would all be flying together in one aircraft, a Sunderland Flying Boat of the British Overseas Airways Corporation (BOAC), that the window shades were all closed and were to remain that way, that we would fly in at low altitude, that we were to be escorted by the Royal Air Force, and that the BOAC was sorry if this seating inconvenienced anybody. No seats were assigned for the reminder of the flight and there were double rows facing each other. I found myself seated next to a tall Britisher who looked very much like pictures I had seen of the King of England. I made a couple of attempts at conversation which were ignored with a supercilious sniff and then I happened to glance at Major Arnold, who was seated facing me but a couple of seats to my right. Major Arnold, who was a perfect gentleman, was flexing his right fist, had caught my eye and wore a mischievous smile which to me said, "Go ahead, Sam, paste the SOB, I'll back you up." Of course, I did nothing of the sort; Arnold wasn't testing me, he was just saying, "Welcome to the British Army". Never, in almost three years around the Brits did I again attempt to strike up a casual conversation with one, but neither did I have anything but the highest admiration for them. In Algeria, Tunisia, Sicily, Italy, France, and the far reaches of the Pacific wars, I was always an Anglophile.

CHAPTER III
LONDON—SCOTLAND—GIBRALTAR

We came in on the waters of the English Channel at Blackpoole after flying in from Foynes, Ireland at 500 feet altitude with at least one R.A.F. Spitfire fighter plane on each wing. Heady stuff, indeed. We were brought ashore to a modest brick building to go through a perfunctory customs admission after setting foot on British soil for the first time. Dick Arnold, now in England for the ninth time in his life, vanished quickly. He was, after all, very near his sweetheart for the first time in months. ..he knew his way around. I found a men's room there in the Customs House and went in to get rid of the Mickey Mouse tee shirt and otherwise return to uniform. In this activity I quickly learned that my spare pair of spectacles (the old fashioned rimless kind, then in style,) lay broken in my suitcase. Oh well, I'll spend the rest of the war in Government Issue (G.I.) glasses. Somehow I got to a railroad station, where there was a train leaving soon for London and that ended my only visit to poor bombed-out Blackpoole.

The train was unlike any I had ever ridden at home. In those days the trains, both at home and abroad, were very important means of transportation. Trains went almost everywhere that one could want to go. Buses had replaced "Interurbans" on a few short hops, but neither the autos nor the roads were anything comparable to those of today. This first British train of my life was full of highly polished mahogany and upholstery. The seats were arranged like booths in an American drug store of that era, two benches facing each other, one facing forward, with a table in between. There were still some like that when I was last in Britain. (1994). We pulled into the suburbs of London shortly, with the frightful damage from the blitz of 1940 becoming more apparent with every minute that we continued. Finally we arrived at some station whose name is lost from memory (I'll guess it was Victoria- but I will not bet on it). The station roof was completely gone. I got into a big high London taxi and he turned on a dime to take me to the Mount Royal Hotel. Checking in at the Mount Royal, I learned that my per diem allowance of $6.00 per day, for everything, was going to be ample. Nowadays the Mt. Royal is far too rich for my blood.

I soon learned the essentials of being a U.S. Army officer (very junior) living in London of 1942. I learned that we were in just about the swankiest section (Mayfair) of London, that we were near the hotel where the Generals stayed (Claridges), that we were within walking distance of the U.S. Embassy and Hyde Park. There was an American Army transient officers mess on N. Audley Street in that area where we could eat and stay within our $6.00 per diem allowance. I forget the address of our first office but we were installed pretty soon in the "Town House" of the Duke of Norfolk (he also had a "country house" (read Castle) somewhere, I guess). We soon learned that the remainder of the Advanced Section, Army Amphibian Command was on the way to "reinforce" Lt. Col. Arnold and Lt. Daugherty who as yet were neither in any danger from the enemy nor overwork. The "reinforcements" were partially coming by air on our Pan Am Clipper and partially on the "Queen Mary" which, as it turned out, was also bringing the First Infantry Division, U.S. Army, unescorted.

The airborne contingent of the bunch arrived first. Colonel Wolfe the first commander of the 1st Engineer Amphibian Brigade was in the Pan Am arrivals, as was Lt. Jack McGrann who turned out to be my good buddy throughout the entire war. A few days later the shipborne group arrived, with some scary tales to tell. Besides having come all of that distance across the north Atlantic with some 20,000 troops and crew aboard, our guys swore that the Queen Mary had managed to accidentally cut into two pieces a smaller vessel of the US Navy during the first days sailing from the United States. I never found out whether or not that was true, but running without escort in those submarine infested waters, the Queen, if she was able to continue, never stopped nor slowed for anything. The entire scheme of her running without an accompanying convoy was based upon the fact that she could move faster than a torpedo could swim and that on a zigzag course she would always be missed by a torpedo. The Queen Mary brought many troops to England during the monstrous build up for D-day during the next two years. The Advance Party, Engineer Amphibian Command now consisted of about 5 officers and 12 enlisted men. McGrann and I were required to share my room, and double bed at the Mount Royal Hotel. In a few days, Lt. Col. Arnold brought word that the entire First Engineer Amphibian

Brigade, of about 7,000 men was on its way to Scotland from New York. Col Arnold directed me to get three first class, round trip train tickets to Glasgow, tomorrow, with sleeping accommodations on the return. Never having slept on a train at home, much less slept on a first class train, I had my work cut out for me. To add to my quandary, I didn't know whence the train left London nor the red tape for getting written orders, which translate into money. (pounds sterling in this case). Anyway, by asking every army guy I happened to meet, especially the more friendly looking (lower ranking) ones; I managed to get tickets and to find out where Glasgow was and how to get to the right station. I was learning fast. Came the next morning at about (it seemed like) five AM, I met with Lt Col. Arnold and Colonel Wolfe at the proper station and away we went to Glasgow.

After a long day of riding in our reserved first class compartment; we were met at Glasgow station by an army driver with a command car (looks like an old time touring car with side curtains if it is raining—which it was -pitch dark too.) Arnold had arranged for the auto with the US Army Port Commander. The way the Army was set up to handle arrivals in the British Isles was a thing of beauty—even in the earliest days of the war. Arnold had given me instructions on protocol for getting in and out of autos and both large and small boats when accompanied by a senior officer. The next thing I knew I was giving a snappy (ROTC) type salute to the Officer of the Deck of the USS Manhattan, then renamed the "Wakefield", to keep the Huns guessing. Colonel Wolfe and Col. Arnold met with several senior officers of the various organic units of the First Engineer Amphibian Brigade while I was given a tour of the ship by a junior officer of the U.S. Coast Guard crew. We had already eaten our evening meal on the train, but I did manage to snitch a beautiful navel orange from a fruit bowl in the officers wardroom.

It finally became time to head back to London. Meanwhile, I had made a fearsome discovery; I had lost my train tickets! Thank Heavens I had given those of Arnold and Colonel Wolfe to their rightful owners before starting out from London! Mine were not to be found and I couldn't tell my companions. Those two paragons of savoir faire would have considered me to be an inept dunce. Come to think of it, I wonder today (year 2002) whether maybe Arnold had purloined my tickets as a prank. He was really impressed with the complexity of the work I had done for him in Washington and I believe that perhaps he regarded me as some kind of a genius and hid my tickets as a joke. Whatever, I had less than a half hour to find a ticket and get back to the train.

Luck was with me. The ticket window was still open. I was not able to, nor did I even try to get a first class reservation; but there was a third class berth still for sale. I quickly dispensed the necessary pounds, shillings and pence to buy it and was soon aboard—just in time. Of course I was in a different car than my two companions, but that didn't worry me too much. They had boarded the train as soon as we entered the station and we had (had) private first class sleeping compartments. A wartime 3rd class sleeping compartment had two two-high bunks on a narrow aisle running perpendicular to the direction of the train. I found myself sharing the compartment with three Brits (we didn't call them "Brits" in those days; we called them "Limeys" or "Johnny Bulls"—but not to their faces). I had nothing but great respect for them (still have) seeing what they had gone through in the blitz of '40—'41. Third class passengers took off their shoes (or boots) and slept in their street clothes; and the only bedding provided by the railroad was one woolen blanket (govt issue I suspect).

The two lower bunks were already taken so I climbed into the remaining upper, took off my shoes, placed them so as not to fall and "brain" the man in the lower, and settled back to see what happened next. I felt the orange bulging in my pocket and realized that I couldn't sleep on a hard lump like that. The only alternatives to sleeping on the lump were to climb down and put it in my musette bag (sort of a large canvas purse you could use as a shoulder bag or a part of your pack.) or to eat it then and there. I didn't feel like climbing down, so decided to peel it and have it over with. Now, I was very skilled at peeling navel oranges with my bare hands. You just have to break the skin with your thumbnail and the rest is easy. So I broke the skin with my thumbnail and a little cloud of orange scent filled our sleeping compartment. Three Britons raised their heads in perfect unison and I realized that, whereas I probably hadn't eaten an orange in perhaps two weeks, these poor guys probably hadn't *even seen one* in two or three *years*. We divvied it up, four ways. The orange sections served as an icebreaker and the four of us talked for quite a while before sleep took over. For all I know, my two US Army companions never realized that I had somehow managed to lose my tickets. They are both long dead now. May they rest in peace.

When we got back to London I had a chance to get a little better acquainted with my roommate and bed fellow, Jack McGrann. Jack was a product of The Ohio State University College of Engineering, Class of 1940, Advanced ROTC. He had stayed out of college one year due to the Great Depression. His degree was in Metallurgical Engineering. He had been called up from his job with U.S. Steel, and having no seniority there, had gone into the army soon after starting his professional career in late 1940. Although my degree from OSU was essentially the same it was dated 1939, and I had three years of armor plate steel-making under my belt, and had to be free from U.S. Steel before the army would call me. So Jack outranked me by over a year and as luck would have it, now became one of my life long friends. I could not have asked for a better comrade at arms. Jack and I maintained contact after the war, had similar careers, and sadly gave up our friendship when he succumbed to Alzheimers Disease in 1995.

McGrann and I didn't have much chance to get acquainted. About our third day at work he had a phone call from somebody advising him that some vehicles shipped from the Port of New York were showing on a manifest for a Liberty ship due to arrive at Bristol Channel Ports later that week and that we had better get somebody over there to receive them or we could lose them. Now, this was long before our SOS (Services of Supply) arm had set up the procedure whereby troops going overseas merely turned in their vehicles in the USA and drew new ones at their destination. This early in the war you had to prepare (waterproof) your vehicles at the Port of Embarkation and ship them to yourself at your destination. Really cumbersome at both ends! Of course neither of us knew what a manifest was nor where the Bristol Channel Ports were, but we had a map and our civilian stenographer had a dictionary—I was the gopher. The distances were short so that afternoon I was on a train to Bristol with all of my gear.

Night had barely fallen when my train pulled into the bombed-out station at Bristol, so dinner was in the station dining room that night.

As I departed the restaurant, I saw the silhouette of a British "Bobby" standing in the gloom. I approached him and asked, "Sir, could you direct me to a hotel?" Before the policeman could answer, a voice came out of the darkness beside him. "Aren't you from Columbus, Ohio?" to which I replied, "Yes, and you are Jim Dusenberry". Turns out, this fellow, an American Soldier, had grown up about three blocks from where I was growing up at the same time. In those pre-television days most all kids ranged far and wide in their after- school escapades so Jim and I knew each other fairly well; not from the classroom, because he went to parochial school while I attended the public version. Our acquaintanceship was mostly brought about by the fact that the play yard at the public school was surfaced with fine cinders which made it perfect for playing marbles in the spring. Came high school days, when we were far too "grown up" for marbles, Jim and I had last encountered each other in the annual Aquinas versus North High School football game. In those days, one played both defense and offense, with only one appearance per half allowed for each player. I played left guard for North while Jim was facing me at right guard for Aquinas and that was our last contact until this one in Bristol approximately eight years later.

The policeman volunteered the information that the hotel nearby was booked solid for the night so it was decided that I would spend the night at Jim's bivouac area. Jim helped me with my gear and we boarded a street car to get to where his Port Company was situated. I got up early after sleeping on the wooden floor, ate in the enlisted men's mess with Jim and his crowd and was on my way to one of their administrative buildings long before it was open for business in the morning. (I wrote of this to my Dad, who was a newspaper reporter without mentioning the location and he had it published in the Columbus, Ohio papers soon afterward.) I never saw Jim again after that and haven't seen him since. I wish him the very best.

As soon as the port offices opened that morning, I entered and reported to a Colonel Mayo, a waspish sort of a West Pointer, very impressed with himself. He seemed to bear a grudge against all reserve officers. (Maybe he just happened to have found out about the one who had slept on the floor of the orderly tent of one of his companies last night, I never did find out).

The Bristol Channel to which I had been sent in such haste to cover for our vehicles is the mouth of the Mersey River and forms the southern boundary of Wales. Wales is a part of England and during WWII every Welshman I talked to was fiercely loyal to England. Cardiff, and Swansea are the larger ports facing the USA on the Bristol Channel and Port Talbot seemed slightly smaller. I spent most of the next month driving a jeep from one of these Welsh ports to the next, taking care of seemingly orphaned 2-1/2 ton trucks for units of the 1st Engineer Amphibian Brigade. By "taking care of" I merely mean signing for their receipt and seeing to it that they were actually on this earth. I kept Jack McGrann advised of their arrival on ships and he 'phoned to our troops at various locations in the United Kingdom for mechanics and drivers to come to the ports to service them and drive them to their proper "owners". Usually Jack waited until I had enough vehicles to make a convoy (20-30), and then the unit would send an officer to shepherd them along.

Some of the troop units had been transshipped to Northern Ireland after arriving in Scotland so Jack had to transship their vehicles after I received them. It was not as messy as it sounds, when you consider that none of the individuals involved had any experience with this sort of work. We all just had to work a little harder and a little longer to get it done. We got plenty of help from the British, too. There were all kinds of vehicles in the mix-everything from jeeps to bulldozers and road graders, with their flatbed trailers to transport them. Another source of a lot of confusion was the fact that all of the Brits insisted on driving on the "wrong" side of the road.

There were a couple of occasions when I had to go to London to straighten out bookkeeping with McGrann, and I kept up with the army gossip that way. I learned that the War Department had eliminated our "Advanced Section of the Engineer Amphibian Command", we were now in the 1st Engineer Amphibian Brigade (1st EAB). I learned that, among other things, the failed "raid" by the Canadian Forces at the seaport of Dieppe in France had proven to the American High Command that an invasion of Europe was out of the question that autumn of 1942, and that we would probably all go somewhere else instead. Captain McGrann knew the "where" of that equation, but I didn't, and I didn't need to know until my present task was completed. That was OK with me.

17

One of the weekends when I was in London, I ran into the fearsome Colonel Mayo on one of the hotel elevators. I do not know what he was doing there, but I knew that, officially, I lived there. Nothing ever came of it, but I worried until I had been back at Bristol Channel Ports for a few days. I had not been on active duty for six months yet and didn't know the "ropes" like an old hand such as he. I never saw the man again. One of the pleasant memories I have of that month at the Channel Ports was meeting Lieutenant Charles Sullivan. I do not know what his job in the Brigade Headquarters was at that time, but he had chaperoned a bunch of mechanics and drivers to take home some of our trucks to Scotland, and had to wait a couple of days while they were unloaded and serviced. "Sully" was a good Christian "boy" from Mississippi, and one of the calmest people I ever met. When I last said good-bye to Sully, we were on Okinawa, both alive, in one piece, and the war was over.

One weekend, when I visited London, McGrann asked me if I was aware of any more cargo that was due to arrive for the 1st EAB. I was pleased to tell him there was none in any of the ships for which I had received manifests, and that because we had not been receiving any in the recent past it was probably safe to assume that we had received it all. So I moved back into what had originally been my room at the Mount Royal Hotel. Col. Arnold was still around but had been assigned to Headquarters, II Corps, the highest army unit then in the European Theater of Operations.

One day when I was walking alone to the Officers Mess for lunch, I was hailed from a large black Cadillac, going in my direction. As it pulled to the curb and stopped I could see that it was driven by a good-looking red headed woman in British A.T.S.(Auxiliary Territorial Services) Uniform, sitting beside her on the passenger side of the front seat, was my friend Col. Arnold.. They both asked me, at the same time, where I was going, which considering the time of day and the direction I was going, seemed rather obvious to me. Dick told me to get into the back seat and they would drive me there. I protested that there were a General's two stars on the front license plate, and that we would all be in trouble if our deception was discovered. Arnold, far more adroit than I at playing army games, as much as said, "Shut up, and get in!"smiling all the while from ear to ear. He introduced me to his betrothed, Kay Summersby. He told me

18

that if anyone chose to salute me, I was to salute in return and to keep my hands on my shoulders to hide my rank. I was riding to lunch in the limo of Major General Eisenhower!

September, 1942 was rapidly gaining on October, and it was announced that Colonel Noce was coming to England to review the training of the 7000 troops of the 1st EAB, and that when he came to London, as he most certainly would, I was to serve as his Aide deCamp. Well, of course he came to London and I filled in for Jim Mueller who was back in the USA. The Colonel spent a couple of days attending meetings at Hq. II Corps and on Saturday he stated that he wanted to visit Dover, on the English Channel to inspect the beach defenses the British had installed at that location. Dover, was the closest point in Britain to Europe and the assumption was that the German defenses on *their* side of the Channel, would be very similar. Colonel Noce was what any man would describe as a good guy. I don't know how it came up, but he prescribed what he called, "The first law of the Ozarks" translation: "Don't take yourself too seriously" as the answer to most problems. Once when he saluted first, while passing a young soldier on the street, he told me, "They are just self-conscious when they're new at soldiering, get them started and pretty soon they'll enjoy it as being members of a gang.

I arranged for a suitable car to drive us to Dover on Sunday, and rounded up some "C" rations in case we got *that* hungry. We needed some kind of a pass to get through the Home Guard check points in case we were challenged. (I didn't know this, I didn't even know the route to Dover but learned this at the motor pool Hq. when I arranged for the limo). We started early Sunday morning from the Mayfair section of London where we had been staying at our swanky hotels, he at Claridges, I at the Mount Royal. The street scene in London early on a Sunday morning in the Autumn of 1942 was encouraging to behold; people were out and about doing their part to win the war. There were air raid wardens coming home from their all night vigil, there were home guard members going to drill, and there were boy scouts out rounding up recyclable materials. It was as though all London had been just waiting for this day off in order to have a day on their own to do something to help bring about the end of Hitler.

Colonel Noce was a great traveling companion, he was observant and curious of all that was going on about us; he had enjoyed his time in London and wasn't afraid to reveal that he was having some interesting experiences in this unfamiliar land. Most of his military life had been in the Rivers & Harbors work on the delta of the Mississippi and, though far from being a country bumpkin, he was not in the same league as my friend Lt.Col Arnold when it came to sophistication.

As we approached the small city of Dover we were objects of scrutiny at a pair of checkpoints which we cleared without any problems. We proceeded according to our written directions and soon found ourselves at several large gun emplacements in the company of three officers of the British Coastal Defense Forces. We crawled around the remainder of the morning looking at the obstacles and the defensive positions created to protect and defend these large artillery pieces. As I recall it, these were a number of guns of at least sixteen inch caliber, all retractable in their casemates and capable of hurling a 16" armor-piercing projectile upwards of twenty miles. We didn't take any notes, we were there to observe how these guns were defended, not what they did. There were no larger guns on American battleships, and we of the 1st EAB had the pleasure of having them firing *over* us in the assaults on the beaches in N. Africa, Sicily, Italy, Normandy, and Okinawa. None of the enemy countries, except Japan, had any battleships left when we got to them, and the American naval assault force against Okinawa was too strong for the Japanese.

When we had our fill of looking at the defenses of the big guns at Dover, the Commandant of the installation turned out the guard for Colonel Noce. He very quickly told me how to behave; (it was simple). We inspected the formation, and went to lunch in their mess, as their guests. When we had finished lunch, the poor souls brought out a presentation on what was one of Britain's (and these particular men's) most humiliating experiences of WWII: the Escape from Brest, France up the English Channel under the noses of these guns by the German battleships Gniesnau and Scharnhorst, which had taken refuge at Brest, months earlier, after being crippled by the Royal Navy in a battle in the Atlantic. Scharnhorst and Gniesnau made it safely back to Germany and were repaired. The British had thought them safely bottled up for the duration.

The afternoon was waning when Colonel Noce and I started back to London with our Brit driver who had spent his day seeing Dover. For the first time since I had left home, I felt just a little bit homesick......just mildly so. I guess it was the fact that it was Sunday evening and fall was arriving and that has always been a wistful time for me. The homes we passed looked so snug and cozy that I really noticed it.

The day following my trip to Dover, McGrann told me that Col Arnold had called and instructed him to bring me and meet him at II Corps Headquarters in Norfolk House that morning at eight o'clock. (Norfolk House as we found out later was the town house for the Duke of Norfolk. It was like a small grey sandstone palace, without any palace grounds, but with very large, high ceilinged rooms, and magnificent hallways and stairways. I never found out how many floors there were, but it was an elevator building. We met Arnold as appointed in the lobby of the town house and walked up a majestic stairway to the second floor. There, Arnold left us and passed beyond an armed sentry to enter a closed room. He soon returned accompanied by a lanky Lieutenant Colonel of about Arnold's age, who proceeded to take McGrann into another room leaving me with Arnold in the hallway. We chatted for several minutes, and then the Lieutenant Col. and McGrann reappeared.

I went with the Colonel back into the same room he and Jack had just exited and he proceeded to give me a lecture on "Security of Information". to which I listened attentively although he told me nothing I didn't already know. We then rejoined Jack and Col. Arnold in the hallway where we proceeded to pass beyond the armed guard into the large super-secret war room of G-2, Headquarters II Corps, ETOUSA (European Theatre of Operations, United States Army). Once inside, Col. Arnold briefed Jack and me on "Operation Torch". "Operation Torch" was the code name for the invasion of French North Africa by three task forces: the Eastern Task Force made up of British Navy and Army personnel striking around the capital of Algeria, Algiers; the Center Task Force striking around the Free French Naval base at Oran, Algeria, by a combination of British and American Forces, from the UK; and the Western Task Force, all from the USA striking around the Atlantic Ocean seaport of Casablanca, French Morocco.

We were engrossed in learning as much as we could about "Torch" when the tinkling of a tiny bell could be heard in the hallway, so we all trooped out into the hall for the morning "tea break", a nice custom, by the way, which we Americans pretty much picked up from the Brits over the years, (coffee instead of tea). As we all stood around the tea cart in the hall eating our second breakfast, my new friend, the lanky Colonel, sidled up to me, saying "What did you tell me was the name of your outfit?" I told him. He responded, "I never heard of an Engineer Amphibian Brigade, how big is it?. To which ("Old Eager to Please Everybody") replied, "Approximately seven thousand officers and men, sir."

GOTCHA!!

The lanky one chewed me out to a fare thee well! I had fractured RULE ONE of the "Security of Information" lecture he had just given me. I had talked about troop strength matters in the presence of strangers including the young lady who brought the tea cart around...I was never so embarrassed in my life! Never! I have not forgotten the lesson I learned that day. Fortunately for me, the Colonel realized there was no harm done, and a powerful lesson brought home to a greenhorn lieutenant.

On the way back to the Mount Royal that afternoon, I stopped in a shop and bought a small second hand camera. McGrann walked home by another route which took him by a bookstore where he bought a number of maps of the Mediterranean area. We reviewed them in our room. I heard much later that the sale of maps of North Africa increased so rapidly in London during that time period that the Germans should have guessed what was going to happen.

McGrann and I set to work in the secure area of Norfolk House creating troop lists for the 1EAB in the Center task force of Operation Torch. It was extremely detailed work but it had to be done—otherwise you had no idea of how many troops you had to get to the scene of the landing, what heavy equipment had to get there simultaneously, what wave of the assault you were planning for etc. etc.. One day, while we were engaged in this detailed work, we heard the unmistakeable sound of a man screaming, as a matter of fact it was the sound of a man utterly, (repeat utterly) screaming his lungs out. I never heard such carrying on. McGrann and I merely looked at each other and kept on doing what we were doing; there were plenty of senior officers around and none of them paid any attention to it. This place was, among other things, the home of G-2 (intelligence) section of II Corps, and G-2 is where the cloak and dagger work is planned and executed, to a large degree. I cannot vouch for it but I'd bet dollars to doughnuts that some spy for the Germans was being tortured to divulge what he knew about something secret. Several times during the war Jack and I reminisced about this experience and it always provoked a cold shudder in me when it came up. I never discussed it with our Brigade S-2, but now I am sorry I didn't. At the time it happened the Brigade Headquarters was at Rosneath, Scotland and the S-2 was a man I didn't even know.

One day at about this time, Colonel Arnold stopped by where we were working and asked Jack and I whether we would like to go on the invasion of North Africa, leaving London soon. Jack said, "Yes". I said, "Wherever the army wants me". One learns that you had better always appear "Gung Ho" to a West Pointer if you want his full respect. Maybe it was my imagination, but I always felt as though Colonel Arnold lost some respect for me because I didn't answer his question the same as my friend Jack had responded. Soon after that, McGrann vanished from the Mount Royal and from London, and I was for the first (and last) time a member of the Rear Echelon 1EAB. I was to remain in London until no longer needed there, and then join the remainder of the Rear Echelon at Rosneath, Scotland for subsequent shipment to North Africa. I moved to a lesser hotel in the Mayfair area of London because the Mount Royal was filling up with officers of higher rank; maybe someone of higher rank told me to move, I don't remember. Almost immediately I fell into my next main assignment; serving as resident guide to London for fellow officers of the brigade rear echelon, and I soon learned that the headquarters had, for the most part, remained at Rosneath. One at a time. I showed the sights of London to guys I had not met before; Picadilly, Saint Paul's Cathedral, Westminster Abbey, the Houses of Parliament, all of the hallowed places we had read about in high school history classes. I also had to make a trip up to Hull to carry orders to our 591st Engineer Regiment which had been left out of the first convoy. About the middle of October, 1942, I was told to close" up shop in London and to join the Rear Echelon at Rosneath Castle. I had not been to our brigade headquarters prior to this, so it was with pleasure that I found the gang with which I was probably going to start my portion of what we now refer to as WWII.

I went to Glasgow by train and then telephoned the Brigade Headquarters Motor Pool to get a ride to Rosneath Castle. I was picked up at the station about a half hour later by an army private named Bohannon driving an army command car. Bohannon was a young man from West Virginia who was about 20 years old, very large, (six feet plus-weight about 250) and a trusted, frequent companion over the next 2 1/2 years. He and/or Pvt. Carl Singer, from Pittsburgh, Pa. were the Jeep drivers who figured into most of my petty adventures thenceforth. Singer was the soldier you always see in the movies carrying a guitar ...I doubt if he weighed half as much as Bohannon... for that matter, I myself scarcely weighed half that much.

We arrived at Rosneath Castle in time for evening chow where I met the cuisine of the HQ 1EAB Cooks for the first time. Pretty good by my midwest cooking standards, but definitely not Mom's Sunday best. I also met some of the officers and men of Brigade Headquarters, although I had met a lot of the officers in London previously while serving as the guide to the big city. I was invited by Lt.Col Blimp to share his large bedroom, so I accepted, and a canvas cot was soon brought in, complete with blankets and a pillow and for the first time in my army career I could consider myself (sort of) a field soldier.

Let me tell you a little bit about Lt. Col. Blimp: He was a southerner about 45 years old, who got his commission from the ROTC program of some Engineering college. His commission was in the Infantry, the army did not seem to have much Engineer ROTC before my class of 1939. Col. Blimp was the executive officer of the Brigade, second only to Col Wolfe, CO of the brigade who was with the forward echelon, now somewhere between Glasgow and the Port of Oran, Algeria. Colonel Blimp had a thin line of a mustache and was the only American Officer I ever saw who habitually carried a riding crop. Most of the enlisted men hated him for his pompous manners. He was also a very heavy drinker. I learned this fact that first night at Rosneath when, long after turning in for the night, I heard the Colonel get up and glug, glug, glug take a big swig out of a bottle from a table beside his bed.

Rosneath Castle was a graceful, gray sandstone building on acres of well kept lawn overlooking the Firth of Clyde, a huge bulge in the Clyde River where large Ocean Liners frequently hid from the German U-boats while unloading American Troops into Britain.The Queen Mary made many such calls during the war, when she was in constant unescorted service filling England with Yankee troops for the final push to end the war. Quite a few temporary army buildings in the form of Nissen huts intruded upon this otherwise idyllic scene. In one of these so-called "huts" a platoon of 50 or 60 troops could find living quarters with a concrete floor and a wood-burning stove to boot. For Brigade Headquarters and Headquarters Company we always needed similar total space. A few stately old oak trees completed the picture of Rosneath Castle. Brigade Headquarters stayed in many other buildings throughout WWII, including another castle, on a high cliff in Sicily, overlooking the Mediterranean, but we didn't stay in anything finer than Rosneath Castle.

During the two weeks that followed we took one all-day hike in the Scottish countryside to make us "physically fit" for the hardships of battles (!) yet to come. During this hike we saw a few of the native Scotsmen working in the fields and were amazed at their ruddy complexions and robust appearance.

When the call finally came to shoulder our gear and move out of Rosneath, I was relieved that we were finally going to start to catch up with our forward Echelon. We had read enough in the daily newspapers to realize that the invasion was a success although there had been more than expected resistance at all three points: Algiers, Oran and Casablanca. Some sniping by the Vichy French forces was continuing, especially at night. Now all we had to do was get down there.

We loaded onto a troop train in the Helensborough Station near Glasgow. There I saw the leader of the rear echelon of Headquarters Company, with all of the confusion of loading a company of men onto a troop train, take on the added responsibility of carrying one of his Lieutenants, dead drunk, on his shoulder onto the train. The leader was a man named Leland Burgess and typified to me the finest qualities of an officer in a bad situation... not life threatening, just bad. Both of these officers were of the same rank, both were from Clemson. The good officer seemed to have to work like the devil to get his Captaincy later in the war, but he did make it; the drunk was sent back to the States a couple of months later as "unfit", and I don't know what happened after that.

We rode all night down to Liverpoole on the train and boarded the Cunard Liner HMS "Samaria" from the train in the morning. On the Samaria we officers ate like royalty (almost) and our men ate like dogs. Fortunately, we had heard of this and someone had brought several cases of C-rations which we officers stowed in our very crowded sleeping quarters. No man in his right mind would order C-rations on a Mediterranean cruise such as we were embarking upon, but on this particular occasion the rations became somewhat popular after a few meals featuring mutton stew or tripe. While still in the busy, busy seaport of Liverpoole we had the privilege of seeing something a soldier seldom gets to see: one of the big Aircraft Carriers. I do not know which one we saw, it was British, all of ours were in the Pacific fighting the battles over what we now call Guadalcanal. The aircraft carriers were so valuable that they did not spend much time in port, and this particular one was outward bound when we saw it.

Having arrived in England by Pan American Clipper,(Ha!) this was my first time at sea. All of my previous seafaring having been confined to the rowboats at Camp Willson when I was 10 or 11 years old, and having matured during the Depression, I had never even thought about being on a luxury ocean liner so I thoroughly enjoyed exploring the ship. After a few days, when we got into the Gulf Stream the air magically turned quite balmy and as many of us as possible hit the decks to get the gorgeous air. There were quite a few Army Air Force Pilots being moved to N. Africa with us, and they had a crap game going on deck most of the time with stakes so high that we poor ground soldiers just watched and shuddered. Our ship was moving as part of a large convoy, code-named UGF 27, destined for the center task force at Oran, due on D+27 or 27 days after the D-day of operation "Torch". We were not aware of any deliberate delay on the part of the convoy but obviously they wanted to enter the straits of Gibraltar in the dark of night because of the danger from German submarines. The ships of the convoy, including, of course, the escort vessels, had to pass through the straits in single file. There were many very small craft which seemed to be "just milling around" in the straits. I, with my wild imagination, supposed that a large percentage of these small boats had spies with clipboards in hand checking off the various categories of ships coming through: personnel, ammo, general cargo, gasoline, etc. etc.. Each small boat had at least a lantern burning.

It was an eerie experience, to say the least, going through the Straits of Gibraltar, under blackout conditions. The "Rock" on the port side, completely darkened and looking like a tremendous black advertisement for the Prudential Insurance Company because of the bright lights of Spain outlining it so vividly. The right side view was a composite of the lights of the city of Tangiers surrounded by the much more sparsely distributed lights of rural Spanish Morocco. Our convoy almost got through unscathed but, as we learned a couple of days later, a minor collision forced one of the smaller troop ships into the British port of Gibraltar for emergency repairs. We cleared the straits quite early in the morning, formed up our convoy, and headed southeast to the city of Oran, Algeria, and its port of Mers el Kebir, on the south shore of the Mediterranean. Mers el Kebir is a beautiful seaport consisting of, among other things, a long concrete jetty, set at right angles to the shoreline, sticking into the sea. Trucks from HQ First Engineer Amphibian Brigade were waiting at dockside, along with transport for some of the other passengers, when we docked late on a Sunday afternoon. I had watched the docking process and was taken aback by the large number of neat signs painted on the jetty stating "defense d' afficher", meaning of course something to do with the defense of French North Africa against the American invaders. It was several weeks before I learned that these signs, which seemed to be everywhere, merely stated, "Post no Bills" or words to that effect.

As we rode through Oran to get started to our destination, I had a whole raft of first impressions; perhaps the primary one being that these people were deprived of the many things that we in the U.S.A. still had in abundance, war or no war. For example, the people all seemed to appear a bit dusty, as did their clothing. Soap was in short supply, but the real reason for the drab appearance of everything and everybody, was the fact that near a desert there is a lot of dust in the air, and Mers was near the Sahara.

Another first impression which we Americans simply had to get used to, was the cruel treatment of their animals: horses, mules, and donkeys, (and I suppose, camels; except that you didn't see many, if any, this far west). You would frequently see animal-drawn vehicles, (the Germans did not allow much gasoline to get into this now drab colony and they were not *highly* mechanized prewar, anyway). One would frequently see an animal-drawn vehicle, piled unbelievably high with whatever, and with a driver, large whip in hand, beating the poor beast as hard as he could. I believe that an occasional American soldier, especially ones from the farm, got embroiled in a discussion or a fist fight over this scene.

As we cleared the outskirts of Oran we found the coast road west of the city to be a good one and soon our small convoy of trucks pulled off to the side to eat our evening meal. The drivers advised us that we had another couple of hours to go and it was easier to pull off to eat when it was still daylight. The drivers had brought C-rations for all of us and I was finally about to get my first experience with this omnipresent emergency food. In those days there were only three varieties; meat and beans, meat and vegetables stew, and corned beef hash. Each of these constituted half of a soldiers meal; the other half consisting of an identically sized can containing several cigarettes, a packet of biscuits, some hard candy, some toilet paper, and most important; a key to open the other can. Of course I was so unlucky as to take the key which was attached to the wet can and use *it* to open the wet can, thus ending up with no key with which to open the dry can. Somebody bailed me out by loaning me a Swiss army knife to open my dry can. Why the army didn't put keys *on both* cans the way civilian companies do is beyond me. Did they ever change?

CHAPTER IV

ALGERIA AND SOME ALGERIANS

After we had eaten our C-ration and remounted the trucks, we continued on the coast road through town called St. Cloud toward our destination: the town of Arzew, Algeria. St. Cloud had the scars of battle but not of artillery or bombs; buildings pockmarked with small arms dents and the like. Arzew, as they now spell it, at least in the USA, was a seaport capable of taking small steamers and also had a seaplane basin for a small formation of single engine and trimotored sea planes owned by the French Navy. The Brigade Command post was established in a modern elementary school building, the school having been closed with the commencement of hostilities on "le huit novembre" (the 8th of November).

It was dark when we arrived at the CP and we lost no time in reporting for duty, although it took someone more steeped in army tradition than any of us to tell us what to do. Fortunately the Brigade Adjutant, Lt. John Steele, got us straightened out quickly, not that he was more "steeped in tradition" than any of us, it was just that he had been there all day awaiting our arrival, and while doing so looked it up in Army Regulations. We finally got to our living quarters and there we found the officers of the forward echelon, Hq. and Hq Co., 1st EAB. I only knew three of them: Col. Wolfe (slightly), Major Adams and Lt. McGrann. We were in a very new and modern building, which I believe was the only building in town more than two stories high. It was about five stories tall and was built as a government housing project. McGrann and I were in the same room, each with a canvas cot. His report to me of the invasion hostilities consisted of five minutes of the hostilities and about an hour of the celebrities; McGrann had seen Ernie Pyle, and one of FDR's sons, and had just missed seeing Ernest Hemingway. In the morning, I learned that the officers mess was on the first floor and all ranks ate together. The only difference from the typical officers mess in the US was the fact that we had wine on the table down here. I never heard of any problems created by this policy, maybe because we always ate our evening meal at 5:00 pm and frequently had several hours more to work. This policy of wine on the dining table disappeared a month or so after the N. Africa landings.

My first workday with my outfit was not particularly memorable except for the fact that I met a lot of good people. Before I get started on that subject, however let me digress for a moment and tell you a little about how the 1st EAB was organized. First, a brigade used to be an important and common unit in ground warfare, it was one half of the basic autonomous unit, the division. Theoretically, a division could survive and make war all by itself; it had a large and well organized force of foot soldiers (infantry) and a staff to take care of their basic needs, ie: people (G-1), Intelligence (Enemy) (G-2), Operations/Training (G-3) and Supplies (G-4). Supporting these basic tasks a division had all kinds of organic units: Medics, Engineers, Signals, Quartermasters, Transport, Artillery, etc.. Every person in the foregoing listing wore the same divisional shoulder patch. Nobody else did. The foregoing description of a division is so over-simplified as to be almost good for nothing, but it lets me write, "the 1st EAB was similarly organized and half as big, but with the principal staff functions labeled S-1, S-2, S-3 and S-4 instead of G-1, G-2, etc." Our main units were Engineer Regiments instead of Infantry, reflecting our intended main job, rather than fighting the enemy.

I went to work for McGrann in the supply section (S-4) under a Captain Herman Bunch. Capt. Bunch was a career soldier from the peacetime army who had worked his way to a reserve officer commission through army correspondence schools. He was good at handling company level supply problems but not too comfortable with the bigger problems of Battalions, Regiments, Divisions and up. Capt. Bunch claimed to be large part American Indian. My first assignment from McGrann was to locate and rent a well (if possible) to provide shower baths for troops in the area. Arzew is on the fertile belt rimming the Mediterranean, farther inland lies the Sahara Desert. We had good maps provided by the French Foreign Legion which showed several water wells in and around the town. Checking them out on foot, I found the first one I checked was already spoken for by the town. There was a fairly modern water purification plant, complete with a concrete block building, offices and flower garden atop the well. (Our maps were not *that* new).

The second well search was more productive. I found a large shallow well within a couple of hundred yards of the brigade CP. It was on a vacant lot owned by a prominent local attorney, who was also a member of the French Chamber of Deputies (Congress) and had been put in jail by the German Gestapo because of our invasion and was there to stay for "the duration". The owner's home was right across the road from the vacant lot and his wife and daughter were in residence, so I dusted off my high school French and went knocking on doors. Bartering for use of the well was a snap. In the first place they had only bought the lot to protect the value of their property. They hadn't wanted some Arab goat herdsman moving in, besides the well water was brackish and unfit to drink. So I closed the deal with a five pound box of army coffee and notified the operations officer of our 531st Engineer Shore Regiment that the way was clear for them to go ahead. They were to install a kit to create a 16 sprinkler-head portable shower unit, complete with water heater and duck boards. I suppose it was model M-1. I do not remember how long that task took, but it was a matter of weeks from start to finish. The actual labor was probably only two or three days, the rest of the time was lost in finding the well and then locating the owner. That was the sort of job the army described as, "in addition to his other duties"

The assassination of Admiral Darlan threw the high command of the American forces in north Africa into a minor tizzy. Admiral Darlan had been the high mogul of the Vichy French across North Africa, but as an expedient, the American high command had held on to him as the best available under the circumstances. Now, at the bark of an assassin's pistol he was removed from the scene forever and we were all on high alert for a few days. That settled down in a week or so, and it was Christmas Season, 1942.

A young French naval aviator came to our office in uniform and was directed to me as the only one in the office who even tried to speak French. I had sent a letter home requesting my mother to send me the "Beginners French" book from home in Columbus, Ohio. She had obliged promptly to my V-mail letter and the turn around time was short. The French Naval aviator merely wanted to invite two American Officers to Christmas Dinner at his home with his family. I accepted for McGrann and myself, knowing Jack well enough to know he'd be receptive. We went the next day to a 2nd floor

31

apartment, in a courtyard building next door to our office in the school. Had a fine Christmas dinner with roast goose instead of the turkey provided our forces. Lieutenant Du Pont and his attractive spouse had a little girl named Monique and another on the way.

I met several other French people as a result of my effort to speak French: Mr & Mrs. Geoffriot, Madame Jeanmot and daughter Paule, and a couple whose name I've lost: Dr. & Mrs. X, he a Parisian and a French navy doctor, she a Vietnamese upper, upper class. While I didn't get to spend much time with these people during the seven months we lived in and around Arzew it was fun to talk to someone once in a while besides my soldier buddies.

Other officers in the brigade were interested in learning the language and somebody found a teacher!! Right there in Arzew lived a lady, American born and raised, who had been there since the WWI armistice, or thereabouts. She was the middle-aged lady-friend of a middle-aged American, a Captain Hamilton of the French Foreign Legion. He had also been there since that same armistice (what a story that would seem to make). She was a teacher in the school in peacetime, so someone tracked her down and hired her to come one evening a week to try to teach the brigade officers to parlez francais. That lasted 3 or 4 weeks and then deteriorated into a monthly Brigade Officers Meeting.

At one of the monthly meetings we had a speaker fresh from the Tunisian front. I think that he had been a battalion commander in our 1st Armored Division which the Germans had nearly destroyed in the battle of Kasserine Pass. That was the first big battle for American forces in the European theater; and the Germans, under General Rommel, had shown us that the war was for real. The Germans were now fleeing North Africa despite Hitler's orders to fight to the death. We came away from the meeting thoroughly impressed with the seriousness of the situation and increased respect for the German army's fighting ability.

At about this time we began to get hints of something which was going to happen to the brigade several times throughout the war. "They" were trying to break us up. The fact that we now had about 5000 troops, specially designated to help make large scale invasions, was just too much for some of the "high brass". Some of them were still fighting World War I, and those were the ones who gave the top command the most trouble, they hadn't given thought to the type of war that the Germans had demonstrated so ably under the blitzkrieg way nor General U.S. Grant in his share of the Civil war. Others in the top echelons couldn't tolerate the way we had to be specially trained and prepared to do the "special work" required to assault a beach under heavy defensive preparations: Example; when do you want to bring in your mine clearing capability, your summerfelt matt, your beach marker signs, your demolition supplies for that 9 foot thick sea wall, your defensive personnel, equipment and supplies to make it a real "beachhead" in case the assault infantry ran into trouble and had to seek a place to regroup (ala the invasion at Salerno, Italy), and on and on. The question was not only "when?" to this myriad of detail, but also "who?" and "how many?" and "where?" and the like. In any assault it would be nice to have everything at your fingertips, but sometimes, unlike an assault on dry land one could not hold up for half an hour waiting for a certain capability to come forward. True, every assault is a mass of confusion; nevertheless there is such a thing as "organized confusion" and that is what we hoped to provide.

We had left the United States with a troop strength of approximately 7000 and were already whittled down to 5000, as a result of the Navy getting the job of providing the crews for the assault landing craft. Our 591st Engineer Boat Regiment had been downgraded to an Engineer General Service Regiment. In the Pacific fighting, the army won the argument and so the 3rd, 4th and 5th EABs all operated their own landing craft in the smaller, "island hopping" landings vs the Japanese. This sort of argument was the domain of the career officers..Not mine.

During January and February of 1943 we lived about as close to normal garrison duty as at any time during the entire war, only we didn't realize it because few of us had experienced life in a stateside army camp anyway. As assistant S-4 of the Brigade, I had some unusual experiences which would have made a peacetime supply officer's hair stand on end. For example, there was the matter of the .50 caliber machine guns. Now, recall that the brigade had arrived in Scotland from the USA with two Regiments of Combat Engineers, to wit, the 531st Engineer Shore Regiment and the 591st Engineer Boat Regiment. At that time the thinking was that the masses of Canadian,

British and American infantrymen plus those from various other allied nations would be ferried from England to French beaches by the small boats of the eight Engineer Boat Regiments of the eight Engineer Amphibian Brigades slated to become available magically "in the near future". (Sort of a "Dunkirk in reverse" operation) Upon arriving at the far shore (French, "hostile") the attacking infantry would be greeted by the eight Shore Engineer Regiments of the eight Engineer Amphibian Brigades, and the War would resume from where it had left off on June 3, 1940. The disastrous Canadian "Raid" at Dieppe, thank the Lord and Bless the Canadians, had put an end to that kind of thinking, and so we found ourselves pursuing a more reasonable military objective in French North Africa. Meanwhile, the U.S. Navy had won their little battle over which branch, Army or Navy, would operate the landing craft in (hopefully) upcoming invasions of the German-held continent. Hence, the First Engineer Amphibian Brigade had lost its 591st Engr. Boat Regt., along with its boats (then abuilding in New Orleans). BUT, the Brigade had NOT lost the .50 Caliber Machine guns and mounts, which were on order for the lost boats, and they began to arrive at our simple warehouse in Arzew. They were packed in the old reliable Cosmolene, two per crate.

I do not recall how many of the crates we had stacked up in our small overcrowded little warehouse before we finally got an answer as to how to turn off the seemingly endless stream of crated machine guns, but it was a matter of weeks. Getting rid of the 2500 officers and men of the 591st Engineer Boat Regiment was much simpler matter, unfortunately. The War Dept. merely wrote an order redesignating it the 591st Engineer General Service Regiment and it went from the glorious future of assaulting hostile shores to that of building bridges and the more mundane (but no safer) tasks of typical engineers at the front with the enemy. Getting rid of the Landing Craft of the 591st was even more simple. They were in demand in the Pacific theater.

I waited and waited for orders as to disposition of the crated machine guns, they being more or less my responsibility as assistant Brigade S-4. At one point, one of the battalions of the 531st Engineer Shore Regiment was ordered to the Tunisian front to provide additional trucking. So, as I recall it we issued some of the crated guns from our warehouse to the battalion for mounting on their truck cabs on the theory that the guns were of more value against the Huns than sitting in our tiny warehouse back in Arzew. I also managed to trade a crate of guns for a worn-out British motorcycle and a case of two British bicycles at the suggestion of the First Sergeant of Brigade Headquarters Company who felt that his outfit could use same. When orders came to turn the machine guns over to the II Corps Ordnance Officer, nobody questioned the disappearance of the several missing crates. Case closed. (Almost)

About the end of our stay in Algeria I heard a rumor that a Sergeant in the 531st Engineers had been nominated to receive the Distinguished Service Cross (second only to the Congressional Medal of Honor) for having shot down *two German Stuka dive bombers* from an army truck in which he was "riding shotgun" during the Tunisian Campaign. I was never in a position to verify this story which went kind of like this: The truck was one of several running in convoy, when one of the leading trucks suddenly halted while driver and guard "hit the dirt". They had sighted a pair of Stukas, flying at treetop height, strafing the road with their machine guns. The truck bearing the heroic sergeant screeched to a halt to avoid striking the vehicle ahead and the sergeant grabbed the gun mounted in the truck cab above his head. Leading one of the slow flying Stukas by just the right distance, the sergeant fired a burst and brought the first plane down.. The remaining dive bomber continued up the road a short distance and turned to make a second pass at the convoy, or perhaps to avenge his fallen comrade. As you have guessed by this time, the brave sergeant observed the returning foe and proceeded to give him a well aimed burst too. I always believed this story and liked to fantasize that the gun was one that came from the Brigade warehouse in Arzew.

As the Brigade settled in for the winter months in Arzew, Algeria, the supply section of the headquarters found a lot of ways to be useful, and the several thousand men of the Brigade found a few more things to wish for, seek, crave, and demand. Imagine if you will, please, hundreds of American men, with only a few months of Army service, put down in a flat, muddy plain in the middle of a nowhere called "Algeria", sleeping on the ground, two men to a "pup tent", eating from hand held mess kits, performing tasks ranging from the supervision of Arab gangs of street cleaners to unloading ships like stevedores. With the German and Italian enemy armies about five hundred miles to the east in a place called "Tunisia" there was no danger except perhaps loss of sanity.

There were several things which could be done to help make life more bearable for all of us; the Army Mail Service came up with "V-mail" whereby if the writer chose to use a prescribed form, his one page letters would be microfilmed and sent via air mail to the USA, thus beating the boat delivery by a matter of weeks. Individual units could scrounge living quarters in some strange places too. For instance our Quartermaster Battalion took over an ancient fortress of the French Foreign Legion while its rightful occupants were off in Tunisia. Even the stevedore troops were able to scrounge wooden dunnage from the ships to build tent floors and miscellaneous niceties. The little matter of food, always a morale factor, was not terribly serious... nobody starved. We received canned mutton from Australia (reverse lend-lease, I suppose). It never tasted like lamb, always like mutton. Spam and more spam. Canned hard biscuits, and the omni-present meat and vegetable stew of the C-ration family of delicacies. Fresh Oranges were available from street vendors. Local wine was plentiful, in fact I once sat on a Special Court (the Army equivalent of a local Justice of the Peace Court) where the accused testified that he had "*only*" purchased a "helmet full of wine" from an Arab passerby while guarding the "Ammo Dump".

One of my own assignments became a considerable challenge. Somehow or other, we got a sizable shipment of wheat flour from the USA. The army, at this stage of the game had only Coleman gasoline stoves for cooking in the field, we did not do any baking, so my boss, Captain McGrann, told me to see what I could do about getting fresh white bread baked locally for the thousand or more troops we had scattered around in the vicinity of Arzew. Now in those days it was customary for the citizens to go to the local bakery every day to buy their loaf of bread so there were plenty of small street corner bakeries to be found. The Gestapo under the Vichy government (or vice versa) had long rationed everything worthwhile, so the locals were as starved for decent bread as were our troops. So the job of arranging for the baking of the flour into delicious loaves of genuine French bread was going to be a simple bartering arrangement: "You bake me so many loaves of bread per day for my troops and I'll give you so much extra flour to make loaves for your patrons" Alas, nothing is ever as simple as it could be; we had no yeast! To avoid total embarrassment of the S-4 section, (especially me, who had carelessly let word of the coming of Manna from heaven get out). In the face of this bad public relations faux pas we arranged for the bakers to produce baking powder biscuits. So I had brigade kitchen helpers, in their unit jeeps at eight local bakeries at 4:00PM one day picking up hot biscuits for their evening mess. They had to pick up their share of the biscuits in barracks bags (clean, I hope), and keep them warm with army blankets—paper bags and the like were unheard of in wartime. As I recall, we got yeast from somewhere after about a week and were able to make at least two more batches of bread before the flour was used up. We never got any more flour.

While we are on the subject of army rations, here's a word about fresh sea food. Now, we were on the shores of the beautiful Mediterranean Sea, where the populace had lived off of its "fruits" since prehistoric times, where it had always been a toss-up as to whether Neptune ("King of the Sea") or Jupiter, ("Ruler of the Heavens") had the final say. On only one occasion did I see the efficiency-conscious U.S. Army take advantage of that ocean of goodies to feed the Mutton weary troops. That one occasion came in early February, 1943 when I first met Lieutenant James Ralph "Shug" Jordan. Jordan who was in the supply section of Headquarters, 531st Engr. Regt., drove up in front of the Brigade Command Post in L'Ecole Maternelle, in Arzew in a Jeep. The only other living object in the Jeep was a huge Tuna fish in the passenger seat which was then taking its last gasps. Shug, who played a big part in my later war-making, had located a fisherman unloading his catch, and brought the big Tuna around to alert the Brigade supply people to the possibilities. Unfortunately, by the time we found the fisherman his catch had all been sold to the locals—who probably needed it more than we did anyway.

One other rather atypical anecdote about ration problems encountered while in Algeria deserves mention at this point; one day along about mid January, 1943, in my capacity of Assistant S-4 of the Brigade I received a phone call from the Corporal on duty at the Ration Depot that some meat had arrived by rail and that it had a strange odor to it. I called the Medical Battalion to see if I could get somebody from the medics to go with me to investigate this strange report and, lo and behold, who should join me on my way to the Ration Depot, but the Medical Battalion C.O. in person, Major Merle Smith. Major Smith was a former Infantry Reserve Officer who was a Medical Doctor in Civilian Life and one of the nicest, most unpretentious guys I ever met. We teamed up on this occasion to check out the Corporal's comment about the smelly meat. Major Smith and I were both expecting to smell some canned Mutton from our ally, the Australians but what the corporal had to show us was one of those dinky little French railway four-wheeled flat cars with a side of beef chained down and fully exposed to the elements. It had come all the way from the USA under refrigeration, I am sure, and then been forwarded from the Port of Oran in this manner by the native stevedore gang. That was the only fresh meat the army ever tried to provide us while we were in the Mediterranean Theater, and Major Smith had to condemn it as unfit for human consumption. Maybe it ended up being fed to the Arab dogs—which probably needed it more than we did anyway.

One time while I was Officer of the Day and everyone else was at noonday mess, I received a phone call, from someone hunting for First Sergeant O'Brien, the "Topkick" of Brigade Hq. Co. who was also responsible for the Brigade stockade, where minor lawbreakers were incarcerated while awaiting trial. I finally called the stockade, where the Corporal on duty advised me that Sergeant O'Brien was indeed present, but was busy at the moment, beating some respect into a member of the 1st Rangers, who had challenged O'Brien's manhood when brought in for drunkenness the previous evening—so it went with our neighbors the First Ranger Battalion, predecessors of all of the most elite troops in today's army. One additional story story to illustrate what the Rangers were like, comes to mind. One day a kind of short (I'm not very tall myself) Ranger Lieutenant with a big Walrus mustache came by our Hq and asked if I would go with him to OK his admission to our warehouse area. I went with him, and found out that he was interested in a huge sea mine which he had noticed on the ground outside the warehouse, and he wanted to know how it worked. All I knew was that it's very large explosive charge went off when a ship hit one of the "horns" which protruded its spherical body. That was all I knew, or ever wanted to know; but the very likable Ranger with the huge handlebar mustache wanted to pursue it further. So we proceeded to debate the question. At one point I said, "I always heard as a child that one couldn't have flame in the absence of air, and that if you dropped a lighted match into one of the tanks at a gasoline station, the match would not ignite the whole tank full but would merely go out. I never knew any one who tried it; but I imagine you would have done so, had you heard the argument." The Ranger's reply was, "Oh, I heard that one and I tried it and it is true." I cannot believe that I talked him out of trying to take that horn off of the mine so he must've succeeded. Anyway we both survived. The Rangers moved up to Tunisia shortly thereafter so we sort of lost contact with them; I saw some of them again before we all invaded Sicily. Many years after the war, I heard from a golfing companion who had been at Anzio that the 1st Ranger Bn. had been in on the ill-fated Anzio end run, and had been virtually annihilated in trying to break out. They were a great bunch to be around. May they rest in peace.

While we were still in Arzew, maybe it was late February, the Germans decided to pay us a visit. It wasn't much of an air raid, however, but to those of us who had never before had the Huns trying to kill us it was, as they say nowadays, kind of a wake-up call. A six plane formation came out of the setting sun at low altitude, seeking what target we never managed to figure out. Our units had .50 caliber machine guns set up on the long quays in Arzew harbor and a friend of mine got a Purple Heart medal for severe burns on his hands received when trying to turn the gun around by picking it up by the barrel. We had a similar attack a few days later when I happened to be at the home of some of my French friends for dinner. They had an air raid shelter in their yard, but by the time we got out there the shelter was full of people, mostly Arabs. We returned to the house and sat on the floor behind a large overstuffed sofa and with an interior wall of the house at our backs. I decided before long that it wouldn't do for an officer of the United States Army to be cowering behind an overstuffed sofa with a bunch of French people, so I got up and went outside. It was still broad daylight, and though most of the people were off the streets, there were still a few like myself whose ego forbade them to take cover. I had learned that it was more

Sam Daugherty

fearsome, when you couldn't see the enemy planes than when you could see them. After that, my "cover" usually was to "hit the deck" when it got *really scary* otherwise, just watch and hope for the best. I saw some of the German planes when I got outside and it turned out they were only fearsome when they were flying in your direction and close.

During this Arzew period, Captain McGrann and Major Adams had the honor of attending the Casablanca conference between the allied heads of state, Winston Churchill, Franklin Roosevelt, Chang Kai Shek, etc. They participated in some discussions on amphibious warfare and at least got to see our leaders. My activities were less impressive during that February, I did trade a few potatoes for a ride and lunch aboard a beautiful yacht. One morning when I was alone in the office in the school a very sharp looking Royal Navy Lieutenant came in and asked if we had any potatoes to spare. Now it was our job to operate the supply dumps in the area, and we had few, if any, requests from our Navy for food and had never even heard of the Brit Navy needing rations. It was within our charter to provide any ally with whatever he needed if we had same. Turns out, he was the commander of this beautiful large yacht, which was called by some Royal sounding name, probably that of it's peacetime owner who had loaned it to the King for wartime use. (like the "Duke of Wales" or somesuch). It rode unbelievably nicely in the water, and the crew kept it so spotlessly clean that it was a joy to behold. Its purpose in life was to perform hit-and-run attacks on Axis shipping in the Mediterranean. It had, in addition to it's crew, a gaggle of British Commandos aboard to liven things up when raiding. It was quite an experience for me. Incidentally, we still had the American First Ranger Battalion bivouacked nearby, and their escapades kept our MPs on their toes most of the time. Colonel Darby, a dashing young West Pointer was their founder and Commander, and I had the pleasure of helping him several times when the Rangers needed something.

Later in the spring, some one managed to make it "hit the fan", and Brigade Headquarters was "broken up for good" and we all moved in to downtown Oran to work in the supply offices of the Mediterranean Base Section. I was quartered in a seedy, second rate hotel and had an office on the third floor of a modern office building nearby. That lasted about two weeks, then we moved into a small beach town, near Arzew, called "Port aux Poules". The Brigade was alive once more!

Now we were living in a very small resort town scarcely a stones throw from the sea. It consisted mostly of a single row of two story beach cottages, all facing the sea, all with balconies such that one could walk from house to house on the second floors merely by climbing over the small balcony railings. The beach road and some low dunes were the only barrier between land and sea, and the "beach road" was only the track in the sand left by the most recent vehicle to pass. Porte aux Poules translated literally means (I guess) "Port of Chickens", although I never found the "Port" and I never saw one "Chicken" during the several months we were there. We were practicing Assault Landings with our 531st Engineer Shore Reg't, first with engineer company landings, alone; then with (simulated) infantry battalion landing teams. The 1st Infantry Division, the "big Red One," with whom we were going to make the next landing, was at this time all tied up in the Tunisian fighting. We practiced night landings and day landings.

The nearby town of Mostaganem was a thriving Arab community with several American units in and nearby. I ran into a young soldier named Bennet Nau, who was a neighbor in Ohio, in Mostaganem one Sunday afternoon when we both had free time, I took off my Lieutenant's silver bars and we had a couple of beers and a long chat. Bennet was the second acquaintance from home I had seen overseas. He had come into Africa with the Western task force at Casablanca.

When "they" broke up the Brigade in North Africa "they" had forgotten to appoint a commander to take charge of the scattered remaining units. The "break up" lasted such a short time, we did not know what in the devil was going on. Looking back, I now have come to the conclusion that maybe General Patton had a hand in it. When they started the Brigade up again they gave us a new Commanding Officer, Colonel Eugene M. Caffey, West Pointer, class of '13, who had dropped out of the army because he couldn't support his family (ten kids) on Army pay, got a Law Degree and had a good practice started in Atlanta when WWII erupted. He came back into the Corps of Engineers, whence he had previously resigned; and very soon commanded the 20th Engineer Regiment which he made so

41

outstanding that it was used as the Guard of Honor at the Casablanca Conference.

The 1st Engineer Amphibian Brigade was renamed the, "1st Engineer Special Brigade" for obvious security reasons at about the same time Col. Caffey arrived. He lost no time in letting us know that we were soldiers in the U.S. Army and that he was strong on military discipline. He had a remarkable effect on the spirit of the entire 5,000 man brigade and it was noticeable almost overnight. We knew him and both revered and hated him as "the old man" long before the Brigade *really was* broken up for lack of any future large scale landings. Colonel Caffey was a fairly tall, trim looking man for his age (about 60), with medium mustache, piercing black eyes, a broken nose and in general, a very fierce demeanor. Most of us were scared to death of him most of the time. One day, when we were just getting used to Caffey, after almost a year under the mild, quiet Colonel Wolfe, and most of us had heard a few General Patton stories, of which there were new ones almost every day, I had my first and only "one on one" encounter with "old blood and guts" himself. It happened like this: It was my turn to serve as "officer of the day", which basically meant that if any thing came up while there was no one else present to take care of it I would either handle it myself or get someone to handle it. I was serving as OD this particular day in the brigade HQ operations office on the second floor of the beach cottage we used as our command post, all of the other people had gone to lunch when I heard the "clomp..clomp..clomp" of boots running up the stairway. I went to the head of the stairs to see what all the noise was about, and who was coming up that stairs but General George Smith Patton himself. As soon as he saw me, the only human being in sight, he sort of grunted in that high pitched voice of his, "Gene, where's Gene?" To which I managed to blurt back, "Chow, he's at chow SIR!" to which he responded, "Chow, where's CHOW?"

By this time, I guess we were both operating on instinct, he kind of lunged at the screen door to the deck, pushed it open, and exited to the deck with me right on his heels. I answered him by pointing and talking, "third house down, on the ground floor, SIR!" General Patton was off like a shot, vaulting the guard rails that separated the four decks each as he arrived at it and then entering into the third house through the open screen door to the porch roof deck, still calling, "Gene, where's Gene?". Although General Patton was famous for his flamboyant dress, among other things, I am not sure what he was wearing that day. It happened too fast for this citizen soldier to tell.

Speaking of army clothes, at about this point in the war, the men of the Engineer Brigades were authorized to wear the same boots as the Paratroopers, the reason for this expensive change was being given that most of us spent a lot of time walking in the sand, which was true. With this change to a more distinctive foot protection you could just see the esprit de corps of the troops improve. I rather doubt that Col. Caffey was in on the chicanery needed to get the new boots, I rather believe the impetus came from General Noce, because Jim Mueller had mentioned it when I first got into this amphibious troops business.

We had incredibly sad news at this time. Colonel Arnold had been killed! I was saddened to a degree I had never experienced in my life. He was such a good guy, a real sense of humor and yet a really dedicated officer. I believe that it happened this way: when Colonel Caffey was made Commander of our Brigade, the top position in the 20th Engineer Regiment became open, and Dick Arnold was promoted to fill it. As I understand it, the first day after his promotion, Arnold was in the field getting acquainted with his troops in a mine clearing operation. The Tunisian campaign was completed, but there were hundreds upon hundreds of German, American and Italian antitank mines all over the battle area. Colonel Arnold was on foot in an area where his new troops were working, and someone pulled on a rope tied around a mine to dislodge it. As was frequently the case, that mine was tied to another mine by means of an underground trip wire and, unfortunately Colonel Arnold was on top of that undetected second mine; it was what was called then and now, a "booby trap." Germans were expert at all kinds of Booby Traps, many Allied Soldiers were victims despite intense training on the subject. General Eisenhower's chauffeur, who had been Arnold's betrothed, mentions this heart-rending turn of events in both of her two postwar books. The General himself comments on the event in one of his books. My own recollections of Dick Arnold are some of my most treasured of my own WWII memories. After 59 years I can still hear his voice and see the twinkle in his eyes. May he rest in peace.

Soon after learning about Col. Arnold, I was summoned to the office of Major. Adams, the brigade Operations Officer. Capt. McGrann was already there. Major Adams said that since our preparations for the invasion of Sicily were practically completed, he was going to give us new assignments for the invasion itself. I was to go on Temporary Duty with the Third Infantry Division as liaison officer, to bring a status report to Brigade Headquarters on the 3rd Division's situation after the first few days. McGrann was to serve as liaison officer to the 45th Division.

CHAPTER V

TUNISIA—THIRD DIVISION—36TH ENGINEERS

I knew that the Third Division was in Tunisia where the fighting with the Germans had just been completed with victory for the British 8th Army and the American II Corps. The 3rd had passed through Arzew not over three weeks previously and had barely had time to catch the finale of the Tunisian Campaign. It is approximately 800 miles from Arzew to Bizerte in Tunisia, where we learned that the Third was encamped. I was cleared for air travel to get as far as Algiers so I got my field soldier gear, went to the Oran Airfield very early the next morning, and was soon on my way. It was interesting to look down from the plane to the ground and just gawk at everything. I had not flown over much inhabited land before, with all of the lush vegetation one sees along the intensely cultivated Mediterranean coast, and certainly hadn't seen that many goats before. We flew at quite a low altitude, I suppose it was because the Luftwaffe was only a few miles away, in Sicily, and was just looking for an opportunity to "get even" if only a tiny bit. We were far from having the air superiority we enjoyed later in the war. And I do mean "enjoyed."

We landed at Maison Blanche Airport in Algiers, where I saw my first camels. They were hauling some kind of freight from a small warehouse near the airport out into the wilds of Africa. There wasn't another plane flying to Tunis, my destination that afternoon, so I had to spend the night in Algiers. I arranged to stay in a casual officers accommodation for the night, and, since it was only early afternoon, decided to try to locate John Adams. John Adams was a new friend who had transferred out of the Brigade when Colonel Wolfe was relieved of command; he was a close friend of McGrann also. Adams was a few years older than Jack and I, and used to regale Jack and me with tales from his law practice in North Dakota. I spent the rest of the afternoon with Adams during which we called upon Colonel Wolfe to pay our respects. We had dinner at the Alletti Hotel before going our separate ways. John gained a degree of fame after the war as Counsel for the U.S. Army in the highly publicized McCarthy hearings.

Early the next morning I was at the airport and caught the C-47 to Tunis without incident. I saw a lot more camels this time and some mountains to boot. At the Tunis airport, war damage was everywhere; a lot of German planes had either been caught on the ground or destroyed in landing. It wasn't open to commercial traffic yet and the baggage claim was merely a pyramidal tent beside the runway. I was surprised and pleased to find my bedroll there, it having made the trip yesterday when my body had failed to make the same connection.

I made arrangements to leave my bedroll with the baggage at Tunis airport until I could get a way to haul it to Third Division headquarters. Then I started hitch hiking on the road to Bizerte, where there was steady bumper to bumper military traffic, and was soon at the division CP. The division headquarters motor pool very obligingly told me they'd pick up my bedroll and bring it from the airport. The funny thing was that, after so much fuss about getting my bedroll, you'd think it would have been more simple just to get another from Division Hq. supply, but I had an excuse: it would have embarrassed me to death, to get another, and besides, mine was all marked with paint, per army regulations, to identify me as the owner.

After bumming a ride from the airfield at Tunis to Third Division Headquarters near Bizerte, I pitched my pup tent in an olive orchard, near some other guys of similar rank, and settled down to await whatever was going to happen next. I hadn't long to find out. While lying on my bedroll on the ground, I happened to notice a large black ant crawling along at antlike speed toward my tent and my bedroll. It did not take me very long to discover an anthill within about ten feet of my as yet unslept- in bed on the ground. Numerous black ants were to be seen coming and going to a hole in the ground the size of a nickel. While pondering this situation and its potential for disaster (mine) I happened to notice a tiny red ant crawling along, also near my bedroll. Here was a challenge. Here I was, among total strangers, at the highest field headquarters I'd ever been near, the proudest outfit, dating back to World War I, the "Rock of the Marne," selected by General Patton for the left flank of the assault on Sicily. The last thing I wanted to do was attract attention to myself. I guess that necessity is truly the mother of invention. I am proud to state that this soldier won the skirmish with ants. Here's how: first, took a piece of tablet paper from my Dispatch Case and folded a sharp crease lengthwise. Next, got out my emergency "D" rations, bit off a corner (almost broke my front teeth), wetted the chocolate with my saliva and placing, it in the center of the paper, put the paper on the ground near the red ant hill and settled down to let time pass. In about an hour, I jolted the ants off of the chocolate, made a little chute of the paper, holding the chute over the entrance to the black ants' ant hill, gave it a flip with my middle finger and sent a couple of hundred tiny red ants cascading into the domain of the black ants.

Pandemonium! To arms! Ants to the ramparts! The black ants began to tumble out of their ant hill. Some were carrying large white cocoon-like objects which I took to be eggs. The remainder seemed to be empty handed, but all were in a desperate hurry to get away from the tiny red ants. You never saw such a scramble! Naturally, I didn't want to sleep near such carnage so I spent the better part of that afternoon finding an ant-free spot and moving tent, bedroll and sundries to a more secluded spot in the orchard. My own personal first battle with the enemy was a draw…I guess.

Spent a couple of hours the next day being briefed by one of the Captains from the division staff. In the course of our conversation he dropped the news that General Eisenhower was coming to inspect the division the next day and to have lunch with General Truscott and his key staff members…and that I, along with most junior officers on the staff, was to find something to do, including eat my lunch elsewhere—out of sight. Of course I had already seen General Ike, even ridden incognito in his limo when I was stationed in London. Curiosity over the army's way of entertaining a big shot got the better of me in the morning so I thought I would just sneak by the mess tent while preparations for the lunch were taking place. I managed to get up there about 10:30 the next morning, and I got the impression that most of the preparations were already under control (completed). That's the way the old army frequently prepared for an important pesonage. Each link in the chain of command took a safety factor of 10-15 minutes with the result that the "grunt" at the bottom of the chain had some time on his hands. (Hurry up and wait!) I'm not saying this was the case, but it sorta looked that way to me. What really caught my eye, though, were the clouds of houseflies settling down to enjoy the General's lunch even before he arrived. I am confident that sombody caught hell and that probably some poor private stood there and shooed the flies, oriental royalty style, until the General arrived. (to take over the fly detail himself?) The tables were set out in the open.

I came by the luncheon scene, at much greater distance, at about one PM, and heard strains of soft music of a regimental band emanating from a small tent facing the head of the table. The luncheon was underway in grand style.

My stay in the olive orchard with the 3rd Division wasn't all that long—about a week as I remember it. But I had no assignment, only to be there, and to be able to report on their situation after the first few days ashore in Sicily. The headquarters people were all completely occupied with last minute plans and preparations for the assault landing over the beaches around Licata. Very wisely, in my opinion, I simply stayed out of their hair. One afternoon during this idle period I decided to visit the 36th Engineer Regiment, which was slated to become subordinate the 1st EAB after the landings. Their HQ was located within walking distance of 3rd Division HQ where I was living so I set out on foot to call upon the 36th, with which we had been practicing our assignments all that month. As I was proceeding through a freshly plowed field, adjacent to my olive orchard, I noticed the body of a man very close to my projected path, he was clad in what seemed to be rags. As I drew nearer I decided that he was alive, probably overcome by the extremely hot sun. When his feet were within reach, I gently tapped one of his sandals with my army boot. He sprang to his feet in a flash and jabbered away like a madman. I was every bit as scared as he was for, you see, I had committed the unthinkable, the deed we had all been warned to avoid before we ever set foot in Africa. I had disturbed a Moslem in his midday prayers. I think he was intimidated by my uniform and I know that I was afraid of starting a holy war. We both backed off—me to continue my journey, he to get back to his work.

When my business with the 36th Engrs was concluded that afternoon, they offered to send me back to 3rd Div. Hq. in one of their jeeps. I quickly accepted the offer and away we went—just the driver and me. As we proceeded along I noticed that the truck in front of us, an army Weapons Carrier (it was all military traffic- the civilians had long since ran out of gasoline), bore the bumper markings of the First Ranger Battalion. They pulled out from us with greater speed and were soon far ahead. All of sudden, their truck came to a stop, two soldiers baled out, ran into the adjacent field, seized a small calf grazing there, carried it back to their truck with its throat cut, threw the calf aboard, and went on their way. ...Supper!!!! We had been around the rangers quite a bit in the winter of '42-'43 and I had talked briefly with Colonel Darby when he came to our Brigade Hq in Arzew, but I had never seen this action before. They had been ordered to "live off of the land (ala Sherman's march to the sea during the Civil War).

The last evening that I was ashore in Tunisia with the 3rd Infantry Division, I went with a bunch of headquarters type officers, who seemed to know where they were going, to a large natural ampitheater in a pasture nearby. In the audience were to be seen the square blue and white shoulder patches of hundreds of officers from the various infantry, artillery, engineer, and miscellaneous units of the Third Division. There were many officers from the 2nd Armored Division, part of which was to land with us at Licata and part of which was to land at Gela. You couldn't miss the armored people with their big multi-colored triangular shoulder patches. (General Patton always insisted that both officers and enlisted men wear the authorized recognition symbols of parent outfit and rank at all times. It is my humble opinion that General Patton wrote the book on military morale.) Eventually somebody shouted a command and we all took seats on the grass facing a small platform and microphone which were (obviously) facing us.

Unfortunately, I didn't take notes on that occasion, 57 years ago, but his words were pure Patton at its best. This was before the infamous "slapping incident" and before his breakout from Normandy and his magnificent sweep across France terminating only when Ike started rationing his gasoline. It was long before his rescue of the valiant 101st Airborne Division at Bastogne during the Battle of the Bulge. General Patton was already somewhat famous for his flamboyant manner in Commanding armored troops at the Indio (California) Desert Training Center, for his command of the Western Task Force at Casablanca in the invasion of N. Africa, and for his coming to the rescue of the II Corps during the winding down of the Tunisian Campaign. As mentoned earlier, I had already encountered

49

General Patton one-on-one about a month earlier in Port aux Poules when he came looking for Col. Caffey during the lunch break. I was really looking forward to this exposure to "Patton before the battle".

General Patton in full battle dress, had barely opened his mouth to speak when a warm breeze swept softly over the assembly, he immediately pronounced it a good omen; "a hot wind from the desert," which the natives in their superstition believed "swept all before it". Good luck indeed! He started gently, reminding us that we were superbly trained for battle, that we had the finest equipment in the world, that we had the strongest nation in the world behind us and that God was on our side (or something like that)...Then he went into the fact that in battle we should never "freeze up", no matter how scared or bewildered we might be. He said better to do SOMETHING than to just stay there and be slaughtered. "Don't be eager to die for **your** country, make the other poor son of a bitch die for **his** country". He went on like this for a few more "Pattonisms". Then, as I recall it, he told us a little bit about the battle plan. How we comprised I Corps, (Eye Corps), the First Division on our right, was the assault unit for II Corps, and the 45th Division, (Oklahoma National Guard) was coming directly from the States to be on the American right flank. The British Eighth Army would be to the right of the Americans. If memory serves me right, he then told us that all of the American units would be melded into a U.S. Seventh Army when the beachhead was secure. I do not remember whether the assembly closed with some sort of a benediction or not. It was dusk by that time and we returned whence we had come.

The morning after we heard General Patton's inspirational speech to the officers of the invasion force, we started getting ready right after breakfast. I was determined to get ashore earlier than McGrann this time to sort of get even for his having beaten me by 27 days in the North African invasion the previous autumn, so I went as a combat soldier; leaving behind my ubiquitous bed-roll. My personal costume consisted of woolen olive drab shirt and trousers, combat jacket, steel helmet and liner, field glasses, first aid kit, canteen w/ cup and pouch, mess kit, musette bag w/harness, dispatch case, extra socks, 3 C-rations, 1 D-ration, gas mask, .45 cal Thompson Sub Machine Gun, 3 clips of 20 rounds each .45 cal ammunition, fountain pen, 2-pencils, spare spectacles, cigarettes, and compass. Of course my uniform also included my underwear, socks and paratroop boots. What the heck? It was July and this was (Gonna be) Sicily, besides who needed a bedroll for this climate? We turned our bedrolls in to 3rd Division Hq. supply to have them brought ashore with the rear echelon.

The 3rd Division motor pool trucks delivered all of us odd-ball liaison officer types to quayside in Lake Bizerte where there were many, many LCIs all tied up together side by side. You could actually climb from one to another, there were probably more than a hundred LCIs and there were many different types of landing craft. Lake Bizerte is not really a lake, but rather a sort of a bay of the Mediterranean sea on the shores of which sits the city of Bizerte. Our contingent of officers boarded LCI No. 110, which if I remember it right, was operated by the U.S. Coast Guard. Then we settled down to await developments. We were fed our evening meal and were just goofing off getting acquainted with the layout of the little transport ship, and with each other. Evening came and went, and I was thinking about crawling into my top spot of the three-high hammocks when I heard the deep throated cough of large caliber antiaircraft artillery range firing for the evening. Only this evening they didn't merely range in, they kept right on firing, with more 40 mm guns joining the 90 mms every second.

Most of the passengers on this, as yet still stationary LCI, scampered quickly to the deck to see what was going on. There by the light of several large chandelier flares dropped by the enemy and thousands of tracer bullets sent skyward by the ships on Lake Bizerte and their protective ring of antiaircraft batteries on the shore, one could see the start of a genuine German air raid. Almost immediately our big high powered searchlights came on and began sweeping the dark night sky. Soon one of the searchlights caught a tiny silvery image of a twin engine German bomber, the famous Ju-88 from aircraft recognition class we had attended in an earlier life. Instantly many of the other searchlights jumped over to the now illuminated plane, and my thought was, "how eerie it must be in that plane with all of those very powerful lights shining on it". Armed Americans had more vicious thoughts, and soon there was a huge cone of tracer bullet paths ending in the sky at the plane and starting from all over and around Lake Bizerte. By this time, we American spectator fans had gotten into the act and you could hear cheering from all over the lake. The cheering rose to an absolute crescendo when smoke began pouring out of one of the engines, (you could barely see it at that distance). Within seconds the plane began to spiral down in flames, just like in the movies, and the crowd went wild.

CHAPTER VI

SICILY—OLD "BLOOD AND GUTS" PATTON

In the morning about dawn, our LCI began to make noises like it was getting underway. Sure enough the cluster of five LCIs, all tied side by side, came loose from the pier and soon were maneuvering to get out of the harbor. Before long, we were out in single file headed south in exactly the wrong direction to find the island of Sicily. I guess they were just getting us out of the way so they could load more ships in Lake Bizerte. Our little file hugged the Tunisian coast all day and managed to get as far south as the harbor at Sfax, where we put in to escape a storm which had arisen. I'm hazy on how we spent the next few hours, but suffice it to say that I did not get seasick, although many did, and by midnight we were in position off the coast of Sicily south of Licata. The 82nd Airborne division was dropping amid light antiaircraft fire and the Third Infantry Division was landing on the shores around Licata. We could see AA fire in the sky down the coast to our right at Gela where the First Infantry division was landing as was our Hq 1st Engineer Brigade and its cohort the 531st Engineer Shore Regiment. I imagined that I could see similar signs of activity farther to our right to where our 45th Infantry Division was landing.

Landings went well, except at Gela, where German tanks caused considerable concern as some almost reached the beaches late in the afternoon. Fortunately, the U.S. Navy came to the rescue and a beautiful destroyer scooted up to the very edge of the beach and proceeded to give the German tanks a lesson in marksmanship by knocking several of them out of the picture, ending that threat. Of course I didn't witness this but heard about it from my buddy "Shug" Jordan over the following two years. We who were waiting to go ashore had the opportunity to learn more about German airplanes as we endured a few low level hit-and-run raids by individual fighter planes. I never heard of any damage they did, but they managed to liven things up for us.

After breakfast our LCI pulled up to the dock in Licata, and Brigadier General Morrie Rose, Commanding Officer of Brigade B, 2nd Armored Division stepped off, dry as a bone, and ready for action.

53

He was an imposing, youngish sort of a man. As I recall, he was wearing tan jodphurs, leather leggings, combat jacket, and steel helmet. None of my friends even knew he had been aboard, but considering his rank, there were undoubtedly private quarters for generals aboard an LCI. I didn't notice any other military types get off with him but presume he was not traveling alone. He didn't appear again in my share of the war.

While we were at the dock several of us "passenger officers" decided we might as well get off too. So I retrieved my back pack and Tommy gun and stepped off on dry concrete. There had been no fighting to speak of in the Port of Licata, and I couldn't hear any nearby; only at great distance. I decided to check in at 3rd Division Headquarters, if I could find them, although I did not have any idea of what I could do for them at this time.

I started walking along what was a main road leading inland and soon found myself going uphill; following handmade coded signs, probably the same ones I had followed from the airstrip at Bizerte. As I neared the top of this first low hill, there came the sound of firing from the huge armada of ships of the invasion fleet lying offshore. The cause of all the commotion was a German ME109 strafing down the shore road. The fact that I was higher than all the ships and that the plane was also higher than all of the ships and somewhere *between me and all of the ships* made my situation unenviable to say the least. I hadn't made any trajectory calculations but it seemed a wise thing to leap into a field beside the road and hit the deck; which I did, as quickly as I could. To my good fortune I escaped unscathed. One ricochet from a nearby tree managed to strike my steel helmet, on the second bounce and end up in the dust under my face. It was a 20 mm bullet fragment and made a good souvenir which I carried in my pants pocket until I lost it somewhere in less than a year.

My path soon put me at 3rd Division (Advanced) Headquarters where I knew at a glance that I would be in the way. My duties only entailed bringing a situation report to my 1st ESB Hq after the landings, so I stood before the latest situation map and saw where "Truscott's Trotters" had reached as recently as an hour ago. That was great, but it was unclear as to the width of the gap between the 3rd and 1st Divisions. It was too early for me to try join the 1st ESB. There had been serious opposition to the landings at both Licata and

Gela (as I found out later) but none serious enough to more than slow the powerful assault forces thrown at them by these two crack divisions. We were also winning the air war, but it was far from air superiority at that time. I walked to one of the beaches of the 36th Engineer Combat Regiment to see how they were doing, and was pleased with what I saw. Their job was essentially the same as that of the 531st Engineers, of my own outfit, the 1st ESB. The principal difference being that the 36th did not have their own medics to handle wounded beyond evacuation, or quartermaster troops to operate dumps, or a signal company, etc. Incidentally, our 286th Joint Assault Signal Company was so capable that 7th Army HQ used them to communicate with the War Department in Washington, D.C. during that first week after D-day when the 7th Army needed that capability. The 36th Engineers had their part of the job under control as much as anyone gets things under control on D-day on a hostile shore. My bed for D-day night in Sicily was in the back of a 3/4 ton truck at the CP of the 36th Engineers.

In the morning of D+1 I went back to 3rd Division (Advanced) Command Post to let them know that I was still there and available for work. There an assistant G-4, a Captain who I had known longer then I knew anyone in the division told me that they were trying to get an LST, loaded with artillery ammunition to come to the Licata Docks for unloading. The ammo was sorely needed to maintain the Divisions advance. He said that when the LST was docked, a platoon of the 20th Engineers was assigned to unload it onto 3rd Division trucks, and that it might be appropriate for me to volunteer to relieve the 20th Engineer Lieutenant in charge when the job was about half completed. I said "OK will do" and spent until noon hanging around the docks waiting for the LST to enter the harbor and dock. It turned out that the 20th Engineers had only assigned a squad of about 12 men to do the job and that the task was still in progress when darkness fell.

The night of D+1 on Sicily was famous for one of the big SNAFUS of WWII. A large number of paratroopers and Troop Carrier personnel were lost in this action. The army had scheduled an AIR DROP of the 82nd Airborne Division Reinforcements, and the Army Air Force had ROUTED them right over the invasion fleet and DID NOT tell the navy, and the ENEMY had scheduled a bombing

RAID at the SAME TIME.. That is a dangerous combination of events at any time and is extra dangerous when a large number of troops, both Army and/or Navy is new at the combat business. I happened to be on the pier at Licata, awaiting my turn at leading the ammo unloading gang, when the whole thing erupted and I took refuge under a jeep along with a couple of other guys. We had heard and recognized the asynchronous whine of the German aircraft engines and had *seen* and recognized one of the paratrooper C-47s flying away from Sicily at treetop height in the midst of the melee. At about this time an Army Dukw came out upon the pier where I was now standing beside the jeep. The Dukw driver said that some of the paratroopers had been forced to ditch their planes at sea and that he was going out to see if he could help them. The two men who had taken refuge under the jeep with me said they wanted to help, as did I, so we all three climbed into the big floating truck and we went off of the pier into the Mediterranean. In less than ten minutes we had pulled a big healthy American paratrooper captain out of the drink. He was only soaking wet with no other injuries. Our Dukw cruised around off the port of Licata for about a half an hour, finding no more people or floating bodies. The sea was quite smooth and the visibility was not bad under our headlights, so we returned to the port and parted. I didn't know any of the individuals involved and we never met again. It was a tragedy of huge proportions due to what is now called, "friendly fire".

The ammunition on the LST was almost unloaded by this time and I stayed aboard the huge craft with the 20th Engineer Lieutenant until it was all loaded onto 3rd Division trucks.

The next day I was able to reach Brigade Headquarters by Army telephone so I took leave of the 3rd Division and started east on the coast road in the jeep which the brigade had sent for me. We were still within sight of the Licata pier when the jeep driver and I both saw a German fighter plane coming right toward us, treetop height, strafing the coast road. We stopped and tumbled out of the jeep in time to get a shot at the underbelly, the most vulnerable spot on a fighter plane in those days. I led the speeding plane as much as I could, considering the terrain, and fired the entire clip of 20 rounds at the belly of the intruder. Of course the entire fleet was firing at him with all guns at the same time as I was, and the plane made an abrupt left turn and flew off the end of the steel pier and crashed into the sea. As a former pheasant hunter, I always had a feeling that I had shot him down. I never carried a Tommy gun again as my weapon of choice after Sicily, despite the much heavier fighting in Normandy and Okinawa. The Tommy gun and it's ammunition were just too heavy and not worth my effort after the Sicilian Campaign. Besides the Tommy gun is harder to clean.

The remainder of the trip dawn the coast road from Licata to Gela was uneventful but gave me a broader picture of the impoverished island. We arrived before lunch time and I learned that the Brigade Command Post was in some temporarily abandoned ground floor apartments just off the coast road which the tanks of both combatants had already ground to dust. I reported on the status of the 3rd Division to our new CO, Colonel Caffey, who then proceeded to give me a new assignment, which proved to be an interesting challenge.

Colonel Caffey described my new assignment as follows: The official borderline between the British and American Forces ran through the town of Vittoria which the U.S. 45th Division had already secured. Vittoria was an important railroad center and it was believed that there were a number of steam locomotives abandoned there. I was to go to that town the next morning and bring as many of the locomotives as possible over to Gela to get them away from the British zone so there would be no question as to ownership while the battle was going on. He then as much as patted me on the back and said "fetch". I had to beg a blanket from the meager Brigade supply tent but that was better than I had the two previous nights. I had not been able to get my bedroll from 3rd Division Hq. because it was on one of their rear echelon trucks.

In the morning after breakfast I went immediately to the HQ motor pool to get a jeep and driver (General Patton didn't approve of his officers being their own drivers). Someone at the motor pool suggested that Pfc. So-and-So would be a good choice because his parents spoke Italian at home in New Jersey and he could serve as my interpreter. Sounded good to me! So off we went.

In about two hours we reached Vittoria and found the Railroad terminus, the same way one used to find the station; "follow the tracks". There was no one in the facility, not a single person, only a stray dog. I went from room to room among the five or so rooms which had been pretty well cleaned out with hardly a scrap of paper in sight. In one room, which I took to be the police department (polizia) I found everything had been removed but a small wooden crate. We used the jeep's shovel to pry that box open (foolishly) and found that it contained six brand new Italian army carbines which were still in cosmolene a gooey protective coating used the world over for long term storage of weapons. We loaded that crate into the jeep like good souvenir hunters.

The Italian Fascist government had had all of the railroad jobs under its control for many years, and the workers, whether or not fascist, were apparently scared out of their wits to see an enemy officer prowling around their workplace. About noon one man came into the office where my driver and I were exploring at the time. He spoke American English fairly well and told us he had lived in Cincinnati as a boy. He volunteered to help us so I told him of my mission and he agreed to help round up some railroaders, he, himself being a brakeman. One by one a handful of workmen, who had probably been watching us from hiding places we didn't know about, put in their appearances One obstreperous individual, who was probably the Fascist equivalent of a Russian Commissar, put in his two lire worth by asking me in rather broken English, by what authority I was seizing the locomotives and planning to move them. I was standing close enough and tall enough (at 5-8") to touch his lips with the muzzle of my Tommy gun which probably still smelled of burned gunpowder from yesterdays excitement over the strafing plane. He shut up promptly but gave me a look which, coming from a Sicilian of the 1940s, should have been enough to stunt my growth, had I not been almost 26 already.

I have often thought of this and wondered what I would have done had he been gutsy enough to stand up to me. I seriously doubt that I would have had the nerve to pull the trigger. We went into the yard and counted five small locomotives, all stone cold. I asked my new Sicilian interpreter how long it would take to bring all of them up to running condition, he said that it would require until midnight to get water and lubrication and to get steam up on all five. I asked how long for just one, his reply, "about the same" made up my mind for me. I asked him if he thought the group of men could be trusted to get a couple of them ready in my absence. He stated that with the exception of the obstreperous one he could guarantee success. I told him that I would go back to Gela for the night and that I expected the five locomotives to be ready to go, with steam up on two of them when I came back early in the morning. Colonel Caffey had advised me to push a couple of flat cars ahead of us in case the Germans had placed antitank mines in our path so I threw that requirement into the mix for the next mornings parade of railroad equipment. I then sought out the bellicose individual again who seemed to know a few words of English and, in his presence, in a conversation with my jeep driver, managed to work in several references to "firing squad" while looking at the bad guy. I didn't want to be on that coast road between Vittoria and Gela after dark; we had seen an artillery observation plane with big black swastikas on it, flying just above the treetops as we came to Vittoria that morning. If the Germans were getting ready to launch a counterattack, it would not be a good idea for a single jeep to try to stop them. No, we couldn't stay here all night just the two of us, there's safety in numbers. So, at about 3p.m., off we went back to Gela.

When we got back to Gela I reported the events of the day to my superior, Lieutenant Colonel Adams, who, though disappointed, certainly was understanding. I rewarded him for being so understanding by presenting him with an Italian army carbine dripping with cosmolene, and I rewarded my buddy Jack McGrann with another as a prize for coming in second in our race to get ashore in Sicily on D-day. I gave another to my driver of the day and have forgotten to whom I gave the other two, that same evening.

In the morning I departed Gela again right after chow, went straight to the railroad yards and in the Vittoria station was met by a whole bunch of beaming Sicilians; one would have thought that they were a gang of triumphant allied soldiers instead of citizens of a soon to be defeated nation. Steam was up, (they blew the whistle on the first locomotive to demonstrate this fact), five engines were on the main line pointed toward Gela with the two live ones at the tail end so they could push the three cold engines, plus the two flat cars, plus the caboose they had added to my list, just as a finishing touch. Our trip back to Gela was more or less uneventful, but I did have to wave my Tommy gun at the "Commissar's" head one time when he was making a last minute obligatory protest, for the record, about the effrontery of the allied forces. I rode in the cab of the pusher locomotive at the tail end of the string with the "bad" guy as my guest, my brakeman friend from Cincinnati as fireman and a man he selected as the engineer . My guest and I rode as best we could, between coal car and locomotive, and the jeep driver brought back the jeep. As we approached Gela I had the engineer "lay on the horn" a bit to announce success. Whether anyone noticed our arrival I never heard. The trainmen rode back to Vittoria in my jeep with two GIs in the driver's seat.

One day after the locomotives were safely in our American barn I called to Third Division G-4 office to see if their rear echelon had caught up with them yet. The answer was affirmative, and after several more calls I learned where my bedroll was, and was told to "come and get it or we'll throw it out". I figured that I could find them, so started out the next morning after chow, in a jeep with Carl Singer, of Pittsburgh, Pa. as my driver. We followed the main road Agrigento - Palermo with its coded Third Division signs as guides, and I was afraid we would go clear into the city of Palermo before the signs turned us into a field beside the road. There was 3rd Div. Hq., ahead of its Infantry by design, ready to take the Capital and principal city of Sicily the next day. Pfc. Singer and I got evening chow at 3rd Div. Hq. mess and spread our bedrolls in the field, out in the open, with the others from Division Hq and loafed around all evening waiting to hit the sack.

I had barely fallen asleep, on top of my blankets, when I was awakened by some slight noise and I opened my eyes to see infantrymen, extended in a skirmish line, just like the book describes it, walking among the sleeping staff people. Maybe the guys from 3rd Division were used to it, but it was really a thrill to me to sit up in bed to watch the beginnings of a night attack by bright moonlight. I never found out which one of the three Infantry Regiments of the Third Division: the 7th, 15th or 30th, we were looking at, and I am pleased to report that there was no severe fighting in store for them at the end of their day; although there was plenty in store for them in the Italian Boot and the invasion of Southern France, etc.

One day while the battle for Sicily was still underway, Colonel Adams sent me back to Vittoria with these instructions and orders, "we have received word that there is an American sergeant of the

45th Infantry Division in Vittoria with a large number of Italian prisoners of war to be taken off of Sicily before they hurt themselves or cause any mischief. Please take Colonel Hill's car and bring them here to Gela so we can evacuate them to North Africa". Now, I had never met Colonel Hill and I didn't know about his car, but orders are orders and I was willing to learn; it was better than sitting in the office. Colonel Hill was a small, dapper man of about 60 who had been brought over to run the railroads for General Patton. His "car" was a gasoline powered interurban type vehicle such as the ones we had here in the USA in those days. I suppose it held about 60 seated passengers, plus 60 standing passengers (crowded) plus 50 passengers seated on the roof. He had a sergeant who was the car driver. I don't know why Colonel Hill didn't go along with us, but we went to Vittoria without him. The "car" ran smoothly over the Sicilian roadbed and we soon pulled into the Station at Vittoria where there was a large throng gathered. In that crowd were a large number of women and children there to see their daddies off to the land of milk and honey. They had large baskets of picnic foods and bottles of the family's best wine. They even had live chickens with feet tied together. None of the men seemed to have a razor or a complete uniform and the story on that fact is kind of interesting: one had to be in uniform for the U.S. Army to take you as a prisoner of war. The, by this time, rag-tag Italian Army soldiers, had made up and the rumor had stuck, that if you had a pair of Italian army shoes or boots or a shirt, the U.S.Army would take you prisoner of war. The sergeant who was guarding this happy crowd for the 45th (Thunderbird) Division told me of this common belief, and also told me not to worry about these POWs; they would fight only in order to get to America. So the driver of Colonel Hill's "car" and the 45th Division Sergeant, and I sorted the POWs, (everyone who had even a scrap of uniform) from the women, old men, and babies, loaded them on the "car" wherever they chose to ride, and slowly took off for Gela. Nobody fell off on the trip, they all wanted to get to the U.S.A.. Evacuating POWs was the last item on our General Mission Statement.

During the two days of procuring the locomotives, the brigade command post had been moved to a beautiful and imposing castle on a cliff overlooking the Mediterranean. It was on our map as Falconara, and had been the property of some solid fascists, friends of

Il Duce, Mussolini. It was only a couple of miles west of Gela on the coast road, and we were in pup tents in a field alongside the big castle. When I had returned from the locomotive deal the first night, my stuff, minus my bed roll, (it was still with Third Division rear) had all been moved to the field and put in a pup tent for me so when I retired for the night I used the little Italian carbine as a pillow. When I returned with the locomotives after the second day of it, the little carbine was gone. I made the mistake of mentioning its disappearance within earshot of Colonel Blimp, the Brigade Executive Officer and he rose to the occasion by ordering a formal "shakedown" of all the enlisted men in brigade headquarters. I was, honestly, never so embarrassed in my life. These men were my friends and it was a humiliating experience to them to be suspected of theft. It was the last time I ever picked up a souvenir, I swore off of that pastime forever and Colonel Blimp didn't find the gun.

The battle for Sicily was winding down, the Island was declared "Secured" by the Seventh Army 38 days after D-day. The supply services of the Army began to take over the handling of supplies from the brigade and most of our headquarters officers were moved into pyramidal tents in the area where the stables had been. McGrann and I shared a tent with Captain Bunch in a yard where goats had been kept, and we all three began to scratch almost immediately. FLEAS!! Whether they came from the goats or the nearby empty hog pen we never found out, but they were the kind of fleas that will stay on a human, as I had learned when as a boy of 15, I had stayed too long in a friends hog lot while shooting at pigeons by the barn when I was there to hunt rabbits and pheasants. The other two men accepted my diagnosis, and we did a hasty search for whatever solution the Army had to offer for his infestation. However he did it, Captain Bunch came up with information that told us that there was a personal kit available for a soldier to use to delouse himself, and as a matter of fact these kits were available to troops on Sicily. Captain Bunch procured a batch of them and the three of us each read up on how to use the kit. It was quite simple, in light of the fact that we were not very busy with our jobs, and had very few personal things to delouse. The kit contained a very large plastic bag, (plastics were just beginning to become common in 1943) a thin necked glass vial containing a bug killing liquid chemical and about one yard of strong cord with which to tie the bag securely closed. You have guessed it: one put every stitch of clothing, etc. into the bag, tied it securely, and then very carefully, broke the neck of the glass vial, which had been placed inside the bag prior to tying it shut. Meanwhile you sat around in your birthday suit, which was easy for us, being as we were less than 100 yards from a rich man's sandy Mediterranean beach.

An interesting footnote to the battle of Sicily, which seems to have escaped the historians all of these years, was that General Patton, who was personally wealthy, gave every officer in his Seventh Army a fifth of Bonded Bourbon whiskey; thus Colonel Caffey told me as he handed me my bottle.

The battle for Sicily had ended with the last of the German army fleeing across the straits of Messina under heavy bombardment from both the Allied Air Force, the Allied Armies, and the combined fleets of both American and British Navies. How they got *anybody across* will always be a mystery to me. Preparations for an allied assault on the Italian mainland were well along, the 36th Infantry Division (Texas National Guard) had been in Africa since early in the year, and the rumor was rife that General Patton had rejected them as unfit for his Sicilian campaign and had brought in the sharper 45th Division (Oklahoma National Guard) direct from the United States. Be that as it may, after 59 years, the rumor was unsubstantiated then and it is now dead.

The invasion of the Italian mainland was now foremost in our thoughts. Colonel Caffey received orders to bring a planning staff to Headquarters Fifth Army at Mostaganem, back in Algeria. He selected Major Jacobsen (S-2), Capt. McGrann, myself, and his aide, Lt. Paul, to accompany him, also taking along eight enlisted men. We were to be picked up at an army air field near Falconara in General Patton's personal C-47, flown to Maison Blanche airport outside Algiers, and there board Lieutenant General Mark Clark's C-47 for transport to Mostaganem. Coming as it did, right after the whiskey present from General Patton, this kind of treatment made us feel a little bit important. Alas! what fools men are! We stayed in Mostaganem about a week; during which time we visited French friends in and around Arzew, read a lot of novels and did not a lick of work. One day General DeGaulle of the French Government in Exile came to call upon General Clark; we were billeted on the second floor where we could observe from above, when Fifth Army turned out an Honor Guard for him to inspect; that was the only thing that broke the monotony of our stay in Mostaganem. Colonel Caffey was busy working to get us into the planning for the invasion of Europe at Salerno, Italy on the 9th of September, 1943. We had no idea what was going on, we were not even classified as to secrecy. Finally Colonel Caffey gathered us together and told us that we were not going to be included in the Salerno Landings. Our Regiment of Engineers, the 531st, would come in at H-hour as was their custom, but the Brigade Headquarters would have no role to play. After coming from Sicily in the two Generals' private planes we were told that all transportation was tied up hauling supplies to the Ports of Tunis and Bizerte to fill the needs of the assault force for the coming invasion, and that we would have to shift for ourselves to get back to Brigade Headquarters in Sicily. McGrann took the situation under control and in 24 hours had found us a ride to Tunis on two of the Army's Work Horses, the ubiquitous 2-1/2 ton truck. These trucks had cargo designated as "RED BALL" freight and would drive continuously straight through to Tunis because they were carrying badly needed tank treads for tanks which needed same after wear in the battle just concluded. There was an extra driver for each truck and all we had to do was to climb on, eat cold C-rations, and be hauled to Tunis, then we'd have to find a way to get to Sicily and to Brigade Headquarters. We had a monotonous long ride of about 3 days, twelve guys in two trucks on top of steel tank treads.

Arriving in Tunis we went right through to where the tank treads were needed and finally got off and stretched our legs. We learned that the 591st Engineer Boat Regiment, formerly a part of the 1st Engineer Special Brigade, was helping run the Port of Tunis. The 591st had been changed to to an Engineer General Service Regiment when the Navy finally won the dispute over who would operate the assault landing craft in the European Theater of Operations. General MacArthur won in the Pacific for the Army, but the Navy won the European side; it made sense to me, considering the differences in the magnitude of the landings in the two theaters. Anyhow that's how the 591st lost their boats. McGrann contacted some officers he knew in the 591st and found out we could get passage for ten people on an Army ferry boat leaving in the morning for Palermo, and Major

Jacobsen said he would look after the eight enlisted men and Lieutenant Paul, the aide, could accompany him. So McGrann and I decided to stay with the 591st and try to fly to Palermo. Turns out that during the time I was working in Washington as Colonel Arnold's gopher, Captain McGrann was at Camp Edwards and had become well acquainted with some of the 591st's top brass. They showed us how to get through to the Brigade Hq. switchboard in Sicily where we quickly learned that it had moved from Falconara to a place called Terimini Immerese on the north coast of the island about 16 miles east of Palermo, we learned further that the entire outfit (except for the 531st Engineers) was sitting there on a hillside slowly going berserk with idleness and with no relief in sight. We decided to hang around with the 591st for a couple of days of R&R after our trip across North Africa as "Red Ball" freight.

The following day in a borrowed jeep, we took off for ancient Carthage by mutual agreement between McGrann and myself. There we happened to encounter a Catholic Priest who was from Ireland and spoke excellent English. He and his Arab looking companion spent about three hours showing us around the ruins, the most imposing of which were the ruins of the stadium where the Carthaginans used to feed Roman prisoners to lions. The next day we went to the Tunis Airport and bummed a ride on an Air Corps C-47 flying into Palermo, and to entertain us dogfaces the pilot circled Mt. Etna, the large inactive (at that time) volcano on Sicily. About ten minutes after we landed at Palermo, we were treated to some aerobatics by a British Spitfire Plane, whose pilot had had a good day. Soon a car came from our outfit to pick us up—and our "fools errand" was finally over.

Jake had arrived safely with the eight enlisted men the previous day and now that everyone was back in the fold we found that the brigade had gone into a training mode. I worked on training schedules for various units of the brigade for a few days and managed to enroll in one where we had to crawl under barbed wire with live rounds of machine gun over the wire and another where we had to jog a couple of miles before morning chow. Almost everyone smoked in those days and except for the fact that the "Huns" were probably heavier smokers than we "Yanks" I'd have hated to engage in a foot race with them, "winner take all". We were all in sorry shape.

65

In all the carefree days we were enjoying I was pleased to learn that I had been promoted to the rank of Captain. To celebrate I was given the dubious honor of disposing of some approximately 400 Italian Army hand grenades which had been stored, loose, under a bed of straw in a small shed on our headquarters premises. These grenades, had been declared too sensitive for issue to troops and were discovered when our own Military Police chased away some Sicilian paramours who had wanted to make some of that easy American cash and hadn't bothered to check out the bedclothes. Sergeant Valentine of the Operations Section Staff and I, hand carried the grenades a few at a time and electrically detonated them ten at a time in a small pit we dug nearby. I stayed with the Sergeant, until they were about half gone, and then retired to other work, feeling that we had demonstrated that it could be done safely. I always regretted not having "stayed the course", but it all came off OK.

As we awaited news of the invasion of Italy and the fate of the 531st Engineer Shore Regiment we found ourselves with more time on our hands, and sought ways to alleviate the boredom of idleness. Several of us went into nearby Palermo one afternoon to visit the Catacombs. That was a spooky experience; it would have been awesome enough in peacetime, down there in the dank underground with hundreds of skeletons dressed in either religious garb or royal robes; but in wartime with many holes blasted through the cave walls and ceilings by our air corps and the fact that the bones were a bit scattered around, it was truly a mess. I felt sorry for the people who had to fix it. The least important people were "buried" standing up; took up less space that way. Around that point in time, Captain Barney Felkner who was our Provost Marshal, (police chief) asked me to go into Palermo for a dinner at the home of a university professor Barney had befriended. The professor, his wife, daughter and mother-in-law, and Barney and I sat down at a lovely table, elegantly decorated and with all of the neighbors standing behind us to watch us eat. I guess that Barney and I were on display too.

September came and after about a week there was a crisis in the Mussolini regime, and the King of Italy took over as head of the Italian government. We heard all of this on the Armed Services Radio Network. Knowing that D-day was scheduled for September 9th, we hoped that our buddies in the 531st Engineers would be able to walk ashore unopposed; and from what I heard later, so did a lot of the assault troops. Salerno turned out to be the roughest assault that any 1st ESB troops were ever involved in, with the defense perimeter of the 531st being put to the test for the first and only time during the war. They succeeded.

Meanwhile, Brigade Headquarters was sitting back there on the north shore of Sicily; fat, dumb and happy, waiting for whatever, heaven only knew. At the same time, our many subordinate units, those which could be of some use to General Clark's 5th Army, were being pilfered away from us, one at a time. Our truck companies, which had been converted to Dukw companies for the invasion of Sicily, reverted back to common truck companies, with, I imagine, consequent losses of self esteem. Our ace 286th Signal Company was called upon to put the main telephone system of the city of Naples back into operation after the Germans had wantonly laid waste to it.

Finally, in late September, we received orders to rejoin the effort to teach the Germans about war, and I was selected to be the point man for the Headquarters and Headquarters Company in a move to Italy. We were to go by road, crossing to the mainland at Messina, opposite the toe of the Boot called Italy. In a movement by truck convoy in those days, on those roads, one normally set the pace at 12 miles per hour, that way the lead vehicle moved at 12 and the last vehicle in a, say 30 truck convoy, found itself whizzing along at about 40 mph just to keep up. Seems funny, but that's the way it was on those miserable worn-out Sicilian roads. I got my stuff all ready to start early the next day, and, because the nights were growing so much colder, I made a special "quilt" by sewing together my two army blankets with several layers of newspapers in between. Very few of us had sleeping bags like most all campers have today, but the Boy Scout in me took over and I was following their motto, "Be prepared". It took several hours to make this quilted beauty but by all that was holy and faithful I was going to be cozy.

One happening over which my old friend Dave Moore and I still chuckle to this day was "The Beard Episode". It seems that the "old man", Colonel Caffey, in his determination to make the Brigade into a well-disciplined outfit, had come across some of his troops who were not up to his standards of neatness. Since by then the battle for Sicily had been won and the Germans were all gone, he decided to crack down a little harder on the dress code. He had Brigade Adjutant, Captain Charles Sullivan ("Sully") write a Brigade General Order, (sort of a Holy Writ), which went something like this:

"Beards"

"Any man in this command has permission to grow a beard. To do so it is required that his name be on the Beard List which will be maintained by the Company Clerk. If, prior to being on the Beard List for Thirty (30) days the individual shall see fit to shave off his beard he will be tried by Court Martial for not having been clean shaven the first day his name was on the list.

All personnel are cautioned that the wearing of a beard interferes with the fitting of the Gas Mask, M-1."

Now, Captain Dave Moore's company was a spirited bunch of rascals, and as could be expected, seven or eight of them, including some redheads immediately had their Company Clerk start the required list. And within a few weeks some of the whiskers were really blossoming. At that time, (maybe the "Old Man" got wind of what was going on, who knows? Col. Caffey let it be known that he was planning to inspect the Dukw Companies the following day. Well, when Dave heard of this development, he immediately had the Company Guard Roster reworked to have the bearded ones on sentry duty the day of the Colonel's visit, so that wherever the "Old Man" went he was greeted with a snappy "Present Arms" by a bearded giant. The General Order was quietly withdrawn late in the afternoon of the Colonel's inspection of the Dukw companies. But the beards came off voluntarily out of respect for the "Old Man".

While we were on the hillside at Termini Imerese overlooking the Tyrrhenian Sea on the north coast of Sicily we had an opportunity to become skilled at "Boot Culture". The First Engineer Special Brigade as well as the Brigades working in the Pacific for General MacArthur were all deemed eligible to wear the spiffy and expensive paratrooper boots, much to the disgust of the Airborne Infantry troops. I guess it was probably the efforts of the old Engineer Amphibian Command still back at Camp Edwards, Mass. which got us the boots on the supposition that walking on sandy beaches so much required special support at the ankles. Be that as it may, the paratrooper boots, as we all called them without shame, did a lot for troop morale, which in my opinion was already high as a result of the "Old Man's" unrelenting pressure on the many facets of military discipline. As a matter of fact, he had transformed us from a scraggly band of rabble into a Brigade of proud American soldiers. We were what you would call "cocky". Given that we had received the new boots just prior to the invasion of Sicily and given that during "an attack on hostile shores" one is bound to scuff one's shoes a bit, it was no wonder that we had made a mess of our lovely new boots during the preceding two months. So, as it was to be expected, we soon went into a frenzy of polishing, and cleaning, and re-polishing, and "spit shining" those beautiful new boots for the first of many such rehabilitations. Officers and enlisted alike.

I was on the road by six o'clock in the morning, with a single goal in mind: to find an area where the Brigade Headquarters could stop for the night to sleep either in buildings or under canvas after the days drive. The Germans had fought a delaying action against our Third Division along this coast road east of Palermo and the road was torn up a bit from demolition, artillery fire and land mines-besides the Fascists under Mussolini had not built for U.S. Army trucks and tanks, but had built roads for two wheeled donkey carts and an occasional 4-wheeled roadster type auto at best. Knowing, as I did, that the brigade would only need to make about 60 miles the first day, in order to end up in Messina for the second night, made my job easy the first day. I found a field, obviously well worn with fresh tire tracks, waited by the side of the road about a mile before the turn off, and caught the lead MP vehicle of the brigade convoy as he came along. Next stop Messina! I did not stay in the brigade encampment that first night, but went clear on into Messina, in hope of expediting our entry into Italy across the Straits the following evening. Arriving in Messina, my driver and I found what turned out to be a well organized effort to get the arriving allied troop units across the straits and on up into Italy where they could help fight the Germans. The British 8th Army was in charge of the crossing operation and they were certainly doing a good job of it. We followed the coast road until we finally ended up at the "jumping off place" where it was obviously necessary to have a boat to proceed further. This was a large open paved area with a row of decrepit brick buildings sitting a couple of hundred feet from the water. One of the buildings had a sign, "Casuals". which my driver and I decided meant us; so we checked it out, and decided to stay there for the night.

We unloaded our gear with the Italian custodians of the obviously British establishment and took off for the loading place to find out the details as to the procedure for getting the Brigade Headquarters across the Straits of Messina. We finally absorbed all the facts we could handle and returned to the "Casuals" sign to get ready for the crossing when the First Engineer Brigade came chugging along in the morning. I ate my evening meal at the casual mess and was soon ready to turn in for the night. I found that my bedroll had been unrolled on a canvas folding cot and to my horror, all of the quilted stitches seemed to be gone... "seemed to be", my foot! The precious stitches *were* all gone! Nearby stood a Sicilian man beaming like a Cheshire Cat, obviously very proud of himself for having discovered a serious defect in the bed of his charge. His "charge", which was me, has not to this day, figured out what in the devil that Sicilian man thought he was doing for me.

In the morning, my driver and I crossed the straits and then returned to Sicily again. The only memorable happenings on the crossing being the extreme stiffness of the British Marine whom I encountered at the mainland side headquarters when I called upon the Officer in Charge of the crossing to learn the procedure of bringing a major military unit from a conquered Island to a belligerent nation. The marine saluted more stiffly than I had ever seen, even at the Tomb of the Unknown Soldier in Arlington. And he didn't click his heels when he saluted, he stomped his hobnailed boots so hard that I looked to see whether he could pull his feet loose from the floor.

Next morning I went back far enough to meet the lead trucks of Brigade Headquarters on the the north coast road and by mid afternoon they were pitching tents on the esplanade alongside the Straits of Messina. I moved out of my berth in the "casual" quarters, where my bedroll had been so desecrated and rejoined Shug and my other buddies in the Brigade Camp. Our MPs had to cordon off our bivouac to keep the townspeople out of our kitchen area. They were hungry. We had set up our camp where people were (or claimed to be) starving. It wasn't our job to feed them but the brigade guys were as sympathetic as you would expect a group of American soldiers could be under such circumstances and soon were to be seen dumping their fresh suppers into the empty containers extended toward them by the hungry Sicilians. It only took a couple of tweets of the First Sergeant's whistle to break up this scene when it became evident that unless someone intervened., the troops would give away their entire supper.

In the morning we had a repeat of the same scene while we were breaking camp preparatory to presenting ourselves to the Brits who were running the operation at the crossing point. I can particularly remember one young mother, dressed in the ever present Sicilian black, who, holding her infant tight to her chest, ran to one of the G.I. cans where our cooks were throwing the left overs, and scooped up a handful of oatmeal which she rubbed across the baby's mouth; force feeding it. It was the job of AMGOT (Allied Military Government) to help avoid such scenes, but they had not arrived yet. Now we had to proceed, without opposition, up the boot of Italy, to the vicinity of Naples a trip of approximately 300 miles as the crow flies, but there were no crows around to advise us; there were only the switch-backs and curly-queues of a very primitive, very mountainous country road. This road was well traveled and showed it. In fact it seemed as though the entire British Eighth Army had been over it since the Italian Government had thought about repairing it, which was probebly true because there was a total collapse of authority in Italy with the absence of the German Army. The art of Graffiti must have been developed at about this time in history because I do not remember seeing so many homemade signs prior to this, but now every large rock seemed to bear a sketch of a rat and words proclaiming the passage of the British 8th Army, the "Desert Rats". It may be my imagination but I think I can recall seeing the statement, "Kilroy was here", which we saw ad nauseum after the war back home in the states. The reason I am so unclear on things seen at that point in the war is that I was becoming ill with Malaria and didn't know it until Dr. Goldstine, the Brigade surgeon, ordered me into a field hospital at Paestum. This was behind the beach at Salerno, the site of the combat assault which had kicked off the invasion of Italy.

My hospital stay was of about two weeks duration and the only thing I can remember is that the ward tent to which I was confined, had a dirt floor with a nice smelling meadow grass growing through.

Almost everybody in the ward had malaria, and we all received treatment with quinine of which our Japanese foes controlled the world's supply. The substitute for quinine favored by both the Axis and the Allied armies was a synthetic drug called Atabrine which all troops on both sides were required to ingest daily, but it had a lower success rate than Quinine, which itself was not a perfect preventive answer to the problem of Malaria. Witness my case.

CHAPTER VII

ITALY - MALARIA - NAPLES

Eventually, as might be expected, the Malaria symptoms began to dissipate in my body, my head began to clear, and the hospital threw me out. They must have discharged the Malaria patients a truckload at a time because my first memories of being a free man are of riding north in a 6 x 6 truck with the top down amidst a group of total strangers. Someone of them must have had a more malaria-free head than mine because my camera was stolen from my musette bag while we were on the outskirts of Naples. The truck somehow managed to find the Brigade Headquarters amid the mess that was downtown Naples after the Germans had withdrawn.

I like to think that Brigade Headquarters staged a wild celebration of my return from the hospital, but the truth was that it was only an eruption of a famous major volcano, named Vesuvius, offshore from Naples that staged the show the night of my return. To professors who study volcanoes, it was no big deal, they had been expecting it for several hundred years,... already.

It was time for us to be declared "excess baggage" again and nobody could do that better than U. S. Fifth Army. We were ordered to move to a village called Messercola, a suburb of Caserta and a hub in the road network leading into Rome. I would surmise that we were destined to be used as a pool of replacements for whoever needed expendable engineer officers. We had lost all of our organic troop units; our 531st Engineer Shore Regiment, our 261st Medical Battalion, our Quartermaster Battalion, our large, skilled Signal Company and the various smaller units which formerly constituted our original 7000 man Engineer Brigade. Meanwhile, we the nucleus (Headquarters), were like lost souls, destined to drift through eternity looking for an assignment worthy of what had once been called "The First Engineer Amphibian Brigade". However, the U.S. Fifth Army wasn't running this show, not by a long shot; and the first thing anybody knew we became *important* again. But I'm getting ahead of myself so let me tell you about our stay in the Messercola school house; which our Inspector General, Major Foster Dunlap, a "Philadelphia Lawyer" if there ever was one, promptly dubbed

"Messercola State Teachers' College" because it reminded him of one of the countless poor, run down, one building "Normal Schools" of that depression era.

I guess we stayed at Messercola about three weeks. "Guess" because I was out of my noodle with Malaria again for a week or more and was in an army hospital for that time living on clear soup, vitamin pills and hard candy. Major Jacobsen (Jake), Capt. Goldstine (Dr. Goldie) and I having been ordered to the Hospital by the Brigade Headquarter's Surgeon (Dr. Goldie himself) who had observed our tell-tale jaundiced eyeballs at breakfast and had scheduled the Brigade Hq. ambulance to deliver us to the field hospital immediately after morning chow. Joining us soon in the malaria ward was our own obnoxious Colonel Blimp showing, the same jaundice symptoms as the three of us. Someone in the headquarters', who knew of Colonel Blimp's fondness for English walnuts had given him a helmet full of them as a going-away present, apparently fully aware that the oil in them was absolutely contra- indicated for a person on a non- fat diet such as our clear soup and hard candy regimen. Walnuts were a ripe, local crop at that time and place, and the helmet was always in place of a paper bag in dirt-poor Italy during those 1943 war days.

Just to keep a finger on the point in time, we had all four arrived in the Malaria Ward in the hospital near Caserta shortly after Thanksgiving, 1943. McGrann and I had gone into Naples and bought some wine for the Brigade Officers' Mess and what with the folks back home providing the turkeys, cranberries, etc., our cooks put together a Thanksgiving Dinner fit for a bunch of kings (unemployed though we were). Our Mess was in the cafeteria of the Messercola State Teachers' College, naturally. After dining in such style, and such quantity, it was a wonder that more than four of us didn't wind up in the hospital the next day or so.

Lying in the hospital, on a cot with a mattress and sheets, surrounded by guys that I knew, I truly never had it so good. Then they moved a stranger into the bed beside mine. I do not recall his name, if I ever heard it, but he was a very interesting person. To begin with, he was an infantry Captain, American, overseas less than three months who had been bitten by a malaria-bearing mosquito. He was not a West Pointer but was a reservist on active duty like I was; and he was gaunt and weary looking but seemed to have a wry sense of humor in his tall, thin body. You say, "What is unusual about that?" Wait! He was also in command of a Company of Nisei soldiers, the (later) famed Japanese-American troops from the Hawaiian Islands who were then denied the "right" to fight against the Japs due to concerns about their loyalty. At that time, all Americans of first-generation Japanese ancestry were locked up, for the duration, in American concentration camps. The Nisei had "raised so much hell" about this challenge to their loyalty, that it had become an issue before the U.S. Congress, until it was finally voted that they could be "permitted" to fight against the Germans, but NOT against the Japanese. He had been with his Company since its beginnings and was very fond of them; he had a number of tales to relate about their legendary bravery in combat. One story, which I remembered all of these years, I will try to relate in the form of a play:

The play opens in the mountains north of Naples as a Nisei squad of about ten men has just overrun a German dugout and the Huns, still firing, were told to surrender or get shot. One German, emptied his machine pistol and then; (shouting):

GERMAN: "Kamerad! Kamerad!"..(Translates, loosely to "I surrender".)
NISEI: (also shouting) "Kamerad, My Ass":......
NISEI'S TOMMY GUN:
"BLAM!!...BLAM!!...BLAM!!...BLAM!!"
NISEI: "..............you kraut son of a Bitch..."
The "End of Niseis in Action"

After about a week on clear soup, hard candy and vitamin pills the army hospital near Caserta decided our jaundice was cleared and we were turned loose. By now, things were really beginning to shape up. Somebody in the War Department in Washinton had put his foot down on General Clark and said, "enough already!...keep your cotton pickin' fingers off of that First Engineer Special Brigade! They're going back to England to get ready for Normandy!" (or words to that effect!).

Anyway, we were back in Prima Donna status again and Brigade Headquarters had moved into the comfortable, new buildings which

Mussolini had been preparing outside of Naples in anticipation of the 1944 Olympic Games (never held). The army transport service had taken these over as the staging area for the Port of Naples. Remember that this was before the era of common air travel (despite my own previous and ongoing good fortune.) Both arriving and departing troops, as well as the thwarted Olympic Athletes could (have been) expected to travel by ship.

McGrann and I, both of us having come into the army from jobs in the Steel Industry, took advantage of the pause waiting for a ship to haul us north to the UK, and visited a bombed out steel mill near Naples. In case you have forgotten, steel mills were enclosed in corrugated sheet iron buildings, and the one we visited outside Naples had really been blown apart. The corrugated, galvanized sheet iron was scattered all over, and the equipment was all twisted and exposed to the elements. It was a totally abandoned mess and obviously out of the war for the duration.

The "lost" units of our First Engineer Special Brigade began to check in from wherever the Fifth Army had posted them. For all I know most of the troops were glad to be back under our wing. I suppose that most of them thought we were to be rotated back to the U.S.A. because after three major combat landings, that might have been a possibility,.. ...but, Dream On! no such policy had been established, nor considered, I supposed. We were all in for the duration. Soon we were hauled to the docks at Naples and, there, amidst the carnage wrought in earlier air raids by the U.S. and Royal Air Forces, we were loaded aboard the Troop Ship, "SS Dickman", a large, new ship under the command of the U.S. Coast Guard. The only noteworthy happening connected with our initial boarding of the Dickman is an anecdote concerning the "good ship Sea Ration", which is related to you herewith: The "Sea Ration", (a 24 foot gasoline-powered cabin cruiser) as I learned that same day, had been "borrowed" from one of Mussolini's favorites by senior officers of the Brigade. The "borrower" was probably dear old Lieutenant Colonel Rand S. Bailey, our signals wizard who was an experienced member of the New York City Power Squadron. He had missed WW I as too old to enlist and had gotten a direct commission as a Major in WWII because of his standing in Bell Laboratories and his boating savvy. Anyway, Colonel Bailey or somebody, had convinced somebody to load the Sea Ration, on board the Dickman as deck cargo, without bothering to tell the U.S. Coast Guard that the "Sea Ration" was loaded with some of Il Duce's finest booze (also borrowed). Somehow, after the "Sea Ration" was aboard the Dickman, and made secure, somebody let the cat out of the bag. and so just as the Dickman weighed anchor, the Coast Guard advised Brigade Headquarters (now aboard) to signal friends ashore (36th Engineers) that "Sea Ration", unmanned, was adrift in Naples Harbor.

The Coast Guard Transport Ship "SS Dickman", bearing the First Engineer Special Brigade and a few elements of the First Infantry Division ("The Big Red One") finally cleared the harbor at Naples, Italy about noon on that cold, gloomy, gray day in November, 1943. There was no gloom among the passengers, however; those who didn't know our destination, probably thought we were being rotated back to the states, where there were warm beds and Mom's pies. Those few "in the know", knew that our destination was England where there was warm beer and beautiful girls who spoke English. And, if this wasn't enough to dispel the gloom, we were on an American ship, where the bunks were sheltered and the "chow" was "World Class." Never mind what obviously lay ahead after a stay in England (!), or that the German U-boats were having their best year (1943).

After our second night aboard, the "Dickman", we awakened to find ourselves in the now familiar Harbor at Mers el Kebir (Oran, Algeria). "Scuttlebutt" had it, that were awaiting to form up a Naval convoy; higher level scuttlebutt had it that the convoy would also load the 9th Infantry Division and the 82nd Airborne Division to put them into the United Kingdom. These two, plus the already mentioned, "Big Red One" constituted a small, war-hardened task force at which Hitler, himself, might be expected to take heed. Now, word went out that we would be tied up for several days awaiting the remainder of the troop convoy and that leave in Oran was free to all troops. I didn't have even an acquaintance in Oran, but, as previously stated, I had some French Colonial friends in the small town of Arzew, 25 miles east of Oran.

In due course, I started out, on a wet November morning, hitch hiking to Arzew. With lots of military traffic to draw from, I was soon in Arzew and I went straight to our old Brigade Headquarters building, which, wonder of wonders, had been returned to its original function as a schoolhouse. They were having some kind of a PTA activity, decorating for a national holiday the next day and the several whom I knew, both parents and their student offspring, dropped everything to make a big fuss over the "returning hero, home from the wars". I didn't tell any of them that about all I had done was to go to army hospitals two times with malaria;—but neither did I tell them any war stories about deeds of valor—in fact they knew better than to ask any questions. I accepted invitations to dine that evening at the Jeanmot's fine home and to stay overnight in their guest-house and to bring Jack McGrann to a cocktail party with French Navy Lieutenant and Mme. DuPont, *in Oran,* the following night.

I bummed my way back to the Dickman at the quay at Mers el Kebir the following morning in the rain, took a very pleasant hot shower, changed to the only dry uniform I possessed, and proceeded to find McGrann to tell him of our social plans for the evening. He was overjoyed, as I had suspected the previous afternoon, when I accepted the invitation, McGrann didn't speak any French but had accompanied me on several social occasions with the DuPonts. As the cocktail hour approached, we arrived by taxi (All of our jeeps were in Italy where we had left them) at the apartment address which I had been given. The party consisted of about two dozen people, all French colonials, some residents of Algeria, the remainder Free French naval personnel. We enjoyed a large table of wartime hors d'oeuvres and a whole lot of red wine; in fact too much of the latter. We were seated on whatever furniture there was in the apartment, but mostly on the floor, jabbering away in a mixture of both of our native languages. I was seated on the floor beside a young Frenchman having a pleasant, if incomprehensible chat about nothing in particular, when a late arrival to the party wafted past. She was a young, attractive colonial clad in the uniform of the American Women's Army Corps. The Army Newspaper, "Stars & Stripes" had recently publicized the creation of this force and the fact that they had been issued American WAC uniforms—only she was not wearing an overseas cap (nor a helmet)—she was wearing a chic little bonnet of Parisian origin. This, to me, a true admirer of General George S. Patton, Jr, was PURE HERESY. To my semi-facetious remark that she was "out of uniform" she replied something like, "Oh, we French do not pay any attention to rules"—to which I uttered (stupidly, I must confess), "Yes, I have heard about Le ligne Maginot" (Referring to the Maginot Line, a long assemblage of prewar fortifications in France which had turned out to be useless, and had been described in the U.S. papers as manned by an undisciplined "lot of Frenchmen"). WHAM!!! the guy I was talking to, punched me in the mouth and had his pocket knife open and at my throat even before I realized my "faux pas". Everybody seemed to be proclaiming "L'honneur Francais", when McGrann pulled my assailant off of me and we retreated to the safety of a taxi and then to the good old SS Dickman, where we unsteadily and sheepishly saluted the Officer of The Deck as we came aboard at about 2:00 AM (GMT)..

Our convoy eventually cleared the Straits of Gibraltar (westbound) in total darkness and we were soon out of sight in the North Atlantic. We settled into the routine of life aboard a troop transport in WW II: i.e.; sleep for the night, get up when told to do so, wash, shave, dress, eat, play poker (then, when the cash ran out; read paperbacks), have "boat drill" at any time, have "General Quarters" at any time; then, to veterans who had some "savoir faire" (and some grain alcohol, aka, "torpedo juice" or "medical alcohol" depending on from whom one had pilfered it), it was time for cocktails. We had long since learned to keep a 5 gallon gasoline can of it on hand for all occasions. I never knew the purloiner nor the custodian, but I always seemed to be included, thanks be! Next came evening chow, followed by more poker or light reading, with an occasional trip to the main deck to get a breath of air. Of course, while playing poker, there was considerable banter about this and that—but never about non-funny subjects. The air was getting colder, this was December, and all but the most naive knew, by this time that our trip was to the U.K. Thoughts turned to England, Scotland, and Northern Ireland; wherever one had been stationed prior to the invasion of N. Africa. Talk was mostly about girls, (The Musical, "South Pacific" ("Nothing Like a Dame") hadn't been created yet, but these were red blooded American Boys far from home!). The English Pubs, took a distant second place in the conversations. There was only one man I had known slightly pre-war serving on the Dickman, and I've forgotten his name.

CHAPTER VIII

BELFAST—CORNWALL—EXERCISE TIGER

As the USS Dickman dropped anchor in Belfast Harbor, I was summoned to Col. Blimp's Quarters for the first time. His orders were brief and succinct:

1. Go ashore and get him a case of Scotch whisky.
2. While ashore, arrange for the off loading of the 1st ESB troops to the "Ben Mycree" for transport to Liverpool.

This meant arrange for several hundred men to spend one night on a huge two decker Irish Sea automobile ferry. Everyone must sleep on the deck.

Inasmuch as I had never before set foot in Belfast, I requested permission to take along someone who had been stationed near there before we had gone on the invasion of N. Africa. Two of my best friends, Captains Dave Moore and Les Kennedy had the necessary qualifications, had a sympathetic understanding of Col. Blimp's problem, could leave their companies to capable seconds in command, and, most important of all their qualifications, knew where to find the distillery of Teachers Scotch Whisky. I decided that Dave and Les were my men. We quickly departed the USS Dickman on one of the many small craft now plying the water between ship and Port Army Headquarters. I knew we had to go there first, to get the troop movement planning underway.

At Port Hq. we returning veterans of the Mediterranean were treated with visible deference. Many of us had three or more battle stars on our campaign ribbon and walked with a jaunty air. At Port Hq. they told me that transshipment of the 1st ESB to Liverpool via the "Ben Mycree" was a "Piece of Cake" (or words to that effect, I don't think they used the term "Piece of Cake"). Anyway, the U.S. Army Port Commander said in effect, "come back in three hours and watch us do our job". That seemed like a reasonable suggestion so we set out for Teachers.

Our cab soon arrived at the distillery. We entered a somewhat stately red brick office building which appeared to be about 300 years old and were directed into the Sales Office. There we found a couple of elderly men in three piece woolen suits in attendance and a middle aged lady who appeared to be a secretary to the men. This was not a retail outlet, nor had I been led to believe it was. When one bought whiskey for Col. Blimp, one dealt in cases; when Col. Blimp drank, he was usually alone. The lady approached me and I told her we were from the U.S. New Hampshire Light Infantry Regiment, up from the battles in the Mediterranean, that we would soon be celebrating a National Holiday, and that we were out to buy supplies for our Officers' mess.

She conferred with the two old gentlemen, and much to my surprise, she returned rather quickly and told me that it was OK. I'd like to say (59 years later) that they *gave* us the case of whiskey, but I do not want to get anybody into trouble with the Accounting Department back in Belfast at the Teachers Distillery.

There was a sort of a lounge attached to the sales office and our new friends insisted that we sit down in a booth and enjoy a little drink while we awaited the delivery of our "purchase". I was not a skilled tippler then, nor ever, but two "little drinks", that afternoon in Belfast sent me off to the docks to witness the off-loading of the 1st ESB. My buddies stayed at the distillery to have "one for the road" and then disappeared into the night. They were to bring the case of whiskey back to the USS Dickman. It took them about two weeks and almost the full case of Scotch to catch up with us again. I am confident that if they hadn't been such competent, outstanding, battle trained officers they would have been in serious trouble. More about Dave later.

When I arrived back at the docks the "Ben Mycree" and the "Dickman" were tied together out in the harbor and the off loading of the 1st ESB troops was under way. There was a wide portable gangplank with stout pipe side rails and canvas sidings spanning the short space between the two ships (shudder at this landlubber's description, you Ex -Sailors!!). Our troops were leaving the big ship, through a sally port (ha!) and entering onto the main deck of the ferry boat, the "Ben Mycree". It was about 6:00 PM, good old British Double Summer Time, and the troops had long since finished supper. NCO's had been designated as guides and gone over to the ferry boat ahead of their troops, who were now spreading out in a sort of orderly manner on the bare steel plate of the Automobile Deck (ferryboat floor). The off-loading, which was begun in the gloomy afternoon of a December day in Belfast Harbor was completed about an hour after dark and we cast off for Liverpool, on the other side of the Irish sea. A couple of thousand men on a small, unarmed ferry boat in the most successful year the German U-boat fleet experienced in WWII. Between the pitching of the boat, the hard steel "mattresses" and the anticipation of coming back to England (where the girls spoke English), I don't imagine that any of these valiant, battle-hardened veterans gave a hoot about the U-boats. As for this gopher, I had to sleep off my visit to the Teachers Distillery.

It was a sleepy, sloppy looking troop of Americn soldiers who got up to zero breakfast on the "Ben Mycree" anchored in the outer reaches of the Liverpool Harbor in the morning. The term "SNAFU" was created for occasions such as now existed: here was a British Ferry boat which had probably made the crossing between Belfast and Liverpool a thousand times, maybe ten thousand times, (it was a venerable-seeming tub); carrying representatives of Britain's staunchest ally, and we were sitting out in the harbor awaiting who knows what. Snafu, indeed!! It wasn't breakfast we were awaiting because there wasn't any. What we did for morning ablutions I do not remember, but for soldiers who have been in the field for over a year that wasn't a problem.

All things come to an end, and this was no exception. We finally pulled up to a railroad dock about ten o'clock that morning and immediately started to transfer to waiting passenger trains. Brigade Hq. was the first unit off of the ferry boat, and within ten or so steps I was on our train. I had been kind of avoiding Col. Blimp in the confusion, but now I ran into him and had to tell him that Les and Dave were in possession of our contraband and that he should look for them. He pouted a little but soon realized his plight. Their units had been assigned to a different train bound for a different destination. Our movement, as it had been since leaving Naples, was in the hands of the Army Transportation Corps; we were merely so many passengers being moved to where the War Department wanted us next.

As the train filled up, the British Red Cross showed up with huge baskets of sandwiches. A welcome treat indeed for all these red blooded, growing young soldiers who were used to eating at 5 o'clock in the morning. Alas, the British Red Cross should have talked to the American Red Cross, (or maybe the butchers union). Kidney Pie, apparently a British favorite in 1943, did not appeal to American soldiers unless they were genuinely starving. These were only ravenously hungry soldiers, not truly starving ones. There were many doors and windows open in these passenger cars and quick as a wink, the kidney pies ended up on the platform floors of the Liverpool station.

The train ride to our destination was uneventful. We detrained in St. Austell, Cornwall County for a truck ride to Truro in the same large county, and then two more miles to Pencalenick, a large brick manor house a few miles from the extreme southwest tip of Merrie England. This "Pencalenick" was, as we say today, "Something else", with at least 20 bedrooms, each with its own coal burning fireplace, a whole gaggle of bathrooms and bathtubs, all placed adjoining each other (probably as later additions); there were also a large ballroom, dining room and numerous unidentifiable nooks and crannies all over the place. On the second floor was a large library room which, as time passed, we kept under armed guard as a "top secret" room for planning, with large wall map and a sand table. Pencalenick was obviously an important estate which had been donated to (or seized by) the military for the duration. There were Nissan (Quonset) huts adequate for Headquarters Company's total enlisted roster; all in all, "we never had it so good." We never found out who owned Pencalenick nor the size of the grounds; but there were large formal gardens of ancient boxwood and camellia hedges bordering the house itself.

We had arrived at Pencalenick in time for a late breakfast. The 29th Infantry Division had been assigned responsibility for our reception and played hosts for us that first day (12-11-43). The U.S. Army had adapted the policy of assigning new arrivals to someone who was already on hand; so, even though we were not new to the UK, we had been away for over a year and were not familiar with this area. It was a great way to handle new arrivals. So, we walked into a clean, warm mansion and sat down to a hot breakfast of Army Class I rations, hot cakes, fresh eggs, canned grapefruit juice, and fried potatoes. The Maryland National Guard (29th Inf. Div.) may have been green when it came to combat landings (they were to be one of our first "customers" for the Amphibious Training School, starting later that month with Exercise "Duck I"; a one battalion affair near the town of Fowey on the nearby coast of the English Channel) but they proved their mettle at Omaha Beach on D-Day in Normandy the following June.

There followed six of the busiest months of our lives; drawing the equipment that we had left in the Mediterranean Theater of Operations, practicing the latest techniques in mine and booby trap removal, getting our mandatory "over strength" personnel on board, refining our own ideas of our jobs, and rehearsing, rehearsing, meeting, meeting—always, as usual, under the highest security classification: "TOP SECRET- BIGOT". For a couple of weeks in February we tried to obey a directive from 'higher up" to take Sundays off; but schedules were just too complicated, at least for the planners, to follow this well- meaning directive. We managed to find some relief, late in the evenings at the pubs or the movie house in Truro; but these were usually not available because we worked too late in the evenings. Our First ESB troops were scattered over Cornwall and parts of the adjoining Devonshire. The troops were billeted in British homes with British families in some cases, some were in Nissan Huts at first then tents, as weather warmed and the Island grew more crowded prior to the big event. My own travels on Brigade business took me to meetings in Paignton, Lands End, Exeter, Exmouth, Falmouth, and at least two dozen other towns in the southwest of England. Once I went overnight, with Colonel Caffey, (the "Old Man") to HQ, First Army, in Bristol, where I attended a meeting with, among others, General Bradley and Admiral Moon, (Commander of Navy Task Force U, for Utah Beach). The meeting was mostly about the upcoming "EXERCISE TIGER", the dress rehearsal for D-Day on UTAH Beach.

It was now late April 1944 and with the date of D-day set as June 5 and H-hour set, for Utah, as 0630 Hours (Greenwich Mean time) one could see that there was no time to spare. But first there needed to be a logistical exercise to test the timing of all of the events which had to dovetail to make operation "Overlord" work at all, regardless of what the Germans had in mind. Of primary importance was the height and timing of the tides at that specific date and time on that specific spot on the surface of the earth. Of course, tide tables of a sort had probably been at hand when the Normans, under William The Conqueror, came ashore in southwest England in 1066 A.D.,to defeat the Saxons in the historic Battle of Hastings; but this was 1944 A.D. and cross-channel invasion had become a bit more complicated in the interim. The tides were as important as ever; but now there was a night drop of several thousand paratroopers and glider troops to be taken into account, thus making the brightness of the moon very important; there were millions of significant underwater beach obstacles, erected by armies of slave laborers, to be disposed of; there were both naval and aerial bombardment to be completed just prior to H-hour when the first doughboys were to come in just as the water began to rise after low tide. There was no mock up of a German (enemy) force planned for this Exercise Tiger, it was complicated enough. It was just to synchronize the timing of the tasks which confronted the Americans on UTAH Beach. Do those things right and the problem with the German Army would be taken care of by our forces.

The whole planning effort was based upon those awesome 25-30 foot tides. The "Assault" Phase of the operation was considered to be the first 24 hours after H-hour, everything after that was considered "follow up". To simplify things a little bit, there were to be three distinct convoys of ships, starting with the First Tide Convoy at H-Hour followed by the Second Tide Convoy, scheduled approximately eleven and a half hours later, with the Third Tide Convoy following the Second by a similar interval. The S-3 (Operations) Staff of the First Engineer Special Brigade was in the First Tide Convoy of Exercise "TIGER", and had made our landings at Slapton Sands on the channel coast of England when disaster struck the Third Tide convoy, then afloat in the Channel.

I was safely ashore and asleep on the beach when the events took place, so I will fall back on my close friend, (then Captain) David D. Moore, who was "In the thick of it" to recount the details of the disaster, as he recalled them, years later, for the Brigade Historian, Howard DeVoe. (SEE APPENDIX B - TIGER)

We returned by truck to our base at Pencalenick the night of April 29, 1944, only vaguely aware that something BAD had happened in the channel. I knew that Major McGrann, my immediate superior had been dispatched to some town near Slapton Sands to help search for BIGOTED men among some drowning victims from the later convoys. So tight was the security that we never really learned the immensity of the tragedy until years later.

We assault units received the last of our mandatory overstrength from bases around the U.S. and elsewhere; some of ours had been in place for TIGER and had been in the Aleutian Islands in the Pacific War. My superior became Major Earl Paules, a regular army officer, Corps of Engineers. McGrann moved over to become Dump Operations Officer. Of course, with so much "high brass" being added, the Brigade staff soon outgrew our posh quarters in Pencalenick and we junior officers were moved into pyramidal tents in the yard - much as had happened in Sicily when we all got fleas from displacing a herd of goats (or pigs).

It was now early May, and we were experiencing a beautiful Spring. Truro is so close to the very southwest tip of England that it gets the full benefit of the Gulf Stream that makes it so warm in our state of Florida. It was no hardship to be moved to the yard at this time of year. One of our units, which I had to visit at this time, was stationed between Truro and Lands End, amidst the burned-out ruins of a large country estate. I have always fantasized that this was the estate that burned in the novel, "Rebecca" a very popular fictional work written by Daphne DuMaurier, an important writer of the period.

It was soon time to close out our "war room" at Pencalenick and, when assured by the Brigade Commander and all of the staff that they had their stuff safely secured, I was given the task of burning "everything else". I nearly managed to do *just that*—literally. In the war room there was a large wood-burning fireplace and we had used it often for warmth during the winter; now, with two sergeant clerk-typists assisting me, we began to pitch in the secret debris of six months of planning effort by about a dozen officers and soon we had a roaring fire. It was too "roaring!!" as a matter of fact, the inside of the chimney was afire! The three of us, veterans of three invasions and two years overseas, went into PANIC MODE. How in hell do you fight a fire in a chimney? All of a sudden, WHOOSH—THUMP!! and a huge ball of twigs and flame fell to the hearth! To add to my general knowledge of trivia, I had learned, as every British schoolboy probably already knew, that those big old chimney tops had been taken over by Storks as ideal for nest building. Fortunately, the fire then subsided and died out. No harm done to that lovely old mansion. All's well that ends well—I guess—but I was scared.

The following morning, bright and (much too) early for me, (I had been up very late the previous night) some trucks arrived to haul us on the next leg of our adventure. Years later, when I told my dear mother of this scene, (which I seldom did) she fairly screamed with laughter, as I knew she would, when I regaled her with the story of how I barely caught the tailgate of the departing truck, as I pulled on the last of my combat gear for the invasion of the European Continent.

We rode for a couple of hours in the trucks, finally winding up in a Nissan hut staging area near a hamlet called "Ivybridge" which was, I suppose, a suburb of the great naval base at Plymouth. We were informed by the Military Police, already on duty there, that this was a "sealed camp". Nobody could get in or out without permission. We of the operations staff lay around on our war gear the rest of the afternoon, mostly re-fighting the American Civil War. Many of the guys were from Clemson University, and loved to discuss that war. McGrann and I, being "Yankees" from Ohio enjoyed baiting them. Soon we ate evening chow in the mess hall, and now faced a long evening of full daylight (British Double Daylight Savings Time) on the eve of the biggest battle of our lives. We decided to give the security of the "sealed" camp a test, and walk into town to get a beer. Much to our surprise, about seven of us walked out the main gate, spent an hour or longer in a local pub, walked back into the "sealed" camp through the main gate, and never "heard a peep" out of any MPs. I am confident, even after all these years, that there was no harm done to "security". We were all too savvy and too scared to blab.

In the morning we started briefing those men who were not up to date on where we were going; when and how. There was also a letter from General Eisenhower to each soldier describing the "Great Crusade" upon which we were starting. I am sure you have seen it, or heard its words, at sometime in your life. We were all quite impressed. (See appendix.)

87

It was the morning of June 4, 1944—tomorrow was the day for which we had been brought overseas in August of '42; the day for which we had we had been prepping ever since. It was time to get on a boat and get going! Now however, some things arose to kill our patriotic fervor: first, after a short march to the boarding quay, we were routed over several LCIs all tied side by side to a Navy LCI our assigned craft, where the voice over the speaker system told us imperiously, "Stay between the lines!! All army personnel MUST stay between the lines" (They had set up stanchions with ropes between, much as the ushers did in movie houses). Who did they think they were yelling at? Didn't they recognize that we were battle hardened veterans?

We returned the snotty treatment by acting as green as possible about things nautical, "Where's the toilet, Sailor boy? Is it on the right or left side of the boat? Nearer the pointed end or the blunt end? Is it upstairs? and on—and on. We all knew that nothing grated the nerves of a kid, fresh out of boot camp, so much as calling a "deck" a "floor", etc., etc. I think that skipper became what Gilbert and Sullivan had in mind when they wrote the Operetta "HMS Pinafore"; ("......and now I am the ruler of the Queen's Naavee, etc, etc").. The other thing that dampened our fervor somewhat was THE WEATHER, though not obvious in the sheltered anchorage at Plymouth, it was beginning to look more and more ugly. Soon we put to sea, and joined a covey of other LCIs more or less holding station in the English Channel. Now we began to feel the swells and choppy waters of that small body, which for thousands of years had been Britain's first line of defense.

I was fortunate in that I never got seasick during the entire WWII, not once during all of the exercises etc., and this was no exception. I could never understand it. They always say, "Never look a Gift Horse in the mouth" and this time I didn't, but it got so rough out there that we finally found shelter in what I always assumed to be Falmouth Harbor, west of Plymouth Harbor. This was, as I've since learned many times via Television, a result of General Ike's famous agonizing decision to postpone D-day.

CHAPTER IX

THE CHANNEL—D-DAY—D + 1

Our LCI with its prissy skipper spent a comfortable night in the harbor tied up with the same bunch of LCIs which we had been with after boarding. There wasn't anything to do, there was not even room to play cards, what with the three-high hammocks so close together. I suppose that most of the troops just talked and slept to while away those otherwise anxious hours. We did not know that the weather would clear enough to go tomorrow or what was going to happen; but you knew somehow that it was out of your hands. I suppose we were given a couple of meals but I've long since forgotten them. I am sure they were eaten in or near your hammock, or out on deck if you could find room to sit, in the gloomy, stormy weather. Shortly after dark, as I recall it, we cast off and pulled out of the harbor. The sea did not seem to be any smoother but the storm did seem to be abating somewhat. The vast armada of ships of all sizes, what one could see of it in the gloom, drizzle, darkness and blackout, extended to the horizon in all directions. We were in some kind of a convoy formation and apparently on our way to start Ike's Grand Crusade. Along about midnight, some of us crowded out on deck to see, (rather, hear) the Air Corps taking in the troopers of the 82nd and 101st Airborne Divisions. We didn't see the troops, their parachutes, or the German flak sent up to greet them,—we were too far out in the channel; we could only know they were there and coming down among the Huns, hours ahead of us.

There was some light showing now from what had to be the coast of France; probably a burning building from all of the hullabaloo the paratroopers were stirring up. (It was without doubt the fire in the town of Saint Mere Eglise, depicted in the movie "The Longest Day", but we only knew it as a glow in the sky on the horizon.) It was time for the air bombardment of the beach front and the naval bombardment of the coastal defenses... so I returned to my hammock to see if I could get some sleep before it was time to debark. (Remember that I was almost 27 years old and had been through this sort of thing before—and, besides, there was nothing to see except flashes from distant explosions.)

89

My slumbers didn't last too long. I guess there was just too much going on. So I got up and ate whatever the galley was offering on this historic occasion, I do not remember what it was and it was not a good scene. Many of the soldiers were still seasick, the channel was still rough, and the decks were slippery with the upchuck of the boys who couldn't find space at the rail. The skipper must have lost his mind at this development, but he had to get rid of us before he could tidy up his boat. We were scheduled to arrive at Utah beach at 9:30 am or H plus three hours, and it was now about 7:00 am, so he had to tolerate us a little bit longer. Soon enough it was time for us to get going, and an LCM (Landing Craft Mechanized) pulled alongside to take us on the remainder of our journey. LCIs, such as we had been floating around on for the last two days, had long narrow ramps extending from the main deck down to the water line parallel to the axis of the ship, so that heavily laden troops did not have to struggle down a cargo net to a bobbing tub of a landing craft in such fashion as in the invasions of North Africa, and earlier. In the wars of today they all seem to be going in by helicopter…maybe drier but just as scary.

Our LCM had come alongside from a pool of LCMs circling in the channel nearby according to their plan; they had no doubt been hailed by semaphore from our LCI according to plan. The U.S. Navy really had this operation "down pat". With three other officers from the1st ESB S-3 staff along with eight Hq. Company enlisted men, I left the side ramp of our LCI and clamored aboard the LCM. Both craft were bobbing around in the (still) rough channel, so it was not a "piece of cake" to go from one to the other, loaded as we were with full combat gear, including life preservers. It was of course much more difficult for the infantrymen or engineer foot soldiers who carried all sorts of extras besides their full field gear—I think it was still a helluva lot better than climbing down a cargo net. I do not know how many other soldiers got into that LCM with our little band from Brigade Hq. Operations staff; must have been a total of fifty or more plus the LCM crew of two or three. Soon we cast free from the LCI and joined other loaded LCMs which now were just dawdling along forming a line parallel to the shoreline still several miles away.

All of a sudden, those LCM engines "revved up" to their highest speed, and though we had all heard that sound before in countless exercises and landings, it was still a heart stopping sound. It was "time to fish or cut bait" the moment we had trained for these many years. We were headed at full speed toward another "hostile shore" True, the Airborne troops had already been there for almost eight hours, and the first waves of foot soldiers had been there for at least two, but it was still pretty much unknown territory to us; due ashore at H + 3 hours. I was perched up on something where I could see the shore and with my field glasses could barely see some of our troops working on the beach; they were of course, from our 531st Shore Engineer Regiment, or the Navy UDTs (Frogmen), or the Navy Shore Party, or our 286th Joint Assault Signal Co., or one of the many Medical Units (including our own) or individuals from some other units who were "just passing through." You can rest assured they were not from the Fourth Infantry Division. Those superb troops were halfway to their D-day objectives, and going like the very devil. No wonder, the "old man", (Col. Caffey) always preached about the "organized confusion" of an assault beach, when indoctrinating newcomers to our Brigade.

As we drew to the shore, I could observe that Utah Beach was not exactly where it was supposed to be and was still under German artillery fire from both the North and South flanks, Steadily, but not too often I could see these shells exploding and blowing up plumes of sand from the busy beach scene. I tried to see as far as OMAHA beach but it was just too distant and around a corner of the shoreline. Knowing what we learned a few days later, I am just as glad that I could not see what was going on at OMAHA. In a short time our LCM grounded the bottom, backed off for another try, and grounded again. This time our very skilled LCM skipper yelled, "down ramp" and it was our turn to get to work doing our assigned D-day task: i.e., "To go ashore at H+3 Hours to establish our initial Brigade Command Post in the location previously selected." We jumped into waist deep, but smooth, cool water and began our long wade up that broad, flat UTAH beach. An occasional artillery round came whistling in from the south; while we were still wading, but we heard no small arms fire from that direction. We had beached at the extreme South end of Utah Beach Sector which now extended almost a mile beyond its original planned boundary. As we later learned, this was due to navigational errors, Germans, and strong tidal currents.

We could barely hear the chatter of small arms on the North flank where casemated artillery was to deny the Brigade the use of the north end of UTAH Sector for more than two weeks.

As we approached dry land, the water became more and more warm and shallow; the tide was of course running in. It seemed as though the German shelling became slightly more intense, (my imagination?), and twice I felt sand hitting my steel helmet as I "hit the deck" in anticipation of meeting "the Almighty". I didn't suffer any harm, however, as we apparently all made it safely to the high tide debris on the beach and turned North toward where we saw the rest of our army about a quarter of a mile away. As we drew closer we could see that a concertina enclosure of barbed wire already contained a couple of dozen POWs, a large gap had been blown in the sea wall and a couple of early tanks were passing through. The bulldozers were hard at work behind mine clearing teams in preparation for putting down more "Summerfelt Mat" to enlarge the embryo road system of Utah Beach, and there were Medics at work just below the sea wall near the gap.The Medics already had a few wounded lined up on stretchers and on foot, and you could see a few Plasma pouches hanging from rifle butts inverted, with bayonets buried in the sand. It was indeed a scene of "orderly confusion".

When we got to the gap in the wall, we went through it into France. The infantry was a couple of miles ahead of us, so we were not exactly pioneers. We were now behind the sea wall exactly where we wanted to be, so we proceeded southward a few hundred yards to the only existing exit road from behind Utah Beach, along which a few vehicles had already passed headed inland. Perhaps 300 yards inland from where we were at this time, we could see a few trees growing beside a dry stream bed and that was the spot previously selected for our first Command Post in la belle France. By now, I was aware that two men were missing from our little band of twelve: Captain "Shug" Jordan and Private First Class Leonce Sonnier; but before looking for the two, we had to reach our objective; maybe they were already there.

We went up that dirt road to the clump of trees where we planned to erect a couple of small wall tents among the trees and stake out parking space for vehicles in the clearing on the seaward side of the CP. The whole area was posted with the familiar Boche signs

"ACHTUNG MINEN" with the terrifying Skull and Crossbones we had seen so often in Sicily and Italy. Although most of our engineer casualties were due to land mines and booby traps, I still knew that the Germans used these signs very profusely for psychological warfare purposes, even when they had neither the time nor the mines in sufficient quantities to create a minefield. But why take a chance? We *HAD* to probe that area. So we formed a line, ten abreast and (mostly with mess kit knives) started to probe that sandy soil, just as we had been taught to do in basic Engineer training school at Ft. Belvoir. Before long, somebody from one of the engineer units on the beach saw our pitiful endeavors, and taking mercy upon us, sent a couple of guys with mine detectors to sweep the area for us.

Meanwhile, I had gone off in search of my good buddy, Capt. Jordan, whom I last remembered seeing somewhere during our northbound journey up the "Uncle Red Beach" about where the POWs were incarcerated. Sure enough, I found him, sitting on the sand, smoking a cigarette and leaning against the sea wall. "Shug" had had a narrow one with the artillery fire from the south, and had escaped with "only" a piece of shrapnel in his upper arm. The nearby Medics had cut out the shrapnel, bandaged his wound, and turned him loose. He seemed to be in a mild state of shock and willingly accepted my advice to "get the hell off of the beach" where most of the, now spasmodic, enemy fire was coming in, and walk with my help to the Brigade CP—such as it was.

We never did find Pfc. Leonce Sonnier, orderly to the Brigade Commander. Although I had a couple of my men look for him all over the Uncle Red Beach Area where we had come in to UTAH. They also checked out Col. Caffey's personal quarters in a huge enemy gun emplacement in the center of our beach front, which the Colonel had put "his dibs on" shortly after he landed at H-hour. They didn't find a trace of Pfc. Leonce Sonnier, or his body and it was finally ruled after many weeks that he must have taken a direct hit by one of those large caliber artillery shells which fell among us as we crossed the beach that first time. There is a road named for him in the UTAH sector. There are a number of roads in that sector named for the Brigade KIA marked on permanent replicas of the 1st Engineer Special Brigade shoulder patch. Incidentally, atop that gun emplacement was where we of the Brigade erected the Obelisk monument "To our Honored Dead" before we departed UTAH for the Pacific Theater in December 1944. After the war the French made a D-day museum out of the cellar of the emplacement, gradually, over the years, other major D-Day units have built monuments nearby, and finally, on the 50th anniversary of D-day, 6-6-94, President William Jefferson Clinton and his entourage of some 1500 Washington, D.C. bureaucrats, now that the smoke of battle had safely cleared, came and gave a speech. It probably will not rank with President Lincoln's short address at the Gettysburg battle field; but perhaps President Clinton had an overly busy speech writer.

Later in the afternoon of D-day, Major McGrann, my good buddy and immediate superior, came riding along in a jeep. After giving our start-up Command Post the once over, said "Let's go inspect UTAH beach". I couldn't have been more surprised if he had ridden up on a dragon, (very few vehicles were ashore for staff officers on that day, and Jack was only a Major). I asked no questions, just got into the jeep and off we went. As we proceeded to the north of Uncle Red, we saw that our Engineers on Tare Green beach were progressing similar to those working Uncle Red. Each of the beaches had been seized by a regiment of the magnificent 4th Infantry Division and a battalion of our 531st Engineers had landed with them to hold and develop the beach to receive and transship countless reinforcements and supplies over the coming months or until the major channel ports could be captured and made operational. When we arrived at the northern end of the UTAH area, we could see that only a small portion of what was intended to be Roger White Beach was being worked by the 531st Engineers. A heavy caliber German artillery piece, amply protected by many tons of reinforced concrete, and mounted on a carriage which allowed it to be withdrawn from sight, while closing concrete doors in front of it, commanded an almost perfect view of what was destined to become Roger White Beach. The Navy had been firing at this large gun intermittently since early morning, but so far, the only way to keep it silent was to try to keep a Navy observation spotter plane buzzing around in the sky above it. The foot troops of the 4th Division had properly by-passed it as they drove ahead to link up with our paratroopers. The gun could only traverse so far toward the south being limited by it's concrete embrasure (or window frame). Our troops had quickly discovered the limits of its traverse and had those limits well marked. The gun went down in our brigade history as the one at St. Marcouf and it was a thorn in our side for many days. Some one of the assault units, (maybe a defense platoon of our 531st Engrs), had stationed a .50 caliber machine gun near the embrasure to fire when the doors were open, but so far as I knew it could not keep the behemoth out of action.

Major McGrann and I were driving back toward our CP when we heard the drone of a large flight of low flying planes coming in from the channel, some were towing gliders, it was the follow-up waves of the 82nd and 101st Airborne Divisions. What followed was one of the most inspiring sights anyone could ever hope to see: there, almost in our laps, the gliders cut loose from their tow planes and the paratroopers began to exit their transport planes. They were all coming in very slowly at what seemed only treetop height, and only about six miles distant; it was such an awesome scene that it made one almost feel sorry for the Huns. These troops were coming in around the village of Ste Mere Eglise, which was less than five miles, as the crow flies, from where Jack and I were peacefully observing them from our jeep. That thrilling scene of the reinforcements for the two airborne divisions probably brought another twelve or fifteen thousand fighting men into the fray on our side in one fell swoop. It was inestimably warming despite the hours-old rumors starting to trickle in from the OMAHA area, where, unbeknown to us on UTAH, the battle had been "touch and go" until early afternoon of that "longest day".

It was now getting on toward dusk, or about 10 PM in those latitudes at that time of year, and I had nothing else to do so I decided to turn in for the night. *Where* to sleep had not entered my mind up till now and that was easily solved. A 90 mm American Antiaircraft battery had set up, close to our CP to defend the area against the German Luftwaffe (which didn't put on a significant show all day, or ever for that matter). As we enlarged the beachhead, the Ack Ack troops went farther inland to a more commanding location, thus giving up their newly-dug gun emplacement. Bedtime! I spread out my poncho, rolled up in my blanket and was soon in dreamland.

Loud Bang! Loud Bang! Loud Bang! Drone—drone—drone. Pretty soon I was aroused from my slumbers by what was to become an almost nightly occurrence, a German air raid. A couple of their medium bombers would slip in after our air cover had retired for the day, drop several so-called "chandelier flares" to light things up brighter than daylight, drop a couple of bombs to make certain we were all awake, and depart. Meanwhile our Anti Aircraft people had picked them up on radar, had turned on their powerful searchlights and commenced firing at them. A recipe guaranteed to *create* insomnia if not to cure it. The troops working the Cargo Transfer Points on the beaches continued their work straight through the night, Luftwaffe or not. This leads me to a brief description of a "Transfer Point" and our "amphibious operations" in general.

After the assault waves had created some sort of a beachhead, if there was not a major port soon available with massive facilities for unloading all kinds of cargo in huge quantities from large seagoing ships, it was necessary to create such facilities right on the only ground you then held: the assault beach itself. Soon after Pearl Harbor, when the need for Amphibious Warfare had become apparent, the Army and the Navy got together with the British and came up with a rationale for conducting same. (I am confident their War Colleges had pretty much worked out the basics many times between the wars). To make a long story short, there were a number of water craft invented and manufactured to solve this sort of problem for WWII: LST or Landing Ship Tank was the largest of the shallow draft vessels. It had a pair of bow doors which opened horizontally to drop a short ramp for disgorging vehicles from the main, or tank deck. It also had a top deck to carry a number of vehicles as large as the standard 2-1/2 ton variety. Early in the war the LST had a ramp leading to the bow ramp to unload top deck vehicles when the bow was open. Later versions had an elevator for vehicles between the decks and behind the bow doors.

LSTs in the Normandy invasion normally grounded themselves about an hour or more after high tide, "dried out" as the 25 foot tides ebbed out, meanwhile having opened their bow doors and gradually lowered their ramp to the beach where the awaiting army engineer bulldozer had tidied up the sand to give the ramp ample backing. That gave the skipper about ten hours to unload and get his ship off of the bottom as the tide made its rounds to low and back to high tide again. When his cargo was mobile, as troops and vehicles, he could, with any luck at all, unload quickly, take on a load of wounded or prisoners (or occasionally, civilian refugees) and still be sitting there on the bottom as the next tide came in to float his big boat free. When his cargo had to be manhandled onto vehicles, like ammunition for example, it might take more than one, or even two, full tides to get off of the beach. It was better than the old ways, but definitely not easy unless you also had good luck.

LCTs (Landing Craft, Tank) was the next craft down from an LST and were of much shallower draft. They typically hauled 2 or 3 trucks, and a few smaller vehicles, or bulldozers. They could most handily beach at or near low tide, drop their one big bow door/ramp, and be free of the bottom as they became lighter or caught the tide. If beached too close to high tide, broached, or otherwise fouled up in unloading they could become a problem.. Our 531st Engineer Shore Regiment and the assault troops in general always counted upon their very early arrival, bearing the indefatigable D-7 bulldozers pulling sled loads of road making supplies, etc.

LCMs (Landing Craft, Mechanized) was a much smaller version of the LCT. Originally designed to haul one M-3 Medium Tank or one 2-1/2 Ton Truck, it was, so far as I know, never used to transport vehicles much bigger than a jeep or a weapons carrier, after the N. African landings. The LCM was ideal for hauling assault troops with their heavy gear, and for very short-haul "end run" amphibious landings around mountainous road gaps (ala Patton on the Sicilian north coast).

LCVPs (Landing Craft, Vehicle/Personnel) were the famous "Higgins Boats" made famous by a tribute from General Eisenhower after the end of the war; there were thousands manufactured and were used by all the armed services for all kinds of tasks in both theaters. Many large seagoing ships carried LCVPs on their davits as lifeboats, which were lowered with a crew of one and loaded with troops climbing down cargo nets or "sallying forth" from Sallie Ports as the transport drew near the hostile (or otherwise) shore. LCI (Landing Craft, Infantry) was described earlier in this book. Numerous other craft were invented and used by the Navy and Marines in WWII, the foregoing were the principal ones in the European Theater. I'll take up the famous AMTRAC of the United States Marines when our Brigade gets to the Pacific and we finally meet some "Leathernecks".

To get back to Normandy: the "Transfer Point" was the center of activity on every beach. At this location all of the supplies being landed for later distribution were sorted into general categories and moved off of the beach to dumps or depots. At first the engineers did it all, but as soon as possible, specialized troops operated the dumps and depots. All troops were supposed to land with three days emergency rations in their personal field packs and the prescribed ammunition supply for their weapon. Troop units carried all sorts of supplies in prescribed quantities in their organic vehicles. Some of the ships in the assault convoy carried a little cargo, some were fully loaded with Ammo or Gasoline in Cans; all of which had to be sorted and dispatched to the right storage place for issue as needed. Cargo was unloaded in the holds of ocean going ships into cargo nets by either Engineers or Port troops. The nets were then hoisted from the hold, swung over the side and lowered into a DUKW (Floating 2-1/2 ton truck) idling alongside the cargo ship under the control of the DUKW driver. He then took off and headed for the Transfer Point on the beach. Reaching the beach he drove his DUKW to one side of the long platform which was itself the Transfer Point. Now a crane on the Transfer Point platform plucked the loaded cargo net from the Dukw, and depending upon whether or not the load needed sorting into the classes designated by the dumps, either landed the load on the platform for attention or, as was much to be preferred, merely swung it across the platform to a waiting, land-bound (regular) truck which whisked it away to its proper destination. The foregoing is a description of a perfect sequence on a smooth ocean, in a mature situation. It was frequently less simple. By the way, WHY the army didn't just call those floating beauties, "Ducks", always seemed to be a tribute to "Supercilious Stuffiness" to this poor dumb engineer. There were many other ways in which supplies were brought ashore in the war. Occasionally, the sorting was done by POWs on the platform under guard. This is not meant to be a treatise on that subject; it is only included to illustrate one method. Now, back to UTAH beach.

Very early in the morning of D+1 (June 7, 1944) I was awakened in my inherited foxhole by the CLACKETY - CLACKETY - CLACKETY - ETC., ETC. of a hand powered POISON GAS ALARM (A government issue, version of a common Halloween toy of that era which, when properly spun by a quick, strong forearm, was guaranteed to "wake up the DEAD"). It was in the hands of the young 2nd Lieutenant of the 90th Infantry Division who was on temporary duty as Liaison Officer to our Brigade. (The 90th Division, which was the follow up to the 4th Infantry Division in the assault phase on UTAH, was to become one of the truly outstanding units of the army as the war in Europe progressed). It turned out to be a false alarm, (we had one on every invasion we made). We quickly managed to put together the explanation, as follows: some American Fighter Planes returning from an early morning raid on the enemy, flew low over Utah beach on their return to their British base. At least one of them properly cast loose (jettisoned) his spare fuel tank into the nearby English channel. Someone on our beach yelled, "What is dropping?." Some more knowledgeable soldier yelled something like "Only gas tanks" to which somebody, more nervous, responded, "GAS?" and we were "off to the races". That scare was over almost before it began, but it got us all on our feet very early on D+1.

It was either on D-Day or D+1 that one of my most outstanding contacts of the war was made. I'm sorry I cannot pin it down any closer, but that's the way it is. I was alone in our CP, a small wall tent, when General Omar Bradley, Commander of all American ground forces in the Normandy invasion, came to the door of the tent, where I saluted him and volunteered to help him. The General replied that one of the transport ships carrying a battalion of 9th Infantry Division troops had been torpedoed in the Channel off of OMAHA, and that the men were coming ashore wet and without weapons, from Dukws, landing craft or even swimming, and that we of Utah should set up drop-off points at the beach exits to collect small arms and ammo from troops leaving Utah, with an excess of same. I saluted, saying that I would take care of it, and he was back in his jeep and gone. Although I had seen him many times in Sicily and in England prior to Normandy, I never saw him again. I sent a runner to Hq 531st Engrs stating his orders, and heard no more about it. We in Brigade Hq had no authority over anybody until D+3.

Later that morning, as we were just beginning to get our wits together, the Luftwaffe put in one of its very rare daytime appearances, as a fighter plane came roaring down the beach,

99

machine guns blazing, at treetop elevation. We all jumped for our foxholes at the same time and I arrived at mine a split second later than the officer with whom I had been conferring; our new S-3, Lt. Col. Elzie K. Moore who had joined us from the Engineer Replacement Depot as part of the required over-strength prior to D-Day. Col. Moore was the unlucky one, all 140 pounds of Captain Sam landed on top of one of his ankles, which despite the protection of the Colonel's paratroop boots, was broken in the collision. My right ankle was the lucky one, getting off with only a sprain. The German pilot was even luckier, escaping unscathed. Somehow, someone took Col. Moore to an aid station on the beach where they took no chances and put a cast on it. He returned to duty, with a pair of crutches and a new Purple Heart Medal issued on the spot. Later that morning my ankle began to swell and my boot became so tight that one of our guys had to slit it above the swelling to get the boot off of my leg. Once the boot was off, "Shug"Jordan, our "star" athlete, wrapped my ankle tightly and skillfully and forced the slitted boot back onto my foot to reinforce his work. I neither wanted, nor was offered a Purple Heart for my suffering. I had the superstitious belief that if you got a Purple Heart without *actually being wounded by the enemy,* then you had a more severe wound coming to you sooner or later.

The big German Coastal gun at San Marcouf was firing with regularity on D+1 and the machine gun which always seemed to fire whenever the big gun did, was chattering away as if to add to the Symphony. After several days of this, even though we knew fairly precisely the limits of its southward traverse, we had all had our fill of that kind of music. Lt. Col. Moore made a classic pronouncement, heard by many of those in Brigade Headquarters who were present at the time. Shaking one crutch in the direction of the big gun, he loudly declared, "If I were a younger man, I'd go get that Son of a Bitch myself!". When one considers that, at least one U.S. Navy *Battleship* had been trying for several days to accomplish just that, it was indeed a gem of a pronouncement. It set the tone for our acceptance of Col. Moore's contributions from that time forward. He was a hard worker, however, and did his best.

One day, early after D-Day, when there was still enemy activity to consider, I observed a bunch of what I assumed to be Norman farm women sitting on the far side of the ditch along the main exit road

100

from Utah. They were dressed like the European peasant women we see in so many oil paintings of farm scenes from the "old country ". They were under control of a 4th Division MP and aroused my curiosity enough that I stopped and asked him, "What is going on?". His reply, to the effect that they were Russians being evacuated from the battle zone to LSTs at UTAH and to England was a new one for me. We learn something new every day, even in the battle zone. Incidentally the billowing skirts of the women were piled high with the hard candy components of army C-rations tossed there by American doughboys as they trotted away from Utah beach in pursuit of the Germans. A few of the women had small children or babies in tow. During our half year sojourn on Utah beach I talked to several LST Captains who told of hauling Russian women back to England from our beach, and they invariably mentioned how the ship fairly reeked of cheap perfume for several cross channel trips thereafter. I read after the war that many Russian women had been sent to countries occupied by the Nazi army to serve as slave labor in various capacities.

One day in April 1944, during the detailed planning for OVERLORD, Col. Adams had told me of the plans to create artificial breakwaters off of Utah and Omaha beaches as well as some even more complicated schemes for the British and Canadian beaches. The one off Utah was code named "Gooseberry" and the one off Omaha was coded "Mulberry". Our "Gooseberry" was to consist of a number of old freighters lined up, parallel to the shoreline, bow to stern, and scuttled to sit on the ocean floor. They were to be at a depth which afforded maximum shelter to landing craft during bad weather. I have forgotten how many ships were to be scuttled, but I seem to recall the quantity, seven. When Col. Adams assigned the layout of this "Gooseberry" to me, I willingly accepted it, despite the fact that as an Ohioan I had never even *SEEN the ocean* prior to my one day assignment at Camp Edwards, Massachusetts; nor had I any combat experience with tides beyond that of the Sicilian Campaign in the Mediterranean. There the difference between high and low tides was usually less than one foot. Alas! Someone had to do the layout, and it might as well be me! So, one April day in 1944, I reasoned that the Gooseberry might as well be placed off TARE GREEN beach, our projected middle one and a few yards inside the low tide line on that very flat beach in that channel of 25 to 30 foot tides. I talked it over with Col. Adams and then gave a simple sketch to Sgt. Valentine, our map draftsman to make another overlay for the map of Utah which we were finalizing.

Now it was D+3 and the Navy beachmaster informed us, by field telephone that the first old ship of our "Gooseberry" was at anchor off Uncle Red and that we had better give the skipper some instructions lest it sink in the anchorage where it sat. Major Paules (or I) sent Lt. Tom Pearsoll, (a Connecticut Yankee on the Beach Operations Staff) with a map and the overlay to get a DUKW and go relieve the anxious skipper. Tom took over the job and, over the next few days put together our "Gooseberry". Whether it was worthwhile or not, I never could make up my mind, maybe some reader could straighten me out on that point. Although Tom had put it where it was supposed to be according to the map, the huge storm of June 19-22, 1944 managed to push a couple of the ships out of line. On June 22nd the port of Cherbourg was captured but it was essentially useless as a seaport; the Germans had it completely blocked with scuttled ships.

One activity to which I became addicted on Utah beach was to be at the dune line on the main exit road when some POWs were being delivered for evacuation to England from the battlegrounds inland. The contour of the land was such that a person on foot couldn't see the ocean until he reached the crest of the dunes. In those earliest days I would occasionally spot a little band of enemy soldiers being marched to the beach for evacuation to prison camps in England or to the USA. This, please remember, was at a point in history when the German Army had only started to lose a few battles and Hitler (plus Goebbels) had them all brainwashed on the subject of Aryan Supremacy. Whenever possible, I would hot-foot it over to the top of the dunes and watch the prisoners faces as they saw that massive horizon-to-horizon expanse of large ships in the channel ahead of them. The more formidable classes of troops, like the incredibly cocky SS of which we were now bagging a few, usually showed the greatest shock. They had believed the German U-boats had put most allied shipping to the bottom of the sea; yet here was evidence that their revered leader had told them a big lie. This addiction may have uncovered a hidden sadistic streak in my brain, but I really got pleasure from their shock.

CHAPTER X

SIX MONTHS ON UTAH BEACH

One thing that seemed to happen every time a new front was opened, was that at least one U.S.Air Force plane was shot down by American troops; and Normandy was no exception. I guess it was about D+3 when the troops on Utah managed to bag theirs. We never knew who was guilty, maybe it was the even the Germans who started the whole thing; but I was driving down the lateral beach road between Uncle Red and Tare Green beaches with my driver, when a trickle of small arms anti-aircraft fire erupted. As always, with so many green troops in the beachhead, the trickle almost immediately became a torrent, and an American P-51 Mustang very quickly began to tumble from the sky. By this time half of the troops on the ground were firing and half were trying to stop them from firing. The pilot bailed out of his doomed ship, his parachute blossomed forth, and, as I am ashamed to relate, even to this day, some of the "trigger happy" ground troops continued firing. Fortunately for the pilot, the marksmanship of the men who were still trying to shoot him, was as bad as their judgment and he landed safely in a nearby field. I was among the first to reach him as he unfastened his chute, and as I apologized for his rude introduction to UTAH, this tall, blondish, Texas cowboy type, merely said, very coolly, "They were shooting at me". I invited him to ride in my jeep and took him to Brigade Headquarters where our Brigade Surgeon, Dr. Ted Kozalka, gave him the once over. The Doctor found one place where apparently a small caliber bullet had grazed his skull, removing a small streak of blonde hair, but finding him otherwise OK. He was thenceforth turned loose to get home on his own. I guess maybe we offered him transportation back to Britain via LST and maybe even a drink of water. I've forgotten his name, if I ever heard it. That was one cool guy.

As the battle for Normandy wore on and more and more troops were packed into the Cherbourg Peninsula and more and more supplies were unloaded, it was time, according to plan, to enlarge the area of Brigade operations; so Brigade Headquarters moved into an apple orchard on the outskirts of Ste. Mere Eglise, abandoning the spot we had selected on D-Day. Our Beach Operations Section stayed near the beach but more central to all three beaches. We moved into an abandoned farmhouse behind the center beach, Tare Green. This large farmhouse, had two stories with two big rooms on each floor. There was a center staircase, a huge fireplace in what was probably the original cooking/dining room, and an attached garage which had originally served as a stable. The only excuses for plumbing were an outside privy and an outside hand pumped well, neither of which we used; preferring an army supplied version for both necessities. We got our rations from one of the companies of the Brigade's own 261st Medical Battalion, who put up a separate little mess tent for our eight officer staff, consisting of Majors Paules and Kellogg, Captains Weir and myself, and Lieutenants Elias, Moore (Wm J.), Pearsoll, and one more whose name escapes after 57 years. We were a 24 x7 operation to use today's vernacular. We also had, in due course, two representatives of the U.S. Maritime Commission whose job it was to settle any labor problems which arose among merchant seamen floating off our beaches. (These two very interesting older men were both retired merchant Captains who had come back to the sea to help win the war. I suppose that similar officials were also assigned to Omaha, Juno, Gold and Sword beaches. Our enlisted staff, which was comprised of clerk-typists, jeep drivers and a couple of table waiters/orderlies, ate in the Medical Company Mess. We all slept in our own foxholes scattered around the farmhouse which was situated at a tee in the main road off of Tare Green and the main lateral beach road which ran behind all of the Utah beaches and a tiny crossroads hamlet named Saint Marie Dumont.

I, as usual, found a clean unoccupied fox hole right in the small front yard of our new Beach Operations office and moved in. All went well for the first couple of nights, and then I made a discovery I never forgot, "Never put your foxhole near a tee in a road net; especially near a beach where they can unload tanks at night". This third night in my newly found foxhole turned out to be a hellish one. I would just get to dreamland when a Sherman tank, fresh off an LST and heading to his assembly area, would come roaring up the road from Tare Green and make a sudden 90 degree turn about 10 yards short of where I was sleeping in mother earth. What with all the dust they extracted from those primitive beach roads, one could hardly see a tank anyhow, and under blackout conditions it was even difficult to see the MP's flashlight supposedly guiding the tank driver. I moved my bedroll to the backyard rear of the farmhouse before dawn. We were now working very long hours trying to get a handle on what had been unloaded, what had been sunk, what was waiting to be unloaded, where the various ships were anchored, what was most needed ashore, what was arriving in the anchorage, what troops were urgently needed ashore, what troops should be held back for later unloading, and etc., etc.. To get answers to any such questions and many more; we needed all of those people I just listed, and then some. The 531st Engineers working the beaches probably had an equal number of men working on the same and similar questions. It was truly "organized confusion" for those first few days, and yet the staffs at higher headquarters had to get all kinds of information in order to plan and fight the next phases of the war. We frequently had to send a staff officer out in a Dukw to get some info. One of our enlisted men put all of the essential information into a formal daily Situation Report known as the "Sitrep", he was S/Sgt. John J. McMahon, Jr. of Brooklyn who earned a Bronze Star Medal for pulling all this together night after night in Normandy (and later in Okinawa).

My move to a foxhole behind the farmhouse was to prove fortunate. As the beaches became better organized, I did the same. First I erected my pup tent over the foxhole, using a second shelter half from Brigade Supply Truck to make a complete tent. Then I put a timber half-roof over the fox hole under the tent and covered it with a couple of layers of sandbags. Thus I had place under the tent to keep my things out of the way and dry, and a reasonably safe place to sleep under my tent and sandbags during the almost nightly German nuisance air raids. At some point during the following month or so, Colonel Caffey our Brigade Commander disappeared. Rumor was that he was in Hawaii, participating as a Defense Attorney in the trials of Admiral Kimmel and General Short. He returned to the Brigade after a few weeks absence. I believe he left Colonel Adams in charge while he was absent.

Before long the 82nd and 101st Airborne Divisions had to be sent back to England where they became more of a potential threat to the German High Command. Colonel Adams assigned me the task of coordinating their off-loading over our beaches and it might have been the easiest job I had during the entire WWII. In the first place these were proud, well disciplined troops returning to a welcoming country after having accomplished a difficult mission. Secondly, they were all in nearby staging areas and a constant stream of LSTs was being discharged daily and available to transport them back to the channel ports where they would find well organized U.S. and English forces to get them back to their familiar pre-D-day bases. It was a "piece of cake". I had Colonel Caffey's Aide, Lt. "Rosie" Charles get two bottles of good Cognac for me. Next, I gave one bottle to each of the Captains who had been assigned by the Airborne Division Commanders to work with me in moving out their respective units. The three of us then found a comfortable spot in the sand dunes from which we could observe the LSTs being loaded with troops and the two airborne outload-coordinators could start planning their next loads one tide hence, as the bow doors closed on the current shipment. It all went so smoothly that Colonel Caffey later received a formal Citation from Major General Matthew Ridgeway, which our Colonel bucked down to me stating, in writing, "To you goes the major portion of the credit". (Really it was the Cognac)!

Having mentioned Lt. "Rosie" Charles, it is probably worthwhile to digress from our tale right here to tell you a little bit about "Rosie" with whom I was often in contact between late Sicily(9-43) and late Normandy (11-44). "Rosie", whose given name was Rosalind, was the only child of a country Doctor, practicing in a small backwoods town in the deep, deep south. The doctor's wife had probably wanted her firstborn to be a girl, so when her baby was born a boy, he had been christened with the feminine name which he carried through life. That was a fairly common custom in the deep south and might have been the reason why "Rosie" went to extremes to prove his masculinity. (In my lifetime I have also known a "Lila" and a couple of guys named "Evalyn" who also seemed to have similar "identity problems". My first awareness of Lt. Charles came in December 1942 when we were fairly new to the scene in N. Africa and very definitely new to having the entire First Engineer Amphibian Brigade all stationed in the same general area. I read on the Brigade Headquarters' bulletin board one morning a notice, required by Army Regulations to the effect that "Lt. Rosalind H. Charles, having been placed under arrest by Civilian Authorities of the City of Oran on

Charges of Public Drunkenness, Disturbing the Peace and Reckless Driving, had been turned over to the Brigade Provost Martial and that upon investigation, additional charges of Removing a Jeep from his Company Motor Pool without Proper Authority and Wrecking a Government Vehicle had subsequently been added and that the aforesaid Lt. Charles was to be tried by Courts Martial" etc., etc., I think it said that Lt. Charles was currently assigned to one of the line Companies of the 531st Engr. Shore Regiment.

Time went by and I didn't think about it again until one day the following spring after Colonel Wolfe had been relieved by Colonel Caffey as Brigade Commander and a Lt. Rosie Charles showed up at our Officers' Mess (still in Arzew, Algeria). Turns out he had been acquitted of all charges (the army needed Second Looeys, I guess); had been reassigned to Brigade Headquarters and was serving as Colonel Caffey's Aide de Camp (general flunky). Most of us supposed that "the old man" was going to try to "save this poor lost soul". In the next couple of months we all took a sort of a liking to Rosie. It seems that he had been trained in Army Flight Schools to be a fighter pilot, had earned his "Wings" but was forced to give them up when he ruptured both of his ear drums doing some absolutely forbidden stunt flying while waiting to graduate from flight school. He usually cupped a hand over his ear when conversing with one and he had some papers to prove his Air Corps background in case you doubted his word. He was transferred to the Corps of Engineers. Rosie was a drinker. His indulgent mother would occasionally mail him a small bottle of Southern Comfort or Anisette in a hollowed out fruit cake and he never passed up an opportunity for a drink of whatever anybody had to offer. One thing we disliked and found hard to believe about Rosie was when he boasted of his extreme hatred for black people. I heard him state that when he was in High School he and a gang of his friends would get a few drinks on a Saturday night and go driving around throwing lighted sticks of dynamite at the shanties of sharecroppers in the countryside. Rosie was a slender, redhead with a pleasant face and a beguiling smile. He always carried a switchblade knife in each pants pocket and could produce them instantly to demonstrate his invulnerability, although I never heard of him actually using them or threatening anybody. He frequently whetted his switchblades on the sides of his boots, which were polished to perfection. While we were encamped near Palermo, Rosie acquired a large leather bullwhip which fascinated him for a couple of weeks; so he rode around the city in the rear seat of a jeep brandishing the bullwhip and, otherwise drawing the attention of people on the streets. I wasn't around Rosie much of the time but only heard of his exploits from him or others at the Brigade Officers Mess.

One anecdote that brings out the "true Rosie", I piece together like this: About two weeks after D-day in Normandy there was a bad storm in the Atlantic Ocean and the Channel. It forced us to suspend operations on Utah Beach and caused considerable damage to the whole scene. Among the many items which were messed up in the allies shipping schedules was the loss at sea of three large rafts being towed by tugboats from ports in England to the Operation Overlord beachhead. These rafts were made up of a bunch of thirty inch cubical welded steel plate containers. These containers floated high in the water and had valves for admitting sea water so that they could be partially submerged in shallow water off the beach to form an artificial reef or quay and were used to build the artificial harbors at Omaha Beach and the British beaches. Only in the case of the three rafts lost in the storm, the containers were filled with *nitroglycerin*, a highly explosive, highly sensitive liquid to be used by army engineers in special demolition's work. Even while the storm still raged in the Atlantic Ocean and the English Channel, both the British and the U.S. Navies conducted an urgent search for these three lost rafts, and as I understood at the time, found and blew up two of the three somewhere off the coast of France. The search for the third raft became almost frantic until finally someone "higher up" must have decided to quit. The storm occurred late in June and along about October, as the allied armies were approaching Germany, someone, somehow discovered the missing raft. It was grounded in the reedy, marshy flat mouth of the Orne River between Omaha and Utah beaches, far above the high tide line of the normal tides. The ever faithful 531st Engineers very quickly built a road into the marsh so that the ever faithful GMC 6x6 trucks could get to the raft and with the help of some very brave demolition's experts, were proceeding to siphon off the *nitroglycerin* into five gallon gasoline cans for shipment to the forward Depots for Engineer Supplies. Meanwhile the rampaging allied armies were considering the coming assault on the famous German Siegfried Line and wanted a supply of *Nitroglycerin* to use on the formidable array of concrete obstacles which the ingenious Huns had built into that long fortification. Enter the heroic Lt. Rosie Charles: A convoy of about eight GMC trucks, each with a relief driver, was formed to go "Red Ball Freight" to the forward depot near the Siegfried line. Rosie volunteered as convoy commander. As Rosie told me about it later; after a lot of hard driving, he pulled the convoy off on the edge of a small city to give the truck drivers a rest before crossing the crowded city. Early the following morning he telephoned the local (U.S. Army) Provost Marshal and asked for a Police escort to help his convoy get through the crowded city streets. The Captain with whom he spoke, barked back "Lieutenant, we've got all kinds of traffic problems in these narrow streets, without being bothered with YOUR piddling eight truck convoy, just HIT the road and get your ass through here as best you can". Rosie's response:"Captain Sir, maybe you'd like to know what we're hauling in our *piddling eight truck convoy?"* To the Provost Marshal's impatient response, Rosie told me it seemed like only seconds passed after he said the magic word, *"nitroglycerin"* and the sound of the MP's sirens was heard out on the road with his convoy.

My last contact with Rosie was when he procured the Martell's Congac for me upon the occasion of evacuating the 82nd and 101st Airborne Divisions over Utah beach. Rosie stayed in Europe with "the old man" his perpetual benefactor when the rest of us in Brigade Headquarters returned to the States preparatory to the Okinawa Landings which will come up later in this epistle. The last I heard of him was through the Army grapevine while on Okinawa. I heard then that he was in the Federal Prison System awaiting trial for shooting a German POW table waiter in an Officers' Mess in Paris. This is the end of the Rosie tale. It's true except for his name.

Around the end of July, while the Allies and the Germans were still fighting over individual farm fields in the "Battle of the Hedgerows", and the Germans were still disputing the area around Caen, and I was getting a midday drink of cold water from our local Lister bag, I heard the deep drone of a flight of heavy aircraft coming across the Channel from England. Soon I was treated to the sight of what appeared to be the entire Allied Bomber Command flying in neat formations and filling the sky from horizon to horizon at a considerable elevation. Their mission was to simply blast a path through the German defenses to let the bottled up allied armies flow out of the Cherbourg Peninsula. There were B-17 Flying Fortresses, B-24 Liberators, and, as I recall it some medium bombers as well. It was called "Carpet Bombing" and it turned out to be a miserable failure simply because so many of their bombs fell on American troops. The planners went "back to the drawing board", corrected some of their errors in judgment on the original plan, and, in about a week, back came the fleet of bombers. I never heard anything about American casualties on the first effort, but our Engineer Brigade did receive a number of "Shell Shocked" soldiers to work in the transfer points as common labor shortly thereafter. The ultimate success of "Operation COBRA" was soon proven by General Patton's Third Army breakout at Avranches and the glorious successes all across France in the Autumn of '44.

At about this point, the nightly German nuisance air raids had ceased, and it began to rain more often. So Lt. Albert Elias, Lt. Willie Moore and I all moved our beds into the hayloft over the attached garage. There was no hay up there any more; I suppose the Huns had cleaned it out for their own captured French horses. Anyway, it was clean, and dry and had a huge open window, through which, in earlier times, the farmers had brought in the hay. It was only a couple of steps from our work place. It was a great place to sleep, the only minus being that you got up there by means of a vertical ladder consisting of 2 x 4 rungs nailed across the studs in one corner and leading up to a hole in the hayloft floor.

The Recreation Officer in Brigade Headquarters, to earn his salt, decided (maybe it was the "old man" who decided) to throw an officers party one evening in celebration of Third Army's breaking out of the Cherbourg Peninsula. Big Hospital Units with many nurses were coming ashore from England and the "States" almost daily now and these nurses deserved an evening of fun and games whenever available. Some of the enlisted men from Brigade Headquarters aspired to become professional musicians and our main office building had a smooth wooden floor, so, Voila!! our party turned into a dance! (It being France we even managed a case of wine).

"After the Ball was Over" and we had returned to our farmhouse on the beach, Willie Moore, Al Elias and I got into an argument out in the stable yard about whether or not it was time to go to bed. I maintained it was the shank of the evening, those two claimed otherwise, and proceeded to try to take me up that miserable ladder to our hayloft. They were bigger and stronger than I and finally decided that if I wouldn't climb that ladder myself, they would carry me up it—feet first. Needless to say Willie and I had both been into the vin rouge early and often (Albert was a teetotaler). After much laughing, struggling, and good natured cursing, they managed to get me into a bundle the two of them could carry up the ladder feet first, Willie in charge of my feet, and Albert in charge of my shoulders. All went well, until with my feet were ready to pass through the hole in the second floor, and my head about four feet above the flagstone garage floor, I decided to reopen the argument about going to bed for the night. I demanded to be properly put down on the garage floor; while Willie and Albert stuck to their original plan to get me upstairs and into my bedroll for the night. One thing led to another, with both of them still holding me tight, until I announced that if they continued to hold me I was going to bite the calf of the leg which the narrow ladder was forcing against my face. They persisted in holding me that way so I bit the calf in my face. They dropped me immediately.. ..**THUMP!!..** My bare head struck the stone floor below with a bang I'll never forget, and I saw a halo of stars such as one only sees in the comic strips. There is nothing so sobering as a dive into an empty swimming pool!

The following morning, I did not have any ill effects from our frolic after the dance, but a funny thing took place: our Brigade Chaplain, Father Ambrose A. McAvoy showed up at our Beach Operations Headquarters wearing his steel helmet without the helmet liner. It was like a small child wearing a grown man's ten-gallon Stetson. He didn't give any sermon on drinking but I got the message. "Father Mac", as we called him, was indeed a character; then (1944) and now (2001). He was the senior Chaplain in the Brigade, and although we had several other Chaplains, of various denominations, including one Rabbi, assigned to the other units, he set a high standard for all to follow. With so many troops ashore, the U.S. Army had all the crime problems of a large city; including

Capital Crimes of Murder and Rape which carried the death penalty after review by the President of the United States. Capital offenses committed against a citizen of the nation where the serviceman was stationed were closed, after final appeals, and for obvious reasons, by public hanging in the locale where the original crime took place. "In addition to his other duties", Father Mac had to attend these executions whenever they occurred in the Brigade's large area of responsibility; to give the last rites when appropriate, and to represent the United States of America demonstrating that Justice was being done. I have included in the appendix a short article on the D-day story as seen from Father Mac's point of view, published for the 50th Anniversary of that important day by "The Witness" the diocesan newspaper covering the area including Dubuque, Iowa where the good Father now resides in a home for retired Catholic Priests.

I would like to include a word or two about the two ex-merchant sea captains assigned to Utah by the U.S. Maritime Commission. As mentioned earlier, their overall job was to represent the Merchant Seamen in a veritable sea of U.S. Servicemen. Such issues as arose between the two groups of men usually included wages and/or exposure to hostile enemy action and from my point of view were virtually nonexistent. It was the prewar experiences of these two old sea dogs which were of interest to us landlubber GIs—especially their tales of "rum running" and the smuggling of aliens. They seemed to know so much about those activities that I sometimes suspected the pair of them of having had a try at running in a little booze once in a while. After all, we did repeal the 18th Amendment, didn't we?

One day in the early Autumn of '44 I was surprised to see my cousin, Arch Priestly, walk into our headquarters. Arch had attended Ohio State a year behind me, and had graduated with a degree in Veterinary Medicine. As I learned, his was an unusual and enviable assignment with the army in France. He was a meat inspector. By this time, the war had progressed to the point where there was actually some fresh meat being sent to the troops in the field, and it was the job of veterinarians like Arch to see that it was being properly handled along the way. As I dimly recall it, Arch was a Captain with a small detachment of men and they were responsible for covering the entire First Army area . His detachment had their own kitchen truck, refrigerators, etc., and were capable of traveling around, behind the front, randomly checking out the movement of meat in the supply system. They also had an adequate supply of famous name French cognac, liberated from the Germans and given to the meat inspectors by grateful GIs for whom they had inspected the meat supply. Long story short: I was the personal guest of my cousin Arch, with his detachment in their small mess tent that evening and enjoyed a couple of Remy-Martin cocktails ahead of the prime steak. I, in turn, rewarded Arch with a paperback copy of "Plutarch's Lives" from the Brigades's recreational library. In the morning they were on their way again. I hope to see Arch at the 75th Annual Morgan Family reunion this fall 2002. He has held it together almost single handedly for the last 30-40 years.

By September the beach was producing like a finely tuned piece of machinery. A division a day had been brought ashore to well organized reception areas on the Normandy coast, ammunition was arriving from the USA by the shipload and placed in orderly dumps by troops well trained for this hazardous duty. Military supplies of all sorts; rations, bandages, tents, locomotives, bridging timbers, "you name it" was brought ashore, either across the beach or via the almost totally destroyed port of Cherbourg. Gasoline, both regular and aviation grade, was being pumped ashore to tank farms. "Shell shocked" US soldiers were being reclaimed by sifting them into the cargo handling gangs at the transfer points where miscellaneous cargo was sorted after being brought ashore by the swarms of "Dukws" (amphibious trucks). These shell shocked troops were products of the earlier bombing by the Army Air Corps in the August massed air assault leading to the breakthrough at Argentan. All in all, the scene was one of a successful army moving rapidly through Belgium and Holland toward Berlin and victory.

Paris had been liberated for a few weeks and the more enterprising of our beach bound Engineer troops had managed to get a few days leave to visit the "City of Light". I decided that I needed a few days vacation myself. Realizing that Paris was probably like a zoo, with so many troops heading there, I didn't particularly want to go there. I wanted to go where it was more civilized; back to England. Not wishing to be officially AWOL, I went directly to the Brigade Exec. Officer, my good friend of two years standing, Colonel Ernie Adams. Together we concocted this scheme. I was to take a couple of captured German souvenirs, rifles were still plentiful, and, bumming a ride on a Dukw, approach a Liberty Ship which was empty and due to sail. I had previously been approached by many Merchant Marine skippers looking for souvenirs, and I was usually too busy to engage in such barter, but this was to be my vacation. Anyway, once aboard a soon-to-sail ship, and having ascertained that he was only going to one of the channel ports on the south coast of England, I was to give the skipper his souvenirs and get permission to take a shower while he made last minute preparations to sail. (We always needed a shower, once earlier I went for five weeks without.) Once showered and certain that the ship was underway, I was to go to the ship's siderail and make frantic signals (with my index fingers only) to shore. These signals would, of course, be of no avail and I would be on my way to Southampton in time for breakfast at a hotel, after a good nights sleep in a real bed on board the Liberty ship.

I didn't leave Southampton for a day but there wasn't much I could find to do there either. On the second morning I checked out of my hotel and headed for Cornwall. Truro to be exact.

I hitch hiked a couple of rides on army trucks to get to Truro late in the afternoon. I checked into the only hotel I knew of in town (I think it was called the "Red Bull", but that sounds more like a pub). I went to a pub and had a couple of pints, and the bartender commented on how fast I gulped them down. (I guess that I must have been feeling guilty about being sort of semi-AWOL) I decided to return to the 1st ESB in the morning.

My night in the hotel in Truro was uneventful except for the very lumpy mattress. Up in the AM at six, breakfast in the hotel dining room (sparse) and I was out on the highway bumming my way to Lands End, clear down at the southwestern most tip of Britain. I had heard there was an army airfield there. I quickly got a ride on an army truck, the driver of which confirmed my understanding about the army airfield, as a matter of fact that's where he was going. Lucky me! We arrived at the airstrip about ten that same morning. It wasn't much as airfields go, but it was alive and in business. In the flight operations tent I was told that I was really lucky; there was a B-17 going to Paris, leaving about two in the afternoon. It was not at Lands End yet but was due momentarily. Apparently non-operational flights from southern England to the continent were controlled from Lands

End and the B-17 was not there as yet. The story went like this: the B-17 was a brand new one which had come up from the Italian front with a load of P-47 Fighter pilots to pick up new P-47s and ferry them back to their base in Italy. Their new P-47s were not ready yet, so they (the fighter pilots) were going to Paris for the weekend, using their B-17 as a taxi. It was some "taxicab"; it's .50 caliber machine guns were still in their crates soaked in cosmolene. The fighter pilots, their "taxi driver" and his sergeant, had been at some assembly plant for crated P-47s up in the Midlands awaiting their new planes.

Now I don't know whether you were ever around a group of fighter pilots or not, but I had been on the boat trip down to N. Africa from Scotland in '42 and there was nothing peppier and more lively than a gang of those birds. This Paris bound bunch of fighter pilots was giddy with the idea of spending their weekend in Paris instead of on some lonesome, muddy airstrip in Italy, or getting shot at in a dog fight—and why shouldn't they be?

The B-17 was not long in arriving at Lands End. As soon as it's pilot had cleared with the control people there at the airfield, I approached him and asked for a ride to Paris. Since I was heading toward the war and not in the opposite direction, he had no qualms about approving my request.

I climbed aboard. I was the only foot soldier among the seven or eight veteran fliers and they outdid themselves trying to make me welcome. They insisted that I sit in the nose gunners seat when we were taking off. That was a thrill I haven't recovered from yet. I had to try out all of the gunnery seats which were accessible when aloft, and then we all settled down and took a nap—with the exception of the pilot, that is. One of the other passengers, a cocky young fighter pilot, announced that he was the Navigator for the afternoon and gave the pilot a compass bearing to go straight in to Orly airport. We had entered heavy cloud cover almost immediately upon takeoff so would remain on the compass route until the pilot picked up Paris on his radio later in the day. From time to time there was an opening in the clouds, but who wanted to see the English countryside after five minutes of looking. At one point the sergeant announced "we are going over the invasion beaches"; but I was dozing and didn't even bother to look. Too bad I did not "bother to look", I would have seen the Pas de Calais area, which had been shown a few times prior to D-

Day, in Stars and Stripes, the army newspaper, as a part of the army's misinformation campaign aimed at German intelligence. We were about 75 miles from where we should have been and heading right straight into Germany. The Sergeant wasn't to blame, I wasn't to blame, if anybody was to blame, it was the fighter pilot who gave our pilot the incorrect bearing. We were lost but no one on the plane was aware of that fact.

We did not have to wait long to find out that we were lost. Apparently the pilot began to think that he had been in the air long enough to reach the environs of Paris and that he'd better take a look at the ground if at all possible. We started a slow descent through the clouds.   All   of   a   sudden,   KERBAM!!......
KERBAM!!......KERBAM!! ......(not anything I had heard before!)

The fighter pilots all began to scurry around, not unlike chickens with their heads cut off, the sergeant pried open a machine gun crate and started to assemble it, when I asked, "What's going on?" Someone replied "That's flak!. .. the damned fools are shooting at us!" The pilot meanwhile was taking evasive action and trying to get the big "Flying Fortress" back up into the clouds. He succeeded or the Lord only knows what would have happened. I can guess several alternative endings for this scenario, none of them good except the real one. Which was perhaps more luck than we deserved. We were in the clouds and no one was shooting at us! We had been flying almost due east. A very hasty conference between the pilot, a couple of the others, myself and our road map resulted in a decision to fly due west for a while and then try again to get a fix on our location. By this time I could guess what had happened. The paratroop assault, made by the U.S. 82nd and 101st divisions plus a British Airborne Division, had been underway for about a week, (I had read about it on our brigade bulletin board before I left Normandy on my (now ridiculous) vacation. I guessed that our pilot had lowered our B17 right into the middle of that mess (I learned later that it was called operation "Market Garden" and even later, I learned that they made a movie of it called "A Bridge Too Far.")

We flew due west through the clouds for about half an hour and then the pilot began, very gingerly, to let her down again. No land in sight! nothing but water! Based on where we thought we had been, we had to be over the North Sea. The pilot turned the plane due south and very soon we could see land on the horizon to our left. Either France or Belgium! Following the coastline, safely out at sea, we pretty soon saw a port, the ruins of a city and a river flowing to the ocean from the interior. Le Havre! and the river had to be the Seine, and up the Seine was Paris! Soon we landed at Orly Airport. All of the fliers got out and began to inspect the B-17, and within a few minutes came up with a total of some 40-odd small wounds the brand new B-17 had received ...and she hadn't even been christened yet.!! The airmen all seemed tickled that I had had such a thrilling trip, now that it was over. But acknowledged extreme satisfaction that we were all alive and unhurt! I came to my senses and agreed.

There was still about an hour of daylight remaining when we all said good bye there on the tarmac. A passing jeep hauled me to the Orly motor pool, and from there I hitched a ride into the "City of Light". I had never been to Paris before, had never expected to be there, but soon found myself on the Champs Elysee—broke, dirty, hungry, sober and sort of AWOL from the First ESB... and adrift in a veritable sea of bicycles. The army bus I was riding made regular stops at a transient officers mess, (there were a lot of transient officers in Paris then and a lot of transient enlisted men too) so I got off, got washed up, ate a good army meal and caught a later bus to a hotel I had learned of at the mess. It was the Prince Charles at the Place d'l'Opera or somesuch. It was 58 years ago, remember?

With autumn approaching and the major ports of Brussels and Antwerp still in German hands, we were given orders to search for locations where cargo might be brought ashore when the winter storms began. A reconnaissance team of Brigade Veterans was put together to check out both sides of the Seine river from Le Havre all the way to Rouen. Lt. Col. Adams was in charge of the team consisting of Major McGrann, Major Harry Jacobsen, Major Bob Humphries, Lt. Col. Rand S. Bailey, Lt. Col. Brock and myself. As a group with a jeep and two command cars (big old fashioned touring cars) we inspected every river town and almost every inch of river bank from Rouen to the English channel. We were gone from Utah beach for about three days, as I recall it, and one rather weird happening comes to memory: in one hamlet far from the main roads, we all thought we sensed a hostility on the part of the few natives we encountered. Since we were about finished exploring for the day, we decided to drop into the only place resembling an inn which we were able to locate to find out about the hostility and to see if we could stay all night. The hostility was easily explained by the proprietor of the inn who was a little less naive than the other natives we had encountered.. They were not certain, but they thought we were Huns and were just not taking any chances. American English sounded a lot more like German than it did like the British they heard on the radio; our uniforms, especially the helmets, looked more like those of the Krauts than those of the Tommies, and so on. The Germans had been chased out of the area two months previously and this little burg had never, ever had an infestation of them anyhow. So the proprietor at least proclaimed us as "LIBERATORS" and we all drank to that.

We were now at the mercy of the weather most of the time and, as usual, higher headquarters, began to break us up. The old faithful 531st Engineer Shore Regiment had already been split into three separate Engineer Combat Battalions and reconstituted so that they could function as stand alone units on their own administratively. The Medical Battalion, the QM Battalion, the massive 286th Signal Company, and The Ordnance Company were similarly taken over and sent to join the victorious First Army advancing across Europe. Who needs an "Amphibian Brigade" when the "Hostile Shores" have all been successfully landed upon? We of the First Engineer Special Brigade Headquarters were (understandably) getting what the old time vaudevillians called "THE BUM'S RUSH", wherein a likable character of a hobo was chased off of the stage by a couple of Keystone Kops after having performed some truly noble deed before the eyes of the theater audience.

We, and the now forlorn "Gooseberry" were still, along with the normal assortment of shore birds, about the only remnants of the once crowded, long expanse of Utah beach. True, we had erected a concrete obelisk monument "To Our Honored Dead" on top of the German coastal gun emplacement at Tare Green beach but, other than that, there was nothing left to commemorate this historic site on the windswept Normandy channel Coast.

Beach operations headquarters had outlived its usefulness and we inhabitants of the Norman farmhouse had moved to the town of Ste. Mere Eglise with the other functions of the Brigade Hq. We now lived in pyramidal tents with small Government-Issue wood stoves to thwart the chill.

It was time for Thanksgiving and we celebrated it as you might expect by this time; most of us attended Church Mass with Fr. McAvoy in the morning, went to a cocktail party at the *house* occupied by Lieutenant Colonels Bailey and Adams, then went to the mess tent for roast turkey and all the trimmings served by German POW waiters. Then we got into a playful but vigorous free-for-all fight. The fighting was all confined to our tent area, and then and now I didn't know what we were fighting about. I remember hitting Captain McStay in the nose so hard that I broke both my right pinkie and Danny McStay's nose, and I remember chasing someone with one of those fifteen inch oaken tent stakes (or was it the other way around, and someone was chasing me?). Anyway we had a grand time of it and I came out with my theory of celibate male drinking "Put together a bunch of normal, healthy, young males who have not had the mollifying presence of females for a long time, get them inebriated, and they will invariably either get into a fight or fall asleep"

So the beaches were all closed, our troops were all doing useful work for somebody else and we were again out of the invasion business; only this time it looked like we had truly outlived our usefulness. Ha! Not so! The small capacity Port of Cherbourg had gotten a few berths cleared and available for unloading ocean-going cargo ships as well as badly needed rolling stock for the French railroads, and Headquarters First Engineer Special Brigade was to be in charge of the operation. Most incredible of all, Col. Adams, now commanding what was left of us, made me the Chief of Operations of the Port. It was sold to me as "My big chance to show my stuff".

I moved into Cherbourg, looked over my human resources, most of whom I knew pretty well, and divvied up the responsibilities according to the talents available. This experienced bunch of men could handle a port three times this big, especially with the former Utah beach dump troops still doing their jobs in the rapidly emptying beachhead. One thing was lacking however, our new higher headquarters, Normandy Base Section, Services of Supply, required that we have a Brass Band for ceremonial purposes! So in addition to taking on a new (and for me) big job I had to procure instruments and find people who could play them. Upon the advice of Col. Adams, I delegated the whole band problem to a Lt. Col. whom I had never laid eyes on but who "came with" the job assignment I had been given. I had organized the Port Operations Section along lines of responsibility as given in Army Field Manuals, and placed the band problem in a separate pigeon hole in my mind for special attention. To get started, I called for meetings of the Section Chiefs every day at 4:00 PM to discuss progress and problems with getting the Port more productive as the scuttled ships were raised. It turned out that we ended up hearing more about the Lieutenant Col.'s problems with finding a tuba on the Cherbourg market than with any more serious supply problem.

We were only on the job in Cherbourg for about a week, when we received startling news! We were to move immediately to Southampton across the Channel, to be shipped back to the good old USA asap. Col. Caffey was relieved immediately as Brigade CO and a Colonel Benjamin B. Talley was to be our Commander. I do not remember the timing of the events during the next few days but I'll betcha that we sailed from Cherbourg in less than 24 hours. We embarked at dusk one day on a British LST which was fitted with railroad tracks for hauling rolling stock to the french Chemin de Fer and we were safely into the big British Port of Southampton less than a day later. I was sent ashore first by Col. Adams to find our Capt. McComb to learn what arrangements McComb had made for our reception. After several hours searching, I found Jimmy in bed in a Southampton Hotel. He *had* made the arrangements and had then found an English woman he had known in earlier days. It was now too late at night to unload the Brigade Headquarters so we all spent another night on the British LST—all but Jimmy, that is..

While in Cherbourg for that week or so, Albert Elias had discovered that our former good buddy, Captain Chuck Boyle, of Homestead, Pennsylvania was a wounded *patient* aboard a hospital train tied up in our dockside yards awaiting shipment to Britain where he would be admitted to an Army General Hospital for additional treatment. Chuck had joined the Brigade Headquarters as part of the D-Day overstrength while we were at Pencalenick, had stayed with us long after D-Day. He had been assigned to a Replacement Depot when we were required to shed overstrength. Chuck had been requisitioned by one of the spearhead armored divisions, assigned to be POINT man almost the next day and went from being an Engineer Staff Officer to being an Infantry Foot soldier in the Battle for the Hurtgen Forest in less then a months time. Chuck was machine gunned and then shot by a German infantryman while on the ground. Chuck eventually lost a foreleg, married his nurse, had a very successful business career and goes to the Brigade Annual Reunion with wife Isabelle. He walks much better than most of us octogenarians; but I would not say that he has had an easy time of it.

CHAPTER XI

ENGLAND—ATLANTIC—STATESIDE

The second night on the British LST was just more of the first, we drank some British beer out of old fashioned bottles with hinged porcelain caps, argued about this and that, and tried to get some sleep. The LST had not been loaded as yet for its next run to Cherbourg with rail cars of ammunition to be shipped directly to forward dumps in Belgium so we had a creaking, ghostly spacious bedroom for the 60 or 70 of us comprising the enlisted and officer remnants of HQ.1st. Engineer Special Brigade. Early the following morning, a sheepish Captain Jimmy J. McComb put in his appearance and we were made knowledgeable of the arrangements for forwarding our bodies to Liverpool over on the west coast of England on the Irish Sea. We were to spend this night in a staging area camp outside Southampton and board a train to the west tomorrow AM.

Sounds simple, ne c'est pas? But nothing turned out to be simple for an army unit headed West in Europe when everybody else was trying to go East. Oh, our problems were trivial indeed when compared to General Eisenhower's problems with the "Battle of the Bulge" which was just beginning but ours were an aggravation. First, we had to wait around all day for trucks to haul us to the staging area where we were going to sleep in pyramidal tents, second, it was growing more cold by the minute, and third we were getting behind on our eating, which is understandable in a combat situation; but was absolutely inexcusable seven hundred miles behind the lines. At last some trucks showed up and we got to the staging area where some army cooks grudgingly ladled some stew into our mess cups. Next, we sorted out our bedrolls and placed them on the double decker steel cot frames, with only a sheet of canvas for an innerspring mattress. We had the little wood burning stove in the center of the tent going full blast but it didn't even make a dent in the cold that was now absorbing most of our attention (and curses). We were in woolen uniforms as we always had been in the European Theater of Operations, even in North Africa, and we had on our wool lined raincoats—but we were still cold. We went looking for wood and found none except the floor boards of the tent which was to be our shelter for the night. So, up it came, and we found ourselves walking on British soil. The real thing this time. From the surrounding tents we heard similar whacks and thumps of other floors being torn apart so we felt "Not so guilty".

During the night a Canine Corps unit moved into the staging area fresh from the USA. You could tell from the barks that these were magnificent dogs, mostly of the Rin Tin Tin variety as German Shepherds were known in those days. Their chief use during the war was to assist the Military Police in the shepherding of large groups of POWs and as I understand it they were very dependable. Something had stirred them up before their arrival at the staging area and they opened up a "Midnight Barking Party" which they carried on with great enthusiasm until the crack of dawn. I never did see any of this bunch; just had the pleasure of hearing them throughout a long, cold night.

In the frosty morning we were hauled by trucks to a railroad yard, where there was a passenger train unloading troops of the 17th Infantry Division (Airborne) to be hauled in *our* trucks to *our* (now floorless) tents in the staging area. One young Lieutenant in the airborne, seeing that we all were wearing the same (Combined Operations) shoulder patch, inquired of Fr. McAvoy, and knowing that we were heading West while his unit was heading East, "Chaplain, Sir, what unit is that?" And Father Mac, looking him straight in the eye, replied in a very solemn tone, "Son, this is all that's left of the First Engineer Special Brigade of seven thousand men". Sad but true.

An uneventful train ride took us to a place called Nantwich which was a staging area in the vicinity of Liverpool. There we were notified that we would be delayed for at least ten days before sailing for the states. The army wanted that much time to get us in shape worthy of men returning as heroes to their loved ones. As I recall it, most of the emphasis was on getting our records and bodies up to date; the records probably were not that much of a problem because Sully, (Captain Charles W. Sullivan from Mississippi) Brigade Adjutant and his staff were always very much on the ball. Our bodies were another matter, however; admittedly they couldn't do a whole lot for our physiques; the time was too short and in those days body-building was frowned upon, as a muscle binder; but they could enhance our immunity to most diseases. So we were given every immunization known to the medical profession, regardless of when we had our last dose of same. (Author's note: count how many times we go through this in the next 60 days!) Like good mommies and daddies, the Army knew that we had not been brushing our teeth twice a day as we had been told to do in childhood, so we had to climb into *that* chair for better or for worse. In this case I was both lucky and unlucky. LUCKY, because I had had a tooth pulled when we were at Pencalenick the previous winter when we were not pushing the army dentists to hurry it up. UNLUCKY, because they missed a cavity that needed attention this time, and I had to have it relieved now under much more primitive conditions. Did you ever see a dental drill driven by a foot treadle operated by a Private, First Class who was the Dentist's Assistant? That's almost as slow as the Chinese Water torture.

The army had fixed my records and my teeth about as much as could be done in the first couple of days and I found myself facing a week of sitting around the staging area with nothing to do. Many of our gang were in the same boat. As a matter of fact, two of our most outstanding enlisted men, Sergeants Stewart and Erickson wanted to leave the group for that week to get married to sweethearts they met and courted during our two previous assignments in Britain. Which they both did. As for me, I wanted to go back to Truro, and I learned that my buddy, John Nathaniel (Pee Wee) Davis of Saluda, N.C. wished to go there too. So Pee Wee and I sat up all night on the British counterpart of an American day coach, freezing our butts off to get to Truro. We got off at two stations along the way to gulp down mugs of scalding hot tea which we both remember to this day. We have maintained contact throughout the intervening fifty seven years. The tea was made with milk added before brewing as it always seemed to be in wartime England. I truly enjoyed seeing Truro and Pencalenick again. They brought back memories of my happiest war years. Pee Wee and I had gone our separate ways after reaching Truro, and only rejoined in Nantwich. At this juncture Shug Jordan's partial denture merits at least a footnote. I don't know that his teeth were any worse than those of the rest of us, but the Army Dentists worked long and hard on his while we were in Nantwich; and yet they never seemed to fit right. He often had to pull them from his shirt pocket when it was time to install them to eat. That didn't seem to keep him from being proclaimed "Football Coach of the Year" while working at Auburn University a few years after war's end. He undoubtedly went to another dentist as soon as he got out of the army.

At last our "phony leave" in Nantwich was over, our shots were completed, and for better or for worse we were all set to go home. By this time we all knew that there was at least one more "Hostile Shore" awaiting us somewhere west of Nantwich; but why worry about that now? We were on our way home after two and a half years away. (In *our war* it was not possible even for Generals of the highest rank to telephone home and, at this point, *Rotation*, was only just getting started.)

Our first surprise of the trip came even before we boarded ship, it was the USS WAKEFIELD. We had heard that she had burned at sea, which was a fact, but the shipbuilders at home had fixed her up as good as when she had originally sailed as the USS Manhattan. They had omitted the passenger liner frills and made her a real troopship. As we settled in, prior to sailing, I went on deck to have a last look at the busy Port of Liverpool. It was about the same as when I had looked at it in November '42 except that this time I did not get to see a British Aircraft Carrier. I did, however, get to see some British troops boarding HMS Argentina en route to duty in India. Among the people loaded with us onto the Wakefield were some Army Air Corps crews which, having completed (survived) the required number of missions were going back to the U.S.A.. Also of interest in our passenger load was a large complement of German POWs and a Company of Dutch Marines escorting them. Rumor had it that there was little, if any, love lost between the Marines and their charges as a result of the two World Wars—and this time the Dutch Marines had the upper hand!

The "Battle of the Atlantic", between the German "Wolf Pack" submarines and the Allied escort convoys had been fairly won by the latter during 1943, so a year later in December of 1944, we were running without an escort. Our ship was receiving news dispatches from the regular news agencies and as a matter of interest to passengers, these were posted at various spots throughout the ship. The "Battle of the Bulge" had become a full fledged battle by this time, and the Kraut POWs became aware of the early successes of

125

their side, with a consequent growth in cockiness. I heard of, but did not actually witness, several instances of cocky POWs getting it with a Dutch rifle butt during these days of temporarily resurgent Aryan Supremacy.

Around the third day out of Liverpool, our table mate member of the ship's officers staff stated that storm warnings were up, and that a North Atlantic storm in December was not a laughing matter. He told us that each officer reported on the quantity of rivets popped by the straining and twisting of the ship's hull during his watch and that this number was the principal index to the ship's survivability following the extensive repairs she had undergone following the fire. This sounded like a "Cock & Bull" story to most of us landlubbers except for the fact that that he told it with such sincerity. That, and the big ship's tossing about in the following storm made all of us plenty nervous, believe me!

We awakened to see the good old Statue of Liberty very early one very cold morning after the scary storm was behind us. With the help of a couple of small tug boats and the music of a half-frozen Womens' Army Corps (WAC) Band, we slipped into our allotted berth on the West Side of the East River and were able to say, "Home at Last". There was some unofficial, non-ceremonial heartfelt ground kissing, as we made the short walk to the waiting Fort Dix trucks.

The trucks from Fort Dix took us down the East river in NYC and through one of the tunnels into New Jersey, we didn't see anything of New York City because the trucks all had their canvas tops in place and it was so cold that most of us were just hunkered down trying to get a little more heat from the next guys body than he got from ours. We knew about and sympathized with our buddies fighting the Battle of the Bulge, but what the hell? We were home in the USA and our troubles were supposed to be over there. Pretty soon, however, we were out of our misery and in the warmth of the wooden barracks of Fort Dix, where we were to be processed for a 30 days "Delay en Route", all reasonable expenses paid trip, to Fort Lewis, State of Washington.

There was of course a mad rush to the pay phones, and then an equally mad rush to the nearby PX to get enough American Coins to operate the pay phones. We had three or four wall mounted telephones all in a row, probably a foot apart, and the queues behind

126

them grew long. The most heart warming story to come out of this scene was Captain Danny McStay's encounter with his four year old son.   Captain McStay's wife and son were living with her Irish mother in Sewickley, Pa. during Danny's overseas duty.   Danny's Mother-in-law answered the telephone when it rang that day and then fainted dead away when she heard Danny's voice. Little Dan picked up the phone and to his father's "Danny this is your Daddy" merely responded, "Oh you poor soul, In the Name of the Father, the Son, and the Holy Spirit. Amen". Fortunately, Dan's wife was at hand to take care of the situation. All's well that ends well, I guess.

My own first contact with Mom and Dad was warm but not as exciting as McStay's.   I had beaten the mail censors by broadly hinting in my most recent letter that IF it was my luck to come home in the near future, I would really like a meal of Mom's pot roast, roast potatoes, Waldorf Salad, and blackberry pie. (Depression raised kids didn't know about *filet mignon* and the only restaurant in town was in the Union Station, in those days). So, my parents were not overcome with surprise when my own phone call came through that evening at the end of December,1944. They were, however, very glad that I was home at last.

The army gave us our shots again the next day, regardless of the fact that we'd just completed a series in England, gave us written orders, authenticating our travel and (the precious) "delay en route" clause, and some ration stamps for gasoline and food, and delivered us, via school buses to the nearest bus or railroad station. I guess, that those of us who needed help in planning travel either got same from the Travelers' Aid Society in the stations or from the army at Ft. Dix. Now we were free from the army until we reported to Fort Lewis late in January, 1945.   My train trip to Columbus, Ohio by way the Pennsylvania Railroad called for a change of trains in N. Philly, a deed which made me feel a little more sophisticated, despite the fact that I was a world traveler: I had seen Rosalind Russell on the stage, in Pittsburgh, before the war, and was still impressed with all the talk about "Main Line", etc., in "Philadelphia Story". Mom and Dad met me at the Union Station on High Street in Columbus later that cold evening. My two sisters were absent at that time; Hanna, my older sister was living in Los Angeles with her husband, Bill, and son Craig (and expecting); sister Mary (spelled Merry), was a yeoman in the newly formed U.S. Coast Guard Auxiliary the "Spars". Merry, an Olympic class swimmer, was stationed at Palm Beach teaching Coast Guardsmen how to stay alive in water covered with burning fuel oil. They were not at home anymore so I got my choice of bedrooms. Sisters are both in heaven now; as are Mom and Dad.

The morning after my homecoming, I slept in until seven AM, and finally arose feeling very guilty about the whole idea; here I, who had dreamed about surviving the war had managed to do so, (thus far) and was spending my day in bed. Shame. I finally arose to the smell of pies baking in the oven and thus was my "delay en route" off to a salubrious start. The dinner of chuck roast, etc. followed at about 1:30 PM after the three of us had a couple of Old Crow and ginger ale highballs (Dad took the day off from work in my honor). Following the blackberry pie, (my parents always canned wild blackberries in half-gallon Mason jars,) we took short naps, after which the parade of neighbors started. All of the former kids in the neighborhood, with whom my sisters and I had played (and/or fought) as children were, for the most part grown and gone, (many in the armed forces and overseas). So, it was with a collection of sixty (plus) year olds that I spent the afternoon, trying to minimize the thoughts of danger running through the imaginations of those with progeny in bad places. Mrs. Gray, a widow, had her only two sons in the Navy; the Hopkins, next door, had their son in the Navy; the Jones's across the street had their son in the Army, and so it went. I am pleased to report that all of these potential casualties came through the war OK; although following the war my class at North High School dedicated a plaque to twelve classmates, mostly airmen, who didn't come back. Throughout my home stay I had visits or telephone calls from friends and acquaintances who, hearing I was home, wanted to talk about the situation of a loved one in the European Theater. I couldn't tell them very much, of anything, about anything, but with General Patton on his way to end the "Battle of the Bulge", it was a whole lot easier to speak reassuringly than if I had come home earlier in the war; like after Kasserine Pass. The husband of one classmate was in the 82nd Airborne and it was hard to assure her of his safety; but I tried my best. I forgot her married name but have prayed that he made it.

One day, early in my visit home, I spent several hours, one-on-one, with the Governor of Ohio. It happened this way: My Dad was an old time political reporter for the Associated Press, and the Office of the Governor was his regular beat. Governor Frank J. Lausche (later Senator) and Dad were the best of friends, despite Dad's being a lifelong Republican. When the Chief Executive heard that I was home from the battlefields he insisted that I come and spend time with him so that he could better understand the returning veterans when they arrived en masse at the end of the conflict. He was deadly serious about this and I hope I didn't disappoint him. I, in fact, hadn't given it a thought as I had my Engineering Degree before the war, and only assumed that I would return to business as usual—if at all. I enjoyed the day, however; enjoyed having lunch with such a thoughtful, brilliant man, and wasn't the least impressed with myself.

My plans for this time-off included going to Pittsburgh to see old friends in the Homestead Steel Works, Open Hearth Dept. where I had served as the General Labor Foreman in Shop No. 4. A nice job with a salary of $185.00 per month, for working at least eight hours every day, and with every 13th Saturday afternoon off. (We salaried bosses were expected to work all Sundays). When I had resigned to volunteer for the Army, and they realized they would not actually have to pay it, they had raised my salary to $225.00 per month, which ultimately caused army personnel clerks to whistle in amazement when I filled out the enrollment forms describing my civilian experience, and earnings. Such was life during the depression. Such was being among the chosen ones at The United States Steel Corporation.

My trip to Pittsburgh, Pennsylvania was a short half day by rail even in those crowded times. I met my old boss, and WW I hero, Bob Fatzinger, at the Open Hearth Shop, and then a gang of us, including Jack McGill and Andy Kurty, went to lunch at a nearby saloon, where I could seldom find money or time enough to eat pre-war. Present at lunch were most of the top supervision of OH#4 as well as Bruce Shields, the chief clerk of the Melting Department, who had served in WWI as a volunteer ambulance driver along with a bunch of his fellow Princeton graduates, before our country got into that "War to End all Wars". Bruce had recently been advised by the War Department of the loss of a son in action in Europe. Late that afternoon I went to my old rooming house where my former landlady made me welcome. That night I stayed at the home of my former immediate boss, and friend "Bud" Hovey whose two daughters had doubled in both size and age since I last saw them, three years earlier. Bud took me to Pittsburgh's Union Station in the morning after his wife had provided a good start for my day with a stateside breakfast of ham, eggs, O.J., and coffee; which probably impinged heavily into their monthly ration allowances.

At home again in Columbus, that evening, Mother, to my delight, had invited Myrtle and Joe Deutschle for dinner and an evening of conversation. Cocktails preceded a nice home cooked meal which preceded another blackberry pie. Myrtle and Joe, who had been friends of my folks for about ten years, were perhaps fifteen years younger than Mom and Dad, and were natives of Chicago, with considerable sophistication. Joe had been a reporter for the Associated Press like my father, and had been a member of the virtually unheard of U.S. Army Reserve Corps since his service in France during WWI. Throughout my boyhood years Joe had been a source of many interesting tales about what it had been like "Over There" in 1917-18. He had also kindly provided me with a free .22 caliber rifle, from the Reserve Arsenal at a time when every kid in our neighborhood imagined himself to be Daniel Boone when it came to shooting tin cans. Joe had been brought back into the army for WWII as a Lieutenant Colonel, and had served with Hq. U.S. Fifth Army in Italy until a few months before my own visit when he had been mustered out because of his age. During the course of the evening I revealed to Joe that our "delay en route" was only a pretext to get us to the Pacific Theater for further "fun and games" against the Axis Powers, which he, knowing the nature of our missions, had already surmised. I told Joe of the resolution we had sworn to get all possible booze while home, and he, being the smart newsman that he was, and well acquainted with every lobbyist in the state told me not to worry.

While home I dropped into a photograph studio to make a record of what I looked like during the war. It came in handy, fifty years later, when our local newspaper interviewed me for their special edition for the fiftieth anniversary of D-day on June 6, 1994. Lastly, I walked across the alley to the home of the Johnson family on Weber Road. The patriarch of the family, Percy O. Johnson had served in WWI in France and his two sons, Bob and Tom, my childhood pals, were now in the Merchant Marine and overseas. Both of them made it to the end of the war OK.

The time of my freedom was getting short now and, just in time to be stowed away in my foot locker, Dad brought home a case of Bourbon, courtesy of J. Deutschle and friends.

Mom and I caught the New York Central to Chicago as the starting leg of our trip to L.A.; she to assist with the arrival of Hanna's second child; I, on my way to yet another encounter on hostile shores. Mother and I arrived by Pullman train in Chicago and were met by her brother, Morgan Smith, who drove us to his home in Hammond, across the border from the "Windy City" in Indiana. Uncle Morgan and Aunt Martha had children, Wesley and Doris, "Wes" was exempt from the service because of ear trouble, Doris' husband was in the infantry in France. We stayed one big night with them and then boarded our train to Los Angeles.

At that time the only choices to get to the west coast from east of the Mississippi river was by ox cart, horse drawn vehicle, "shanks mares" (walking), steamboat via the Panama Canal, or by changing trains in Chicago. Of course you could drive, but both gasoline and tires were under strict rationing because of the war. The fight for continuous passenger rail traffic through the city of Chicago had been going on since the day when someone drove the famous golden spike in Utah on May 10, 1869. At one time the Chesapeake & Ohio Railroad even ran advertisements stating, "A Pig can ride a train through Chicago—but you can't!". So Uncle Morgan delivered us to the OTHER railroad station in Chicago when it came time for us to continue westward.

Our trip to Los Angeles from Chicago went smoothly if you do not try to compare it with the air travel to which we have now become accustomed. I cannot remember whether it was three or four full days. We both had Pullman berths on the aisle, Mom the lower and I, the upper, above. The food was still as it used to be; cooked and served by trained, skilled professionals, and not the micro-waved stuff of today. Our only daytime stop was at Albuquerque, New Mexico, where we saw Native Americans (Indians, as we called them in those days) selling the famous Navaho blankets and other souvenirs in the station. My brother-in-law, Bill Kumler, met our train the evening we finally arrived. My sister, Hanna, "heavy with child" and a three year old son (Craig) in her arms, greeted us at the door of their small home in Westwood Village within the hour. Bill and Hanna had *moved* to Los Angeles as their Honeymoon in 1937, in a second hand Model A Ford. At that time, Bill had recently passed the Ohio bar exams and Hanna had finally made her degree in journalism and graduated from Ohio State University. A handsome, popular couple, it has always been my secret belief that they aspired in the beginning for Hollywood careers.

Bill, who by this time, had been admitted to the California Bar, was right at the start of a very fine career as an income tax lawyer and they treated me royally. We played golf early one Sunday at the Bellaire Country Club, nearby, where the Senior Partner in Bill's law firm had *given* him a full membership the previous Christmas. In the foursome just ahead of us I was awestricken by the presence of the movie super-star, Clark Gable, just out of the 8th Air Force where he had bombed Germany as a gunner on a B-17. We never came into contact but it was impressive to be around him.

One evening the four of us saw a movie, and then dropped in on the famous "Brown Derby" for a drink, the place was not crowded at that hour, so Mother and I merely acted nonchalant when we got to see Robert Benchley and Spencer Tracy arrive together, apparently out on a prowl.

It was time to head for Fort Lewis, Washington. My 30 days "Delay en Route" were almost gone and with considerable regret I had to leave my little family group to head back to the wars. It was late in January 1945, the war in Europe was obviously coming to an end. Hitler had "Shot his wad" in the "Battle of The Bulge", the Japanese had shot theirs too but didn't realize it yet. The Phillipine Islands had just been liberated except for pockets of stragglers. The U.S. Marines were in a fierce battle for Iwo Jima. Bill, Hanna, Craig, and mother all took me to a bon voyage party at a nice restaurant somewhere near the Los Angeles railroad station and after many goodbyes I was en route again. This time my immediate destination was Fort Lewis, Washington.

Two nights and almost three days of riding north along the California, Oregon and Washington Pacific Coasts were enough for me. The train itself was rather interesting though, as we went north, the February weather deteriorated from the sunny and bright of L.A.

to the wet and gloomy of Oregon. We needed heat in the cars and instead of bringing it back from the magnificent big boilers in the steam engine up front, we burned wood! Heat was provided by two pot bellied stoves, one at each end of each car, in the center aisle. Firewood was loaded at each water stop, which of course obviated the ability to scoop water from a trough along the track, the way they picked up their (steam) water in modern (1944) railroading. If I didn't know better, I'd guess that train had hauled troops to the battle of Gettysburg... ...and who can be sure it didn't?

We came into a sunny and bright Seattle at about two in the afternoon. There was an army bus to Fort Lewis in about half an hour so I decided to walk around a little to stretch my legs after the long train ride. The walk was only noteworthy because of the many white foot prints painted on the sidewalk and the fact that I encountered Private "Red" Miller of Headquarters 1st ESB. The sidewalk painting had to do with the local United Way, although they had another name for it in those days. Private "Red" Miller was something else, however. Officers who had been through four major assault landings would almost fight one another (when tipsy) to proclaim him as the best damned orderly in "this man's army". When we were under General Patton, back in the Sicily days, Patton, the discipline man, had decreed that every officer would have an orderly. Colonel Caffey had followed through on that one and as a result we officers were well taken care of in the small housekeeping chores of military life. "Red" Miller was about 20 years old, (perpetually), of medium height and stocky build with of course, a carrot red head of hair. He was reputedly as strong as a bull, and I know that he was as meek as a lamb. He told me that he had been at Fort Lewis for several days and had come into Seattle alone to "see the sights." He was indeed a "loner". Reportedly "Red" would dig a fox hole for anybody, time and situation permitting, for five dollars. "Red" was said to be from a coal mining town in eastern Ohio. A gang of us in the officer's ranks had formed an informal "Red Miller fan club" back in Caserta, Italy, but we never told him.

Eventually I took a bus to Fort Lewis; checked in with the officer of the day, and finally caught up with the Brigade Hq. after the precious '30 days delay en route". They were billeted in a typical wooden officers barracks and someone informed me there was a note on my door. I took probably ten seconds to find my room and rip open the envelope. The note in Col. Adams' familiar handwriting, merely read, "Capt. Daugherty, don't unpack, you are leaving in the morning, early".

When I awakened from a good nights sleep after reading Col Adams' hand written note on my bedroom door I naturally expected to find the good Colonel at breakfast to learn what was going on. I should have known better! Adams and McGrann were already checked out of Ft. Lewis and on their way to Hawaii as the super advanced party, Hq. 1st Engr. Spec. Brigade. As I soon learned, I was to be a member of the common ordinary advanced party of the Brigade HQ, going to San Francisco to assemble there, prior to flying to Hawaii for further instructions. The rest of the personnel of the Headquarters, the so-called "Rear Echelon", of which I had been a member during the invasion of North Africa, way back in November of '42, would follow by troopship right to our final destination— wherever in the devil that was going to be. All this I learned from Captains "Pee Wee" Davis and Shug Jordan as we talked in very guarded tones while waiting in the Seattle Station for our train to San Francisco that morning. "Pee Wee" and Shug had driven with their wives and "Pee Wee"s daughter, Jane, to Fort Lewis from the South Eastern corner of the U.S. and had only bid them good bye the previous evening as their families started the long trek back home to Birmingham, Alabama. Incidentally, I had had to get my shots all over, prior to breakfast that morning!

As our train finally pulled in we discovered that there were more members of the Advanced Party riding with us: Lt. Col. Brock who had joined the Brigade Staff prior Normandy, and Lt. Col. Earl Houston and Major Bob Hunter both of whom had come from the 5th and 6th Engineer Composite Organization on OMAHA Beach with Colonel Talley. Both Houston and Hunter were "good ole boys" who had been friends of Colonel Noce in the Mississippi River flood control projects during the depression. Incidentally, I never met any friend of Col. Noce who wasn't a real guy. As we neared San Francisco we experienced some confusion concerning the Oakland Ferry but soon we were checked into the Saint Francis hotel where indeed we had "never had it so good." The army had put us there, perhaps due to conscience pangs for the fact that they were sending us out again when so many soldiers had never been out of the country for even one day—Be that as it may, we were very proud of our record and glad to be on the move doing our part.

We were on the way to the Fairfield-Suisun Army Air Base early the next morning where some good soul of an Air Corps Operations Chief, sensing our plight, uttered endearing words to the effect that "You guys are out of luck, the weather's no good for your flight today, probably not for several more days either—check back with me tomorrow". (This despite the gorgeous California sunshine bathing everything in sight, and the heavy air traffic in the sky above). On the way back to San Francisco to try to find a place to stay, it was unanimously voted to try the Saint Francis again first, and to let Shug, with his sugary sweet Southern Manners, as compared to my abrupt Yankee Ways, do the talking for the three of us. Shug succeeded and upon the Desk Clerk's advice, Shug and Pee Wee both called the California Highway Patrol to see if they could head their wives to the Saint Francis Hotel in San Francisco. Miracle of Miracles! It worked, and within a couple of hours they had telephone contact, and in less than twenty four hours they were all reunited in San Francisco. And I was the "Odd Man Out"—Whatever *that* is.

We all hung around San Francisco for about four more days when the nice guy at the airfield told us that our luck had run out and we would have to be at the field that evening for 9:00 PM flight. We had managed to "DO" quite a bit of the city including Fisherman's Wharf and the "Top of the Mark" a very famous military watering hole in those days. I even managed to buy 8 cans of stuffed Anchovies for future cocktail parties overseas (about which, more later)

CHAPTER XII

MY TALES OF THE SOUTH PACIFIC

Having "Run out the Clock" on our Delay en Route, Travel Time, and phony Weather Delay, we assembled at the Fairfield-Suisun Army Airfield that evening and quickly boarded our *private* airplane a, C-87, which was a converted B-24 (Liberator) four engine heavy bomber. It was converted, that is, to haul people or materiel rather than to drop bombs. In this case, the people it was to be hauling consisted of Colonel Talley, Lieutenant Colonels Bailey, Brock, Givens, Houston, and Humphries, Majors Hunter and Paules, Captains Daugherty (me), Davis, and Jordan, and First Lieutenant Degnan, and Pfc. Wong, the orderly for Colonel Talley. All of these men have been previously described Except Lt. Col. Givens who was Col. Talley's Son-in-Law.

The sun wasn't very far above the horizon the next morning, a Sunday, when someone spotted land and soon we came in, right over the wreckage the Japs had left at Pearl Harbor that earlier Sunday morning over three years ago. I often wondered if our pilot approached Hickham Field by that route for sentimental reasons or whether it was the common way to get down. We radioed in that we were landing and Major McGrann was at the gate ere we landed. McGrann notified us not to get settled as we would all be leaving as soon as we had our shots and vaccinations! Actually, we didn't leave as soon as we had our shots, we got to stay <u>all day </u>in beautiful Hawaii. We finished the shots in the morning, and spent the early afternoon in a briefing with McGrann, after which we played poker in the Officers' club; high spot of the afternoon was Lt. Degnan's hitting the jackpot on a quarter slot machine. Nearly all of us used these quarters for poker chips from time to time, during the remainder of the war, though most of us were such "Big Operators" that the quarters usually had a "Pretend" value of a nickel or less; like using matches for coins during the Depression. From here on please don't ask me what time it was 'cause I never knew the time zone.

The next stop for our C-87 was Johnston Island, a speck on the map in the Pacific, but a very necessary refueling stop for four engine bombers en route from Oahu to Tarawa. We did enjoy hot cakes and

136

sausage at Johnston, and scenes of earlier struggles at Tarawa as we refueled again en route to Guadalcanal. Arriving at "The Canal", as the local Marines now called it, in time for a nice lunch, now that the bitter fight for the island was finally long finished. We enjoyed a fine afternoon of sightseeing, courtesy of the Sixth Marine Division now temporarily stationed there. This was to be one of the divisions leading us in the assault landing on Okinawa, our ultimate destination, and we left Major Bob Hunter and Captain Pee Wee Davis there on Guadalcanal to serve as liaison officers for the assault landing phase of the planned operation. Incidentally, this was the first unit of U.S. Marines I had encountered during WWII, except for the squad guarding the American Embassy on Grosvenor Square in London, England back in August of '42.

I personally split off from the Advanced Party, Brigade Headquarters at Gualdacanal to take care of some business for Colonel Talley at General MacArthur's Rear Echelon Headquarters in Hollandia, New Guinea. At this big Headquarters I accidentally encountered Lt. Tom Applegate a fraternity brother (Phi Kappa Psi) from Ohio State University. Tom knew of another fraternity brother stationed close by, Lt. Harry Vallery so the three of us had evening chow together at Lt. Vallery's unit, an Anti-Aircraft outfit guarding MacArthur's HQ on the edge of the jungle. After we parted that evening I never saw either man again until we were all back in civvies.

The day after I had met Applegate and Vallery I flew on down to Port Moresby to conclude Colonel Talley's business and then it was time to head again for Leyte in the Philippines, which was to be the assembly area for the Okinawa Assault Force. I didn't have an easy time getting rides to the next island airstrip and sometimes I had to go in the wrong direction to get to one where the probability of gaining some "ground" distance on the *next flight* was cause for hope. It was tough to travel without written orders in WWII but, as in the case of my September visit to Paris the previous autumn, it was not impossible as long as one was "Heading to the Sound of the Guns". The "guns" of course were still quite loud in the Philippine Islands where the Army was "mopping up" in Leyte and fighting a huge battle for the Capitol Island of Luzon.

My first ride north from Port Morsby was to the airstrip at Lae, still on the Island of New Guinea. I was seated in the co-pilot's seat when the pilot made a sudden 90 degree turn to the left. I asked the pilot, "What is going on?" His reply was, "See those clouds on the horizon to our right? They're full of rocks." To my stupid (trying to sound like an airman) comment of, "Oh, you mean there is a bit of turbulence in those clouds?", The pilot replied, <u>"No, I mean rocks!</u> Our flight instructions say that if we aren't at fourteen thousand feet before we reach that little river down there we had better fly around the mountain pass that is in those clouds, otherwise we will hit the mountain." He was so nice about explaining this to me that I swore off trying to talk flight talk, forever.

Our next stop was an island where I was stuck for the night and decided to go to the movies to kill the evening. As in many remote military outposts the Special Services Officer had done a good job with the facilities available to him. It now being a relatively safe rear area, he had set his "theater" in a shallow valley, with the projector elevated on a wooden platform so that very few in the audience were deprived of a good view of the screen. The screen itself was a transparent one suspended high enough above the audience so that persons sitting *behind* the screen could see the action and hear the sounds with perfect clarity, except that, viewing the action from behind, everything merely looked wrong handed. Having arrived at the amphitheater late, I found it a bit disconcerting to see a news reel of my favorite boxer, Joe Louis, fighting some guy left handed.

On the island of Pelileu, in the Palaus Group, where I had landed late one afternoon and was lying around the next morning, hoping for a plane headed toward Leyte, I saw a transport plane coming in from the North. On landing and taxiing to a point nearby where we could see that it was of the Royal Australian Air Force, the two man crew went into the Flight Operations Tent and an American sergeant who worked in flight ops. and with whom I had been chatting, got up and followed them into the tent. After a few minutes the crew returned to their plane and took off; the sergeant returned to his place in the shade and had this to say, "Those guys stop by here almost every week now. They are taking a fairly low-ranking Japanese POW to Sydney for interrogation, he is handcuffed in the cargo bay; it's too bad for him that it's only Monday 'cause if it were closer to the week end they would probably take him clear down to Sydney so they could be with their people over Sunday; as it is, although they didn't say so just now, they'll surely pitch him out of the plane as soon as they're over water again. They will tell their superiors how he escaped. Too bad for him it is only Monday!"

I finally landed at TACLOBAN AIRFIELD on Leyte, Philippine Islands at about 10:00 AM one fine day about ten days behind the forward echelon of Brigade Headquarters......... so much for travel overseas without written orders. I was at least five days behind the rest of the guys, in gossip that is, if not in anything else. They hadn't been doing anything, just lying around waiting to be ordered to do something. I had had to go to XXIV Corps HQ to learn the location of the Brigade Command Post, and while on that minor search, had learned some things I had missed during my island hopping tour from Guadalcanal to Port Moresby to Leyte. I was familiar enough with the "Terry & the Pirates" costumes adapted by the Air Corps from Milton Caniff's syndicated comic strip; heaven knows, those "Fly Boys" deserved to wear whatever they wanted to wear, but after serving under a disciple of General Patton (Col. Eugene Caffey) for a couple of years in a host of campaigns, I saw some sights on that ride to XXIV Corps Hq that made my hair stand on end. For example I passed a fairly large Ammo Dump encompassed by a single strand of barbed wire and guarded only by a lone American soldier wearing a Panama hat while sprawled in his jeep sleeping soundly in the afternoon sun. Patton or Caffey would probably have shot him (or liked to have shot him) themselves.

We were sheltered in the old faithful pyramidal tents and since we had been doing this kind of work for so many months now, couldn't find much to be gained by rehearsing for the next time we hit a hostile shore. It dawned on somebody that we'd better go back to the basics, the way the infantry always does when they find themselves with nothing to do. This didn't necessarily please everybody, but we started a program of physical training—which we sorely needed, if we were to maintain any fitness at all. This lasted either two or three days; I forget which. On one of these three training days we did take a cross country hike along these dusty Philippine dirt roads where I was very impressed by seeing a Filipino girl child about six years old scolding a chicken in Spanish, or Tagalog. It may not have been

Castilian Spanish, but it certainly wasn't my native English, either. It made me more conscious of my deficiencies than ever. Why could a six year old do this; let alone a chicken?

Another thing that would have made General Patton's blood run cold was the manner in which the U.S. Troops in the Pacific Theater used shot-up American Steel Helmets as urinals for open air Parisian-style street Pissoires. Take a 5 foot bamboo stick, about two inches in diameter, drive it into the sand for about half its length, place a bullet punctured helmet upside down atop the stick and behold! If you have the bullet holes in the right places you have created a sanitary urinal connected to nature about 30 inches from the surface of the earth. The war in the Pacific seemed to be just as bloody as the war with the Germans but a lot more crude and primitive.

It was time to board ship for Ryukyus Island Chain from which we planned to seize the largest of the chain, the Island of Okinawa, a scant 400 miles from Tokyo. The Tenth U.S.Army under Lt. Gen. Simon Bolivar Buckner and the VII Amphibious Force, U.S. Navy (7th Phib.) under Adm. Richmond K. Turner were the major Commands involved. General Buckner, as Brigade rumor had it, was the one to whom Colonel Caffey had sold the idea of bringing our HQ to the Pacific; during Caffey's visit to Oahu after D-day in Normandy. I always believed that the "Old Man" intended to *lead us* to the Pacific rather than *send us* as it turned out to be.

Instead of calling it D-day, as we "always" did, the Navy insisted on calling it "L Day", (for Landing Day) and it was scheduled for April Fools' Day, 4-1-45 (also Easter Sunday). A minor advanced action was scheduled for L minus 6 to clean up some tiny islands of the same Ryukus chain. Major Earl C. "Bill" Paules, my immediate superior, and Lt. Degnan, Assistant Adjutant of the Brigade were the only members of the brigade staff on board APA 125, a seemingly brand new Assault Troop Ship, named USS LANIER. It seems to me as though we were aboard more than two weeks getting loaded and forming up the assault convoy before we met our first Kamikaze (suicide) dive bomber several hours from our target. If you thought my memory was bad about events heretofore, please do not even try to make sense out of this first experience with the Kamikazes. They would appear over the fleet, fairly high in the sky, with the fleet "making smoke" beneath them, then they would seem to just hang there for a second or two and then, having selected their targets commence a power dive in that direction. It was when they were "Just hanging there for second or two" that I found them to be incredibly difficult to understand; here was a human being making the last and most significant decision of his life out in the open for all the world to see; truly the epitome of what General Patton had in mind that evening Pre-Sicily when he told us, the assembled officers of his Seventh U.S. Army "Don't be eager to *die for your country*, make the other poor son of a bitch die for *HIS country.*" Please keep in mind that from here on, throughout the remainder of this little book, the Kamikazes, if not a part of the story, were at least a *potential part of the story,* because the threat of their showing up in the sky over the fleet off shore was forever with us.

Getting back to life aboard ship, we had spent most of our time hanging out in the Officers' Wardroom playing poker, using Lt. Degnan's now famous sock full of quarters as chips with varying denominations represented from game to game depending upon the state of affluence felt by the dealer of the moment but *never* as much as the true face value of the coin itself. I don't remember why such miserly bets were the rule, maybe we were impressed with the true solemnity of the scene and didn't wish to take any chances that gambling might be considered a *sin in the hereafter.* Whatever the cause, I know that I was getting a little bit "jumpy"—the pitcher that goes to the well too many times is bound to get broken sooner or later—(ancient Hebrew Proverb, I guess).

CHAPTER XIII

BLOODY OKINAWA

The Landings on April Fools' Day (also Easter Sunday) came off as virtually unopposed. No Japanese units of any size, shape or form, worthy of the name, were found on any of the beaches and the Marines were heading northward toward their main objective, while the U.S. Tenth Army was starting toward Naha, the Capitol city of this Japanese province, in the south. With the damned Kamikazes so actively working over the fleet, it seemed as though it might be safer on the island than on the water. So Major Paules and I decided to go ashore. We, of course had to find transportation to get to the dry land we now so eagerly sought, but that wasn't too difficult. Our Troop Ship had an LCVP standing by, already in the calm East China Sea and it took merely a toot on a bosun's whistle to bring it alongside at one of the sally ports (No more climbing down the side of the ship on cargo nets in the modern (1945) version of things). The next thing we knew we were on Hagushi Beach where we had been trying to get since leaving Utah beach in December, 1944.

The First Engineer Special Brigade Okinawan Command Post, did not exist until L+3, so Major Paules and I didn't have any special place to "hang our hats" (excuse me, helmets) on the nights of L+1 and L+2. For some reason or other, we found a place to sleep in a pyramidal tent with four Navy Officers. One of these was a delightful gentleman who as I recall it, was a Lieut. Commander, name of James K. Vardaman, with whom in that short time, I seemed to "hit it off" as well as I ever did with a Navy officer. We had a good time talking, half the night of L+1 about things in general and nothing in particular. In a few days, I went back there to look for him, and learned that our brand new Commander in Chief, President Harry S. Truman, no less, had ordered him to the Nation's Capitol to become Naval Aide to the President of the United States of America, with the Navy rank of Captain (equivalent to a full colonel in the army). Captain Vardaman, it turns out had been a banker in Missouri and a long time, poker playing "crony" of our 33rd President.

Okinawa was so close to Japan that we had a lot of air raids. It seemed for a while like we were getting continuous attention; not massive fleets of heavy bombers flying high in the sky the way we used to see the 8th Air Force, in the newsreels on their way to bomb the German cities, but rather, a few bombers at once to reconnoiter in advance of the fleets of Kamikazes, or as just old fashioned nuisances to keep us from getting any sleep. When the sky is black with night it is very difficult to remain abed when bombs (or shells) are whistling, especially if there is no local enemy nearby and if caves which offer good cover are everywhere, as they were on Okinawa. The caves, which were used to hold the remains of the dead in Ceremonial Urns, after cremation; were quite conspicuous and were very quickly accepted as air raid shelters by the irreverent G.I.s of 1945. On the night of L+1, the Nipponese air force, on one of its soon to be commonplace nightly nuisance raids, had chased ten or so of my compatriots and me into one of these burial caves, where we had found comfortable seats on the burial urns or on the floor. Little bits of conversations had sprung up, when someone probing the cave with his G.I. flashlight suddenly focused in on a *huge black cockroach* high on the cave wall above. No one ever saw a dozen heavily armed men wearing steel helmets all go through the same single exit so quickly. It was a scene fully worthy of Laurel & Hardy...Spooked by an insect.. So much for Yankee Doodle Dandy!!

Our First Engineer Special Brigade Headquarters was very quickly able to assume responsibility for operation of all the unloading and out loading (wounded and POWs) as well as all of the U.S. main supply dumps and depots on Okinawa with three shift, seven day operations.

(Because only the Headquarters and Headquarters Company of the 1st Engineer Special Brigade had been moved from Europe to the Pacific Theater of Operations, it might be interesting to learn how it was possible for the Brigade Hq. to "assume responsibility" over a myriad of highly specialized Army and Marine troops we had never seen before. In the first place, the war was in its fourth year for the USA and a lot of these units had already been "in business" in the Pacific for several campaigns. Secondly, in addition to our original (European) roster of approximately 5000 *assigned* troops: engineer, medic, signal, quartermaster, etc., we normally picked up quite a few *attached* units as the beachhead enlarged. For example, as the Sicilian Campaign progressed, our assigned and attached troop strength grew to over 30,000 men. In the Army and Marines a man was a member of a squad of 8 to 15 men usually under command of a corporal or sergeant. Three or four squads made up a platoon, usually commanded by a lieutenant. Three or four platoons plus a Headquarters normally were banded together into the basic *administrative* unit, or company, usually under a captain, who had a couple of lieutenants and non-commissioned officers to assist him. Companies were formed and trained in a specific *branch* of the service (engineer, medical, etc.) and were so named and/or numbered. For security reasons company numbers were deliberately not assigned sequentially as the companies were created back in the United States. Companies, Battalions and even Regiments of service troops could be called upon by the higher command (in this case U.S. Tenth Army) to serve in their specialized roles as needed. Thus, in the battle for Okinawa the Brigade Headquarters was coordinating the efforts of 185 service units totaling 27,353 officers and enlisted men. (After Action Report, 1st ESB, 1945.) Enemy air activity continued with most, but not all, of the Kamikaze mass appearances in the daylight hours and most of the "special efforts" at night. As our Marine and Air Corps Land Based Fighter aircraft numbers grew with the readying of more of the existing airfields, the enemy daylight air activity seemed to diminish somewhat, in favor of more nighttime work. No-gunned Kamikazes had slight to no chance against the heavily armed Corsairs and Mustangs of Uncle Sam. At Brigade HQ, the S-2 (Intelligence Officer), Major Harry Jacobsen, had set up, mostly for our entertainment, radio monitoring of the Fighter Control broadcasts, and when off-duty we would often hang out in the S-2 tent listening to the pilot to pilot chatter of our guys chasing "bogeys" and "bandits" and miscellaneous meaner critters. Our HQ was right next to KADENA air field, GROUND ZERO as far as the fighter control was concerned. In other words all enemy activity was given a compass bearing (vector) and an approximate distance from KADENA, much as the air controllers keep track of where planes are in today's commercial air travel. One night, as a bunch of us were watching Jake's plotting board the crowd suddenly grew and grew. Three medium bombers were approaching ground zero from the north at low altitude and they were without doubt unfriendly. All three, still in formation, quickly skidded to a halt, and (according to guys who were much closer than we) 15 or 20 Japanese tumbled out of the bomb bays of each plane, each clutching a hand grenade to his chest and each man blowing himself to "Kingdom Come" almost as soon as his feet touched the ground. Meanwhile, a platoon of American medium tanks, stationed at the Airfield for the purpose of guarding same, cut loose with its own .50 caliber machine guns, firing horizontally, with enough force to destroy or severely damage some of our own planes parked for the night on nearby runways. Alas, 'Twas ever thus!

As I mentioned, now with three shifts operating and the logistical problems of the Okinawa landings under control, the Brigade Hq. had an almost peacetime, garrison situation to contend with, ...except, that is, for the fact that the fleet offshore was under almost continuous Kamikaze attack, (see Appendix F, "The Bunker Hill Story" for one example of what was going on with the fleet. The brochure describing "The Bunker Hill Story" was given to me by my friend, Dr. John Hayes, who earned a Bronze Star Medal serving as a Lt. JG, Gunnery Officer, on the Bunker Hill during that battle.)

One of the largest (six infantry divisions) and most bitter battles of the Pacific War was less than ten miles to the South. We ourselves were subject to occasional long range heavy artillery shelling from big guns down near Naha. So, as always seemed to happen, the Special Services officer, bless him, rummaged around in his bag of tricks and came up with some "toys" to keep us out of trouble. ("An idle mind is the devils workplace, etc., etc.) He dug out for us the usual softball paraphernalia, (but no flat ground to play on), boxing gloves, and, believe it or not, Horseshoes (the pitching variety, not the kind for old dobbin.) After a few days of a few guys spasmodically throwing them at the pin; sure enough someone almost got hit, ...complaint made, order issued to only pitch in the rec. area half a mile away, many disgusted at such trivia when other men were fighting the Japs nearby for their very lives. That night came a heavier air raid than usual. After a heavy bomb came too close for comfort; I heard Al Elias' unmistakable New York accent shout from somewhere in the blackout, "You guys get rid of those (blankety blank) horseshoes or take them to the rec. area."

After a few weeks on Okinawa, 2nd Lt. "Junior" Hall, who slept in the same tent as Elias and Willie Moore, bought a small Rhesus monkey from a sailor who had undoubtedly procured it in the

145

Philippines. It was scared to death of pipe cleaners, don't ask me why or how we found that out, if I knew, I would tell you—maybe it told why in the Owners' Manual (nobody reads it.)

The monkey was always kept on a very light leash and loved to sit on a man's shoulder and rummage through his shirt pockets, which were usually full of all kinds of junk. If it found a box of "penny" matches. (Wooden safety matches, common in those days) it would slide open the box and break the matches in two, one at a time. It was fun to watch but we were running out of matches and, besides, we had to pick up the pieces; so we designed a strategy to defeat the little bastard. We removed all the matches from a box, maybe the monkey had already done it for us, I don't remember, placed a pipe cleaner in the box, put the box in Willie's shirt pocket, (He was the tallest of the bunch.) and all walked out to where the monkey was perched on one of the low branches of a nearby tree. We feigned conversation, while peeking sideways to see what the imp was doing. Sure enough, five college trained, commissioned army officers had outwitted a small, solitary Rhesus monkey, tied to a tree as he was. He climbed on Willie's shoulder, started to dig around in his shirt pockets, found the bait, slid open the box and leaped backward from the tree limb, meanwhile emitting a shriek that was more befitting a wildcat. I do not know whether or not we had succeeded in weaning him of that particular bad practice but it sure passed the time for a few minutes. I believe it was Shug who (informally) Christened the creature, "Monko".

The easiest way to get the little beast's attention was to pretend we were fighting each other. One of us could punch the other fellow on the upper arm, as young men are almost constantly doing. and "Monko" would immediately denounce both of us, screaming and glaring at each. As soon as he began to calm down a little bit, he would commence beating his chest vigorously with his tiny fists while lecturing us in more moderate tones and threatening us with quick and total dismemberment if we chose to continue the fight. Shug used to let Monko crawl inside his wool shirt on cool days—of which there were quite a few on Okinawa. With the two bottom buttons invitingly left open on a cool morning, Monko would crawl in, leash and all, then turn around and extending a long, scrawny monkey arm, reel in his long tail, leave only his head out to breathe and observe the crazy humans.

When I returned home, following the war and after being away almost continuously for seven years, my own Mother commented, "Didn't you do anything but play with that monkey while you were away?"

As stated earlier while we were in the U.S.A. on our "Thirty days delay en route to the Pacific theater of War", we all had an unofficial, carved in stone, assignment, to wit: "Procure all of the Alcoholic Beverages you can and bring them, and all of the snack food you can beg, borrow or steal in your foot locker, to the next place we stop at long enough to get our foot lockers". Now, I took that assignment very seriously, especially the part about the booze, and with the generosity of my Dad's good friend Joe Deutschle, had stowed a case of bonded Bourbon in my foot locker before leaving Columbus. The Bourbon rode around the U.S.A. and the Pacific Ocean, in my foot locker from late January, 1945 until May of that year, when foot lockers and owners met again on Okinawa. Only a couple of bottles had been broken, and miracle of miracles, the booze had evaporated, leaving only a musty smell in my reserve duds. Unfortunately, for our expectations of high living, we were not now in the sumptuous quarters we had enjoyed, at Thanksgiving, 1944, when we had made our lavish commitment to get booze while home. Then we were in substantial houses in Normandy about seven hundred miles from the front, *now* we were in pup tents on Okinawa about ten miles from the front. So we didn't put on much of a party. I did have about six cans of the stuffed anchovies I had bought in San Francisco, and which had been a hard lump in my bedroll ever since, while awaiting party time when our foot lockers, and the sour mash bourbon, caught up with us. It finally boiled down to Shug and a few selected "buddies", each having a couple of swigs from one of the bottles in the evening before chow, while we snacked on anchovies and "C" Ration crackers. It wasn't as much fun as if we could have had one big party, but I guess the whiskey lasted a little longer.

One morning, while we were all asleep in our pup tents, neatly aligned on a small hillside, we were awakened about dawn by incoming heavy artillery rounds from the direction of Naha, about twelve miles south of us. This was unusual, we got our share of incoming artillery every now and then, but never this early in the morning. Were the Nips preparing to start some idiotic, hopeless final Banzai attack of which this was the opener? We were all up and out of our beds, clucking like a bunch of scared hens, when a lone guy, still abed, asked, "What is going on?". To which someone replied, "The Japanese are shelling us way back here". The sleeper, Captain Wallace Treadaway, listened for a second or two, then in tones of utter contempt, said, "Hell, that's at least three hundred yards away". We clucking hens crept shamefully back into our beds. Wally who had come over to Brigade Hq. from our 531st Engineer Shore Regiment had been wounded at Salerno and was the only company grade officer who could have embarrassed us so badly, and he didn't mean to do so; I am absolutely certain of *that*. He's a heck of a nice man.

One morning after a particularly heavy rainstorm, Shug could not find his dental appliance which the army dentists had made for him before we departed Nantwich, England, and which was so ill-fitting that he frequently removed it and put it in his shirt pocket. We found it flat in the mud outside our tent. Brigade Headquarters had moved us junior officers into small-wall tents, of the two or three man variety. These were just about perfect for two men; a little crowded when you tried to sleep three men, with the third man's cot running across the back end of the tent. They were no protection whatsoever against aerial bombardment or artillery. Shug and I were getting tired of lying in bed wondering when, if ever, the nightly nuisance air raids would end. We decided to make a more simple solution to the sleep problem. It required several days of spare-time, two-man digging but we settled on a two man dugout set into the side of a low hill, with a ceiling of timbers covered with sandbags and protected from the rain by our pup tent. You could almost stand up in it between the two canvas cots running along the middle aisle. We were even able to erect our mosquito netting supports properly. One night when I crawled into my cozy little nest and had almost finished tucking in the mosquito netting around the edges of the blankets I discovered that I was not alone. A big Okinawan rat was scrambling in the netting trying to get out. I was glad to help him escape.

We soon discovered that this bomb shelter was handier than the more distant burial caves, during the nightly air raid. Standard occupancy during an alert was six men and one pet monkey. To make matters worse, we were almost all cigarette smokers in those days and we had to put a smoking ban into effect during air raids. The little dugout "served with distinction" until late in the war, when the Air Corps erected a tank farm for 100 octane gasoline on top of the hill (virtually right over our heads). Then we just could not bear the thought of trying to swim in 100 octane aviation gasoline when some Jap artillery man found out about the tank farm. We abandoned our shelter and returned to living in the open.

During the construction of this treasure, we had devoted all of our spare time to scrounging the timbers for the roof and in that search we had a noteworthy adventure. One afternoon, starting out in a jeep, we saw an elderly civilian native walking along the road. Civilians were a rarity in that area of the island, (they seemed to have been evacuated before our arrival), so we offered him a ride in sign language. He was either confused or afraid, but he would not get in the jeep with us. We continued on our way with one of the three of us (Shug, Sam and Albert) commenting on the fact that this old man had a fortune in gold teeth in his mouth. To make a horrendous long story short, later that afternoon on the way back to our area, we found the old man, shot in the head, with his mouth a bloody mess. Someone had shot him and pulled most of his teeth for the gold. Rumor had it, at that time that a few of the old timers (regular) Marines carried a little tobacco pouch and a pair of pliers as standard battle gear.

The scarcity of timber on Okinawa was as apparent as it had been on Sicily. What few telephone poles they had were of concrete, rather than wood. They were truly an impoverished nation. The more affluent Okinawans kept a pig in a shallow concrete well, connected to the house by an open concrete trough. With this arrangement, all of the sewage from the house, was available to the pig. A short time after the initial landings, when it was discovered that there were many starving pigs on the island, due to the enemy having evacuated most of the civilians, our army mercifully issued orders to shoot all such captive pigs.

Towards the end, someone suggested that we put up a sign proclaiming our vast experience and sure enough one soon appeared. It was a great archway spanning the width of the entrance to the Brigade Heaquarters Command Post parking area, was well made of heavy dunnage lumber, and, contrary to army and security regulations, proclaimed, to all the world, something like: "This is HQ., First Engineer Special Brigade, D-day Veterans of N. Africa, Sicily, Italy, Normandy, and Okinawa." The painted background was sky blue, the 12 inch letters dark purple. At one end was painted in blue and gold, a large replica of our Combined Operations shoulder patch; at the other end was found the oval shaped red, white and blue sea-horse, chosen by my friend, Mueller, back in 1942 even before the Brigade was activated. I think the builder of that sign even found space for a big representation of the European Theater of Operations campaign ribbon with the battle stars most of us had won, and for the Asiatic-Pacific ribbon and its recently acquired two stars. The whole sign was professionally done and made one very proud just to see it. I'd give a lot for a color photo of it now. We had left a large concrete obelisk atop Col. Caffey's personal quarters/command post on Utah beach in Normandy, bearing the inscription "In Proud Memory of Our Dead" with large, colored porcelain enamel replicas of the brigade shoulder patch, as I have mentioned earlier, and it is still the centerpiece for European Theater ceremonies (2001 AD), but no such memorial to the Engineer Amphibious Brigades exists in the vicinity of Japan.

One final anecdote about the wee "Monko", if you'll bear with me, please. One morning after breakfast, as a bunch of us were returning to our tents, someone called attention to the little imp, sitting on top of the mosquito net support frame of Al Elias' bed, eating a piece of painstakingly hoarded Christmas (!) fruit cake with one hand and holding a copy of Readers' Digest with the other. On the tent floor, directly beneath him, spread the remains of a carton of Chesterfield cigarettes, with each cig broken in two by his little hands. If only he could have been caught onfilm in this situation, maybe peering over his bifocals, we would have had a classic. He always tried to imitate humans in his actions. Maybe he found second hand smoke so offensive that he was trying to tell us something!

As the fighting continued to advance to the south on Okinawa, the high command back in the States gave us orders to look for ways to vastly expand the logistical capabilities of the island. The War Department wanted to make 28 air fields out of Okinawa to take B-29

Bombers and to support the coming invasion of Japan. Our job was to find places where the troops and equipment could be brought ashore to handle this stupendous task. I was given one assistant and an Air Corps Crash & Rescue boat and told to make an initial study of all of the beaches north of our own Hagushi Beach to determine what, if anything, was available in the way of beaches to satisfy the War Department inquiry. I think my assistant was either Lieutenant Tom Pearsoll, of Norwalk, CT, or Irwin Degnan of Keokuk, Iowa, I've forgotten which—if either. We had one day of training in operating the boat, which was a "dream boat" for those days, and then with our maps and instructions took off for the north beaches. It would be nice to say that we found several perfect beaches—but it would not be true. The original planners of the invasion of Okinawa had found the best to be found, in their preparatory work the year or so before. We did at least learn one thing; we learned that the native kids could swim rings around us when they got over their shyness. Events now moved so fast that nothing came of our work.

CHAPTER XIV

MISCELLANEOUS EVENTS & EPILOGUE

We had of course learned of the death of our President and Commander in Chief, Franklin D. Roosevelt, a couple of weeks after our landing on Okinawa. They say you always remember the exact circumstances under which you hear important news: in this case it's true, for my memory at least. We were all eating our noon mess, sitting on the ground in a sort of natural amphitheater listening to armed forces radio broadcast of the days war news, when they interrupted the war news to tell us of his passing. We all felt saddened by this event, regardless of politics, we all knew that the war had drained him of his life. In a similar way, I remember the first news I had heard of the Japanese sneak attack on Pearl Harbor: It was Sunday afternoon, and the 4-12 shift was just beginning to straggle in to work at Open Hearth No 4 shop at the Homestead Works of the Carnegie-Illinois Steel Company in Pittsburgh. I, as General Labor Foreman, had been on the job since 8 AM and knew nothing about the happenings outside the mill (we were working seven-day weeks in those days). All at once the 4-12 shift labor foreman showed up with the startling news, and my life was changed forever.

The news of Hitler's demise, was confusing and, to say the least, not wholly accepted by the "man in the street". Even to this day, there are without doubt a few souls who believe that he is alive and living in Argentina or in the Bavarian Alps. This despite the fact that he was born in 1889 and would thus be 112 years old. Similarly, when I was a boy, in the 1930s there were those who would swear that President Lincoln's assassin, John Wilkes Booth, was still living and over 100 years of age. Actually, Admiral Doenitz, appointed by Hitler himself to be his successor, announced der Fuhrer's death, on May 1, 1945, and it was confirmed by the occupying Russian Army shortly thereafter. I believe that forensic studies, ad nauseum, have long since established the truth about Adolf Hitler's passing.

Colossal events piled one atop the other in 1945, following, but not because of, the deaths of Roosevelt and Hitler. Victory-Europe day (V-E day, of course) was celebrated in even the most remote of the victorious Allied Nations; not so for the troops on Okinawa. We did of course get the American announcement on August 6, 1945 of the dropping of the Atom bomb on the city of Hiroshima followed almost immediately by a movie purporting to explain the A-bomb.

Meanwhile, the Brigade Headquarters as I knew it, had gone to pieces: Colonel Adams, Majors McGrann and Jacobsen, my fox hole buddy, Captain Shug Jordan, and M/Sgt Albert Crawford Sheldon Dobson Clough, III, had all gone home on points due to the wars' end in Europe. I was paying the price for not being in the army long enough, for not having any kids, etc., etc. I had heard of the Navy's Training School for Amphibious Landings and knew that they needed a few Army guys to help out in spite of the old Army-Navy rivalries. There was still one more **Hostile Shore,** namely the Island of Japan. So after Hiroshima and before the second A-bomb was put on the city of Nagasaki, I applied, through channels, for assignment to the Navy Amphibious Warfare Training Center, Subic Bay, Philippine Islands. My transfer was approved quickly.

Between the time my transfer was approved and the Second Bomb hit Nagasaki on 8-9-45, I cleaned up my affairs at Brigade and was ready to fly to Clark Field, outside Manila, which I did on 8-12. So on August 14, 1945 which was declared to be V-J day, I was driving out Dewey Boulevard in Manila, P.I. when the fireworks started. Nobody had any *real fireworks,* I would guess, but there was an abundance of anti-aircraft protection, with tracer bullets galore, and it's a wonder we all did not die from "friendly fire" that night. **The war was over!!!**

Points still counted, when it came to who got to go home, and while I had just missed the magic number of 85 points, when McGrann and Shug went earlier, I now knew that I had plenty of points at 80 to get an early ride to the USA. I reported to the Subic Bay Navy School, where I was supposed to be, and settled down to await my orders to go stateside. I was bunked in a big Quonsett hut, with screened sides, cement floor and overhead electric lights. Mess was close at hand in a fine Navy "Galley" (I slipped and almost said, "kitchen"). I wasn't there long enough to make any lifelong friends, but I did get to know a Navy Lieutenant in the next bunk well enough to know that he had grown up next door to Katherine Hepburn, my all-time favorite Movie Star.

153

I've saved the best to last in this description of the amenities at Subic Bay: each afternoon about 4:00 PM an LCVP would show up at a nearby dock, and most of us would ride over to the Officers' Club across the bay where, in one convivial happy hour, we'd fight the war all over again. In those few afternoons, I ran into one man I knew from home, "Junior" Welch from North High School Days.

In a few days I received my orders to go by railroad train to Lingayen Gulf in Northern Luzon to board a ship which was loading troops of the 37th Infantry Division, (Ohio National Guard) to haul them home. We boarded a Filipino string of railroad coaches just at dusk and set out on an all night ride to the port of embarkation. The glass of all the windows was missing and we got a bit of smoke from the coal burning engine. I shared my narrow coach seat with a Navy Lieut. and we got along well, especially after he produced a bottle of rum from his duffel bag.

At the port, our entire contingent of train riders, was shooed aboard, by soldiers of the *Second Engineer Special Brigade* and we were soon on our way to Oakland, California. We were on one of the newer merchant vessels, a sort of upgraded Liberty Ship, called a "Victory Ship." These were introduced in 1944 and 534 were built. They were cargo ships, but this one whose name I forget, was *sort of* adapted to transport troops. We were advised, over the ships intercom, that we would get two meals per day; one steamed and one cold, and that the trip was estimated to take five to seven weeks. Homeward bound, we were undaunted by this news—at least we were not being shot at and we had time on our hands.

As I remember it, we passed under the Golden Gate bridge five weeks out of the Phillipines after a lot of bridge playing, reading, napping and sunbathing and zero significant problems. We were transshipped by ferry boat to some army staging area near Oakland, where we spent about one day being split up into train loads aimed in the general direction of our homes. We were free to go to Oakland to get our money changed to U.S. currency, which arrangement led to booming business for the local bars.

In the army, someone always has to be in charge, so I was honored to be appointed the Train Commander for a bunch of G.I.s from my state of Ohio for the train going to Camp Atterbury, Indiana. Of course the Army Transportation Corps had real honest-togoodness staff officers to really run the show, so I guess my title was merely an honorary one; but I did get a roomette to sleep in, whereas the other passengers got Pullman berths along the aisles. Every time the train stopped for water or switching, the troops would get off and inundate whatever poor merchant was within sight. I particularly remember seeing a GI from the 37th Division running with a whole stalk of bananas over his shoulder, as the train whistle blew the "all aboard" signal for the umteenth time. Our train broke down repeatedly, including once for half a day in the middle of the trestle across the Great Salt Lake and then again in the enormous rail yards of Chicago. We did, however, finally reach the siding at Camp Atterbury one night well after midnight, when we were all asleep, or at least too tired to do any serious celebrating.

In the morning, after chow, they started the business of mustering us out of the service. As I recall it, they did it in one-on-one interviews, with guys from the separation center at Atterbury doing the interviewing. First, after some chit-chat to put us at ease, they asked us questions about our Service Records to be certain they were current, next they made sure we knew where we were going from Atterbury after discharge, next they gave us a little sales pitch about staying in the Reserve Army. I signed on to do that, having been in either the CMTC (Citizens' Military Training Corps) since 1934-35, the ROTC-1936, 37, 38, 39 and a Reserve Officer since graduating from college in 1939. The years from 1934 through 1939 didn't count toward retirement, but nobody worried about *that* in those days; you worked until age 65 and then you died of old age—that was the plan. Besides, military retirement wasn't that lucrative unless you were Regular Army, with continuous active duty. My interviewer, another Captain incidentally, was pleased to sign me on to stay in the Army Reserve and, with that, he dropped some news I wasn't aware of: he told me that I was promoted to Major and should keep my pistol, watch, and binoculars. I wasn't certain that he was authorized to do all of this—but, what the hell?

I departed Camp Atterbury late that morning by train which was so crowded that I sat on the floor, between coaches. The train was so long that I had to get off way out in the Columbus rail yards and ask a worker there, "Which way to the station?" I finally trudged into the depot, up the stairs and took a cab to the home of my Mother and Father. The 28 year old Major, home from war.

The last word: (7-30-01) Don't let all of the anecdotes about drinking and drunkenness fool you. Probably, if the war had lasted a couple more years, many of us might have ended up as alcoholics, but I cannot think of anybody in the First Engineer Special Brigade who had such a problem after the war was over. Most of the guys had successful careers, nice families etc. And of course, Albert Elias, Sully (the Adjutant), and some others didn't even drink.

****

Only as an afterthought and only for whatever it's worth in proving that "staffies" were occasionally "where the action was", let me add that recently (2001 AD) by way of the Internet I stumbled upon the fact that I had personally made two (different) D-day landings with **the only** two Division Commanders who were KIA in Europe in WWII. Neither were struck during a landing nor in my presence, but I landed on the pier at Licata, Sicily along with Brig. Gen. Maurice Rose; at that time CG Combat Command "B", 2nd Armored Division, about 10:00 AM on D-Day, 7-10-43. I never saw him again. He was KIA on 4-1-45 near the end of war in Europe as he led a column of tanks as Commanding General, 3rd Armored Division. On D-Day in Normandy, 6-6-44, I landed on Utah beach at 9:30 AM at about the same time as my (temporary) Brigade CO, Brigadier General James E. Wharton who was KIA by a German sniper within weeks after he had been promoted to Commanding General of the 28th Infantry Division......This staff officer was with a few of the true heroes at one time or another.

APPENDIX A

ORDERS - PASSPORT - TICKETS

AG 210.31
(7-22-42)OA

July 22, 1942.

Subject: Orders.

Thru : Commanding Officer,
Camp Edwards, Massachusetts.

To : Officers Involved.

1. The Secretary of War relieves each of the following-named officers from assignment and duty at Camp Edwards, Massachusetts, and assigns him to permanent station outside the continental limits of the United States, temperate climate, Headquarters, European Theatre, London, England. He will proceed not later than August 1, 1942, from Camp Edwards, Massachusetts, to New York, N. Y., thence to London, England, reporting upon arrival to the Commanding General, European Theater, for duty with the Engineer Amphibian Command. TDN FD 31 P 431-01, 02, 03 , 07, 08 A 0425-23:

Major Richard R. Arnold   016663   CE
Second Lieutenant Sam P. Daugherty 0275437   CE

2. Travel by military, naval or commercial aircraft (Sec IV Cir 12 WD 1942) Army transport, commercial steamship, belligerent vessel or aircraft and rail is directed. TD by air from New York, N. Y.; to London, England, is necessary for the accomplishment of an emergency war mission.

3. In lieu of Subsistence a flat per diem of $6.00 is authorized while traveling by military, naval or commercial aircraft in accordance with existing law and regulations. A baggage allowance of 77 pounds while traveling by military, naval or commercial aircraft is authorized.

4. Prior to departure from his present station he will be equipped for extended field service, including steel helmet and gas mask, and will have in his possession WD MD Form 81, showing inoculations and immunizations required before leaving the continental limits of the United States, and will require physical inspection as prescribed by par 14, AR 40-100, as amended by Sec III Cir 31 WD 1942.

5. Officer should advise his correspondents that mail will be addressed to him at APO 81, c/o Postmaster, New York, N. Y.

6. Attention is invited to Sec II Cir 200 WD 1941, regarding the preparation and distribution of extract copies.

2 Incls: Pay Guide
Instr. Memo.
Distribution:
Officer (4)
Officers Record Section, AGO   Chief of Engineers, SOS
CG, APO 887, c/o Postmaster, New York, N. Y.

J. F. Ruth
Adjutant General.

Sam Daugherty

No. 18021

Special Passport

United States of America
Department of State

I, the undersigned, Secretary of State of the United States of America, hereby request all whom it may concern to permit

SAM PERSHING DAUGHERTY

a citizen of the United States, safely and freely to pass and in case of need to give to HIM *all such aid and protection as would be extended to like citizens or subjects of Foreign Governments resorting to the United States.*

S   11609

158

The bearer IS A GOVERNMENT OFFICIAL PROCEEDING ABROAD ON OFFICIAL BUSINESS.

_____

_____

The bearer is accompanied by his
Wife, X X X
Minor children, X X X
X X X
X X X

Given under my hand and the seal of the Department of State at Washington on
JULY 23RD
1912

Description of bearer

Height 5 *feet* 7 *inches.*

Hair BROWN

Eyes BROWN

Distinguishing marks or features:
X X X
X X X
X X X

Place of birth COLUMBUS, OHIO

Date of birth OCTOBER 3, 1917

Signature of bearer.

2

3

Sam Daugherty

Photograph of bearer

This Special passport is valid only for travel in the countries designated and in connection with, and for the duration of, the official business indicated herein. If the travel on official business for which this passport is issued extends beyond 2 years the passport is subject to renewal.

This passport to be valid must be submitted to the Department of State for endorsement after each return of the bearer to the United States.

SEE PAGES 6, 7, AND 8 FOR RENEWAL, EXTENSIONS, AMENDMENTS, LIMITATIONS, AND RESTRICTIONS.

4

5

8

*Renewal, extensions, amendments,
limitations, and restrictions*

CEADÚNAS EADARTHURAIS   Uimh _1.3.3./.4.2_
TRANSIT PERMIT   No.

Éifeachtach suas go _2.4/.8/.42_ le haghaidh aon
Valid up to   for a single

túirlinge amháin ag Aerphort na Sionainne (Faing)
landing at Shannon Airport (Foynes)

chun athbhárcachta i gcúrsa turais dhírigh
for the purpose of re-embarkation in direct transit

6

ag Aerphort na Sionainne (Rinneannaigh).
at Shannon Airport (Rineanna).

Ar n-a thabhairt amach i
Issued at the

Leagáideacht na hÉireann
Irish Legation, Washington, D. C.

ar an   JUL 24 1942
on the

Secretary of Legation.

Visas

161

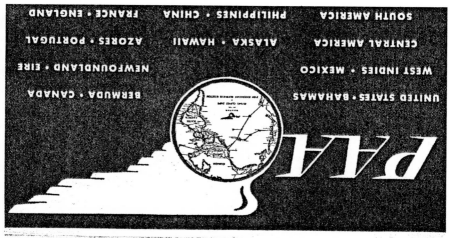

PAN AMERICAN AIRWAYS SYSTEM

& Associated Carriers

SPEED • COMFORT • DEPENDABILITY

TICKETS FOR MR. *Sam P. Daugherty*

(FULL NAME)

EXAMINE YOUR TICKETS: Read the contract conditions, and check routing, expiration limit and other details
DEPARTURES WILL NOT BE DELAYED FOR PASSENGERS ARRIVING TOO LATE FOR INCLUSION IN FLIGHT DOCUMENTS

EMBARKATION NOTICE	AIRPORT DEPARTURE TIMES		
Before any departure can be made to a foreign country, documentation for entry must be completed. This necessitates all passengers arriving at Airport at least minutes before scheduled departure. Earlier arrivals will be appreciated.	From	-	at M.
	From		at M.
TELEPHONE HA-4-8400 IMMEDIATELY UPON ARRIVAL IN NEW YORK CITY. SEDAN FOR LAGUARDIA FIELD DEPARTS AIRLINES TERMINAL 80 E. 42nd ST, AT D:	From		at M.
	From		at M.
	From		at M.
	From		at M.
(USE ABOVE SPACE TO STAMP OR ATTACH SPECIAL NOTICES)	From		at M.

PAN AMERICAN AIRWAYS SYSTEM

Form S

DS1916

PASSENGER CONTRACT TICKET
Not Valid Unless Officially Stamped
IDENTIFICATION COUPON
NOT TRANSFERABLE

MR. *SAM. P. DAUGHERTY*
(Print Passenger's Name)

ORIGINAL PLACE OF DEPARTURE *NEW YORK*
ROUTE VIA *DIRECT*
FINAL DESTINATION *FOYNES*
PASSAGE MUST BE COMPLETED BY *JULY* 19 *43*

Each of the annexed Flight Coupons, if and when officially stamped, and if presented attached hereto, will entitle the person named above, but no other person, to one passage between airports at or in the vicinity of the points and in the service of the carrier therein respectively designated, the address of which carrier is the airport at the place of departure thereunder, and also to transportation to and from such airports in local transfer services operated by or on behalf of the Companies (as hereinafter defined) but only in the cases and to the extent that such transfer services are included within the fare for the aforementioned passage and as provided in the published tariffs, rules or regulations of the Companies, subject, however, to the terms and conditions of such Flight Coupon, which are hereby made a part hereof, and subject also to the terms, conditions and provisions stated on pages 1, 2, 3 and 4 of this Identification Coupon and to the published tariffs, rules and regulations of the Companies, all of which are hereby made a part hereof, and all of which shall be deemed, and are hereby made a part of each such Flight Coupon, and subject also to all applicable laws and governmental regulations, orders, demands and requirements.

Such terms, conditions, provisions and regulations shall be applicable to transportation under the annexed Flight Coupon(s) and to all services and operations relating to such transportation performed or to be performed by, or with respect to which any liability may attach to, any of the Companies, including (but without limitation) surface transportation (either land or water or both) and the receipt, custody, handling, checking, transfer, transportation and carriage of baggage (including both checked and unchecked baggage as hereinafter designated, and both accompanied and unaccompanied baggage) transported or to be transported under any such Flight Coupon or under any baggage check of any of the Companies, and such terms, conditions, provisions, rules and regulations shall inure to the benefit of each of the Companies and its respective affiliated and subsidiary companies.

Transportation under the annexed Flight Coupon(s) is subject to the rules relating to liability established by the Convention of 12th October, 1929 unless (1) the original place of departure and the final destination stated above are in any one, or in any two, as the case may be, of the countries listed at the end of this Identification Coupon, or (2) either of such places is in any one of such countries, or (3) both of such places are in the same country, other than one of the countries listed at the end of this Identification Coupon, and there is no agreed stopping place as hereinafter defined in another country, Great Britain (excluding New Zealand, Australia and Canada) and all territory subject to its sovereignty or authority, France and all territory subject to its sovereignty or authority, the Netherlands and all territory subject to its sovereignty or

Continued on pages 2, 3, and 4 of this Identification Coupon

FOR INFORMATION ONLY — Not Part of Ticket
ROUTING: O.W. ☒ Circle ☐ R.T. ☐ R.D. ☐ A.S. ☐

NYK
(Routing)

PAA-A
(Carrier)

PRIORITY

Foy

BAGGAGE WEIGHT WITHOUT EXCESS CHARGE

PUB. FARE(S) $ ____ CY
FARE(S) PAID ____ CY
____ KGS EXCH RATE

U.S. TAX EXEMPT

I.C. FORM No.
CTC No.
T. RULE No.

AG210.31   WAR DEPARTMENT   BDC/cd/lr/1515
(7-22-42)OA   The Adjutant General's Office
                   Washington, D.C.

Subject: Amendment of Orders   July 22, 1942.

Thru   : Commanding Officer,
             Camp Edwards, Massachusetts.

To   : 2nd Lt. Sam P. Daugherty, 0375437, CE

       The Secretary of War amends so much of classified letter orders,
above classification, of July 22, 1942, as pertains to 2nd Lt. Sam P. Daugherty,
0275437, CE, to read: "2nd Lt. Sam P. Daugherty, 0375437, CE."

                            Ben D. Culleton
                            Adjutant General

Distribution:
Officer (4)
Officers' Record Section, AGO
Chief of Engineers, SOS

Sam Daugherty

APPENDIX B—TIGER
(DAVE MOORE'S LETTER)

Excerpt from Dave Moore's Letter to Brigade Historian Howard DeVoe, (January 14, 1988)

Dear Mr DeVoe:

Thank you for your recent letter regarding information regarding "TIGER EXERCISE'. I will try to answer your questions and to give you my best recollections as to the events, but after almost 44 years some of the incidents are hazy at best.

For your information, I was Company Commander of the 478th Amphibian Truck Company and as the senior army officer on LST 289 was in charge of all army troops on that ship. These personnel consisted of my company (less the 1st Platoon consisting of 2 Officers and 47 enlisted men who were placed on LST 507), a Quartermaster Co. of about 200 men, the medical unit of the 4th division, and several miscellaneous groups including, counterintelligence personnel.

At the time of TIGER EXERCISE the 478th had about 220 enlisted men of whom about 50 per cent had been through the North African, Sicilian, and Salerno Campaigns; and 6 Officers all of whom had been through those campaigns.

As you may know, LST's can only store 22 DUKWs on the tank deck, so it was necessary to utilize two LST's for the transport of my company. Consequently, I placed my second in command, 1st Lt. Herrel K. (Jake) Powell, 1st Lt. Lawrence D. McDaniel, and my 1st Platoon (Platoon Sgt. Rollie Yound, 2 Section Sergeants, and 44 enlisted men) on LST 507. The balance of the company, four officers (Capt. D. D. Moore, and 1st. Lts. Leland H. Burgess, Thomas J. Logan and Glenn A. Davis*) and about 170 enlisted men boarded LST 289. As I recall, there were between 400 and 425 army personnel on LST 289.

For my operational plan in case of an emergency, I set my CP in the Officers' Wardroom. Officers were placed for and aft at the top and bottom of the gangways in order to control the evacuation of troops, if such a course of action became necessary. The captain of the Quartermaster Company was assigned to one of the bottom aft gangways and Lt. Davis* was assigned to the other. Lt. Logan was at the upper forward port gangway and officers from the QM and other units were at other exits or in the CP. Lt. Burgess was in charge of the CP when I was not present. My enlisted men were bunked in their DUKWS and other army personnel were in the transient quarters on each side of the tank deck. Navy quarters were in the stern section of the ship.

At about 1:00 A.M., April 28 1944, general Quarters was sounded and we assumed our stations. Our feeling was that it was just another dry run. However, several minutes later there was an explosion that jarred the ship. Shortly after Lt. Logan burst into the CP and stated that the LST to our stern had been hit and was on fire. At dusk this had been LST 507 and we presumed it still was. I told Logan to resume his post and sent runners to notify all posts to be on the alert. Word was received from the bridge that the convoy was under attack and that the orders were to scatter and run for cover. Shortly there was another explosion that jarred our LST and word was received that another LST had been hit and exploded.

I decided that should go to the bridge in order to minimize any delay in the execution of orders from the ship's Captain, Lt. Harry Mettler. I was on the gangway leading to the bridge when our LST was hit. I was holding on to the chain on each side of the gangway and was able to hang on, landing back on my feet. I returned to the bottom of the gangway and checked the aft passages both of which were blocked in the galley area.

One of the contingencies that I had discussed with the Skipper was the possibility of taking the troops off the LST in the DUKWS in case it became necessary to abandon ship. At this time, the ship's Executive Officer joined us in the CP and informed me that the ship was without power and on fire but not listing appreciably and that they would undog the front and let down the ramp if I wanted to take the army troops off of the LST. Before making a decision, I wanted to know our location and if there were any defense craft in the area. (Several DUKWS were scheduled to have 50 cal. machine guns mounted but none had been received at the time of the exercise.)

The Executive Officer and I went to the Chart Room and scanned the Radar screen (which by some miracle was still working). As best we could tell there were only four blips, which we assumed were LSTs. In plotting our position the Exec. Officer could only mark where we had been at the time of the alert because of the evasive actions that had been taken.

Before I had to make a decision, word was received from the skipper that the fire had been put out, and that we had regained power and would try to make port. I was requested to join the skipper on the bridge so that any needed coordinated actions could be taken as promptly as possible.

The torpedo that struck LST 289 hit aft of the tank deck at, or close to, the water line and had carried away the rudder, but both screws were intact and power was regained. The ship's crew quarters were destroyed and the aft gun deck was blown to a vertical position with some debris dangling over the bridge. Naval Personnel who had remained in their quarters because of illness or were stationed at the aft gun position accounted for most of the killed, missing or wounded on LST 289. I did not keep any records of the incident, but as I recall there were 7 naval personnel killed, 8 missing, and about 20 wounded, including the Gunnery Officer who had both legs broken, as he had been thrown over the bridge from the force of the explosion.

No army Personnel on LST 289 were killed and very few received even minor wounds. The most severely injured was Lt. Davis*. Lt Davis was on duty at the rear of the tank deck when the torpedo struck. A piece of metal was blown through the bulkhead striking him in the groin. Later he was visited in the hospital, and as I recall was recovering but was permanently disabled.

The Captain commanding the Quartermaster Company, who was stationed on the opposite side of the rear of the tank deck, was thrown to the tank deck breaking a collarbone. (Incidentally, this Captain was placed in command of the army troops on one of the LSTs in the invasion because of the experience he gained here). Other than Lt Davis and the QM Captain I do not recall any army personnel who were hospitalized.

I would be remiss if I did not commend the 4th Division Medical Team for the fine job they did in locating and helping to treat the injured on LST 289. We were also fortunate that LST 289 had the Naval Medical team for this group of LSTs. Without their assistance I am sure that several of the injured would not have survived.

Upon joining the skipper on the bridge, I observed two separate oil slicks on fire. The skipper had dropped two LCVPs off of the bow and attached them with tow lines to provide steerage The channel was smooth, the moon had set, but it was a bright starlit night so we guided on the North Star and limped back toward England at about 5 knots with a slight list to starboard.

Because of the number of naval casualties they did not have sufficient crew to man all the remaining guns, and I was asked to furnish a crew for the forward position. By dawn, I would have backed that crew, composed of officers and sergeants, against any other crew in the armed services.

Tracers were observed on the horizon once or twice during the night. However, our first sighting of any craft was about dawn when we met a British Corvette escorting several LCTs along the coast. Shortly afterwards a U.S.destroyer came alongside and offered to give us a tow. A line was attached but snapped. By then we were making very little headway against the tide. Some time later a tug arrived. We were taken to Dartmouth Harbor where we docked in the early afternoon.

After a preliminary investigation, my company, and I presume the other units, were ordered to an army camp in that vicinity where we were again interrogated by the G-2s of 1st Army, ETOUSA, and SHAEF. Their primary concern was whether the enemy could have taken any prisoners. We, of course, told them that there was nothing to stop the Germans from taking any prisoners they wanted from the two LSTs that were sunk, or from the missing sailors on LST 289, if any had survived.

Following these debriefings we were permitted to return to our base camp. (We were probably ordered, otherwise I would have joined the exercise at Slapton Sands). A secret classification was placed on any discussion of the incident at that time. I arrived back at my base camp near St.Austell, Cornwall about midnight on April 29, 1944. This was prior to the return of any other personnel assigned to the 24th Amphibian Truck Bn. engaged in the exercise.

As an interesting aside, there was a German air attack on the port of Fowey going on at the time I arrived. I was greeted by the Battalion adjutant and informed that my replacement had just arrived from the U.S. I remarked that he didn't know how close they came to needing him.

The status of the 478th Amphibian Truck Company personnel who were on LST 507 was as follows:

1st Lt. Herrel K. (Jake) Powell—Killed in action (died from overexposure).
1st Lt. Lawrence D. McDaniel—Survived (spent night in water wearing Kapok life jacket—rescued about 6:30 AM. Hospitalized for shock and paralysis of the lower body—recovered and returned to active duty after several days. He had just completed survival school in London.
Platoon Sgt. Rollie Young (since deceased)—Sgt. Young corralled several men from the company and with some naval personnel freed an LCVP that was stuck in its davits, lowered and boarded it escaping without even getting his feet wet.

Six enlisted men - Survived on a life raft -had a horror story of too many personnel attempting to board the raft, of the raft capsizing and of the fighting to regain a spot on the raft.

Two enlisted men - survived by staying afloat -one of these claimed to have survived without his life jacket.

Total Survivors—   1 Officer and 16 Enlisted Men
Killed in Action—   1 Officer and 16 Enlisted Men
Missing in Action and Presumed Dead - 15 Enlisted Men.

In answer to your query regarding the total number killed from the German E-Boat attack I have no direct knowledge beyond those of my company and my estimate of the casualties on LST 289. However, the total number of casualties was estimated to be about 800 army and navy personnel, most of whom were missing and presumed dead. In any case, next to the sinking of the President Coolidge in the Pacific it was the largest loss of army personnel from enemy naval action.

As you pointed out, the Army History, "Cross Channel Attack" gives Navy figures as 638 killed and 89 wounded, and quotes a Jones, historian for engineer units, at a figure of 749 killed. A more recent article**based upon information collected by a medical captain who treated some of the casualties at the 228th hospital gives figures of 424 dead out of 496 aboard LST 531. As I recall there was a QM Service on this ship which had one survivor, and a detachment of the 462nd Amphibian Truck Company on LST 507 had only 3 survivors. The same article** states that on LST 289 "four of Mettler's crewmen had been killed outright in the action, eight were missing and presumed dead, and eighteen had been wounded- -one of whom would die in a nearby hospital". No details were given of the casualties on LST 597, but quotes a former Royal Navy officer, Harry Unsworth, now a historian of a small town in Devon as compiling a total number of casualties for the exercise at 785.**

At the time it was generally held that there was an excessive loss of life because of the lack of training and the absence of discipline in abandoning of ship, improper use of the type of inflateable life jackets issued to the troops, and the mad scramble that ensued in the water. However, in my opinion, many lives could have been saved if there had been a more expeditious rescue attempt. If it had not been for the decision of the Captain of LST 515 to return to the area of the sinkings the loss of life would have been much greater. As it was, one needed to be in top physical condition to survive four or more hours in 48 degree water. Also, as I recall my detachment on LST 507 had a much higher survival rate than any other unit. This would indicate that the maximum number of survivors from LST 507 including navy personnel would not be more than 150. In other words, I believe your estimate of 321 rescued is excessive.

As I recall, I sent Lts. Logan and Burgess to identify the 478th personnel killed in action. They returned with personal effects taken from the bodies. These, together with the effects left in base camp by them and those missing in action, were screened and sent to their next of kin. I sent letters of condolence to the next of kin of those personnel, but I was not allowed to discuss the circumstances because of security restrictions. As I recall, the particular phraseology used was worked out with Brigade S-2 and possibly higher command. So far as I know, the security classification was never lifted. It was still in effect at the time I returned to the States on rotation in July, 1944. Even after the need to keep any knowledge of the incident from the enemy was past, higher command was not interested in publicizing the affair. The U.S. and British Navies were both embarrassed by the foul up in providing escort service and the delay in sending any rescue craft to the scene despite the fact that the U.S. Naval base at Portland was only a short distance away and that an S.O.S. had been sent in the clear.

I do not remember the disposition of the bodies of those killed in the exercise, but I presume they were buried in a temporary grave until a permanent site was selected. So far as I know, none of the bodies of the men who were missing from my company were ever recovered. Certainly, I was never notified.

Sam Daugherty

I do not know of any personnel who were BIGOTED. I do remember that there was concern at the time, but the bodies of all BIGOTED personnel were recovered.

* NOTE: This officer had just been transferred to the 478th from the 531st Engineer Regiment. He was the only army person who was badly injured from the torpedoing of LST 289. He was still in the hospital at the time of the Normandy Invasion and I believe was permanently disabled with a groin injury. <u>I am not positive that his name was Davis.</u>

**What Happened Off Devon", AMERICAN HERITAGE, Volume 36/Number 2, February/March 1985, pp26-35.

****

Author's Notes: This ends the extract of Dave Moore's 1988 letter to the Brigade Historian, Mr. Howard De Voe. I have been a good friend of Dave since we met in Algeria late in 1942, Dave made all four of our European Theatre assault landings with the Brigade. After the war Dave's career brought him to Battelle Institute in my home town of Columbus, OH where he rose to a senior position. Dave and I have been close friends for going on 60 years now.

APPENDIX C
A PRIEST REMEMBERS D-DAY
REV. A.A. McAVOY, 6-6-94

(Author's Note: This is an account of the activities of Reverend Ambrose A. McAvoy prepared for "The Witness", the Diocesan newspaper of the Archdiocese of Dubuque, Celebration of the 50th Anniversary of D-Day, June 6, 1994. It is included to give you some idea of a Chaplain in battle. (The (now) Monsignor McAvoy and I first met during the landings in Sicily in July, 1943 and though we are both "getting up in years" maintain our friendship and occasional contact to this day. SPD 9-2 -01)

Priest Remembers D-Day

(Note by the Editor of the Diocesan Newspaper, "The Witness", 6-6-94): The following article by Msgr. Ambrose A. McAvoy is an account of his experiences just prior to and on the day allied armies made landings on French shores 50 years ago, June 6, 1944. Msgr. McAvoy had also been an early arrival at the invasion of Sicily and Okinawa. His efforts on behalf of American troops earned for him the Bronze Star for meritorious service. He now holds the rank of Lieutenant Colonel in the Air Force, retired. Msgr. McAvoy now lives with fellow priests in the Villa Raphael, Dubuque.)

After serving two months with the 9th Infantry Division during the invasion of Sicily and the route of the German and Italian forces there, I returned to Africa and rejoined my original assignment with an engineer amphibious brigade whose specialty was the direction of amphibious landings. Thence, across the straits of Messina and up through the boot of Italy to Naples. From Naples we sailed for England after Christmas 1943.

We made headquarters in a country mansion of some 45 rooms, with a pretty name of Pencalenick, about three miles from the Cornwall city of Truro. It was here that intense training for the invasion of France took place. A war room with a very long table showed in relief every physical feature in the expanse of beach upon which we were supposed to land. It was not easy to get into this room. Guards were posted at the entrance and about the building 24 hours a day. I was however brought in one day so I could see three churches close behind the beach which I might use someday. And I did, too. One of them was the church of St. Mere Eglise which was featured in the movie, "The Longest Day." I stayed there in the rectory for some time. The pastor tried to teach me French. I tried to teach him English with communication in Latin. Talk about a Tower of Babel!

The most important part of the training program was practice landings. Men and equipment would be loaded and the night would be spent in the channel and the next morning we would wade ashore on an English beach. These exercises were called "dry runs." One of these exercises met with a devastating disaster. German torpedo boats located our convoy and attacked. We lost 800 men. Of one Chemical unit of 215 men, only 15 survived. the somber thoughts which coursed through the minds of the men as we prepared for history's greatest war adventure grew darker still. "We will win but many will die," was the sentiment which occupied the minds of the men as the time for the real thing came closer each day. The atmosphere became more quiet and feelings a bit more tense. I was getting a little somber myself.

Then we moved to another site, close to where we should be loading onto transports for the crossing. Hundreds of units were located in long, narrow areas which resembled, and were called sausages. There, by the day and hour we awaited the orders to move out. The Special Services people did a marvelous job in keeping up morale. They provided reading material, games, music and a different movie every night. I once heard a general give a talk on morale while I was assigned to the 42nd Armored Regiment at Camp Polk, La. He defined morale as "a lot of little things, like a surprise piece of bacon for breakfast". Special Services gave us all "the little things" you could think of and it helped because many spirits were low.

I can't recall how many days it was before we moved down to the ships and found our assigned places. I was in a position to move easily along a row of Landing Ship Tanks (LSTs), which carried the big machinery of war. Mounting a tank or truck or some other high place, I could call for the Catholic men to assemble for prayer and general absolution, explaining they were excused from penance and gave the absolution, except the first time when I became so absorbed in the explanation I forgot to give the absolution. But I happened to be awake that day in the seminary when the professor explained that when the priest goofs, the church supplies. Never did a priest gather a congregation so easily as to this ritual on the eve of the invasion. The Catholics came but the others didn't leave. A little bit of religion wouldn't hurt about now. It reminded me of the saying, "There are no atheists in foxholes."

The weather was terrible, the channel waters rough and choppy. We know now that Eisenhower moved the initial date for the landings from the 5th to the 6th, waiting for smoother waters. Then, after dark, this vast armada of ships took to the sea and the game was on. When daylight came my ship was stopped about a quarter of a mile off the designated landing, area, code name "UTAH" beach.

09:30 Hours

The small ship on which I crossed during the night was called an LCI, Landing Craft Infantry. It bobbed around in the rough waters like a cork and many of the men were very sick. The cereal and milk we had for breakfast spilled and the floor was a slippery mess. I think we were glad when told to go down the ladder on the port side into an assault boat which rushed to the beach. I let down its front ramp and I stepped into the waist deep water. My wool uniform had been impregnated against gas attack and it tightened up around my body. With musette bag, entrenching tool and inflatable life belt and with Mass kit held high and dry I waded ashore. A few shells exploded in the water but well over our heads.

177

10:00 Hours

The first thing I saw upon reaching the shore was six of our men whose war had come to a quick and permanent end. I remembered we had been told in Chaplains School the dead should be removed from the battle field as soon as possible. The sight of the dead is hard on morale. I had had some experience in the gruesome task of removing the dead while with the infantry in Sicily before military became convinced that this task was not really chaplain's work. But inasmuch as hundreds of our men would see these dead I decided to bury them. I asked a colonel in charge of some trucks nearby for a truck to haul the dead. He told me to go to hell. Then, not a little mindful of the repeated warnings about mines, mines, mines, I dug six graves and buried the men. Nothing happened. I guess God was saving me for Postville!

10:40 Hours

I stood on a knoll and surveyed the length and depth of the beach. It was a huge ant hill of activity: men wading ashore, hundreds of trucks lining up to go forward, amphibious DUCKS loaded with ammunition coming from the sea and scooting onto the shore. Then the eerie sound of artillery fire, incoming mail. I made a quick dash and long leap into one of the huge craters made by Air Force bombers in pre D-Day softening up exercises. I landed at the feet of three men from my unit. After awhile things became silent again and I yelled, "OK men, it's time to move." But they didn't move and I realized they would not move until a detail came to carry them away.

11:20 Hours

I don't want to make D-Day sound like 24 hours of continuous gun fire. What there was, was enough for anyone. One more incident and we'll let it lie. I was standing with our CO and other members of his staff when the scary whine of artillery came again. I quickly made it into a nearby drainage ditch shoulder to shoulder with Captain Ralph Jordan who took a large piece of shrapnel in his left arm. Shucks, I was only about six inches from getting that Purple Heart myself. While on this particular subject I would like to say this. American troops landed on two beaches a few miles apart. My beach was UTAH. The other beach was OMAHA. The difference? If UTAH was purgatory, OMAHA was hell. They got it in the guts. We got it in the arm. Neither was a walk in the park but if any old veteran of OMAHA beach happens to read this, I want him to know I'll stand and salute.

16:00 Hours

Remarkably, by four o'clock the medics had erected hospital tents with all equipment ready to go. The doctors were working on the wounded arriving in increasing numbers. The litter bearers lined them up in a long line and moved them up one at a time. I started the real work of chaplain now, going down the line letting each one know I was his chaplain, not to worry, that the doctors would see him soon and saying a short prayer. Most of the wounded were given the quick MASH type treatment and were moved onto ships waiting to evacuate the casualties. Some didn't make it and were removed to a designated area and remained there until the Graves Registration people began their work.

17:30 Hours

What a sight! What a thrill! Suddenly from the sea came planes towing gliders. A huge flock of them flying so low you felt you could reach up and touch them. A short distance behind the beach the gliders were let loose and the low planes made a quick U-turn and scampered like hell back to England. I am not convinced of the value of this operation. Previous to D-Day France, I was in on the invasion of Sicily when bad winds and bad weather caused 47 of 134 gliders to land helplessly in the sea. Now, the planes flew too low, the fields were too short, the trees bordering the fields were too high. Many didn't make it and crashed into the trees. Some got in safely only to have another glider choose the same field and hit the one already landed. Some pilots died and many were hurt and unfit for battle. But, bless the guts of those who took this perilous route to the invasion beach and went on to fulfill their mission. (Incidentally, if I ever fly a glider I want the Gobi Desert for a landing place!)

19:30 Hours

A German plane flew low over the beach and was shot down. The pilot parachuted and landed on the beach just ahead of us. He was

179

taken by the men and seated in front of a tent. He looked very
worried if not totally scared. But a doctor was rushed to see if he was
hurt. The men lit him cigarettes and gave him candy and brought him
food. I don't know what happened to him.

20:00 Hours

About eight o'clock I went to the medical tent and stood by the
surgeons at work. Haul them in, stop the bleeding, remove the lead or
steel, sew a bit and move them out. Hawkeye and his MASH gang
never did it better. How long could they stand, and stand, and sew? I
gave a sign of admiration and went out.

23:00 Hours

At eleven o'clock I decided I'd had it for one day. I found a good
spot and dug a trench about six feet long, three feet wide and a foot
deep and crawled in. Once in a while since the war someone asks,
"Were you ever scared?" Before I could close an eye there came the
sound of low flying planes. They dropped flares which lit up the sky
with an eerie, purplish light. When would the first bomb drop and
where would it land? I hugged Mother Earth, but no bombs dropped.
Their business was only reconnaissance. But was I scared? Yes,
Virginia, I was scared

APPENDIX D

CITATION FROM GENERAL MATTHEW RIDGEWAY

S E C R E T

HEADQUARTERS
ADVANCE SECTION
COMMUNICATIONS ZONE
APO 113

SECRET
Auth: CG, ASCZ.
Init:_____.
Date: 16 July 44

16 July 1944

SUBJECT: Movement of the 101st Airborne Division and 82nd Airborne Division.

TO : Commanding Officer, 1st Engineer Special Brigade.

1. I desire to commend you for the superior manner in which your organization handled the out movement of the 101st and 82nd Airborne Divisions. This move was accomplished during the period when you were receiving a large amount of personnel and vehicles from the UK for discharge including an armored division. At the same time, you were maintaining the required discharge of supplies.

2. From all appearances, the movement of these two (2) divisions was simple and was accomplished with ease. This headquarters has received many informal compliments on this outward movement for which you were directly responsible. The simplicity and the ease with which you handled the situation could only have resulted from an efficient organization under strong centralized control with the details passed to efficient and capable subordinates.

3. Your handling of this movement is typical of the operations of the 1st Engineer Special Brigade since it has come under my command. I am proud to have such an organization attached to the Advance Section Communications Zone. I am most grateful for your full and complete coordination with my staff and with the spirit and energy which your organization puts into its operations.

/s/ Ewart G. Plank
/t/ EWART G. PLANK
Brigadier General, USA
Commanding

"CERTIFIED TRUE COPY"

Charles W. Sullivan

CHARLES W. SULLIVAN,
Captain, Inf,
Adjutant.

1st Ind.   CWS/ldt

HEADQUARTERS 1ST ENGINEER SPECIAL BRIGADE, APO 230, U.S.ARMY, 23 July 1944.

TO: Captain Sam P. Daugherty, Headquarters 1st Engineer Special Brigade, APO 230, U.S.Army.

To you goes the major portion of the credit for this — a job well done.

By order of Colonel CAFFEY:

Charles W. Sullivan

CHARLES W. SULLIVAN,
Captain, Inf,
Adjutant.

Sam Daugherty

Capt Daugherty:

Should you not see this letter, you may be interested:

HEADQUARTERS 82D AIRBORNE DIVISION
Office of the Division Commander

A.P.O. 469, U.S. Army,
24   July   1944.

SUBJECT: Commendation.

TO   : Commanding General, 1st Engineer Special Brigade, A.P.O. 230,
           U.S. Army.

THROUGH: Commanding General, First United States Army, A.P.O. 230, U.S. Army.

1. I desire to express my appreciation for the efficient manner in which this Division was moved across the beaches at the time of our return to the UNITED KINGDOM, 13 and 14 July 1944.

2. Intimate liaison between our units was maintained throughout. Demands for truck transportation, rations, and other administrative needs which arise at such a time were more than fulfilled by your organization.

3. The entire move was accomplished with that effortless efficiency which after close association during the course of three campaigns we have come to regard as normal when operating in conjunction with your unit.

                    M.B. RIDGEWAY,
                    Major General, U.S. Army,
                    Commanding

        Army indorsed the above saying they were "pleased to note and forward this commendation for work exceptionally well done".

182

APPENDIX E

ORDERS TO FLY OVERSEAS AGAIN

HEADQUARTERS
ARMY SERVICE FORCES TRAINING CENTER
FLOOB 370.5   FORT LEWIS, WASHINGTON

MOVEMENT ORDERS)
                 :   29 January 1945
NO.   22)

    1. The following-named officers and enlisted man, Shipment 4441-A, WP to Hamilton Field, California, so as to arrive not later than 4 Feb 1945:

```
        LT. COL DODSON O GIVENS,   0282912, CE
        LT  COL EARL P HOUSTON,    0907654, CE
        LT  COL FRANK P BROCK,     0250777, CE
        MAJOR ROBERT F HUNTER,     0923505, CE
        CAPTAIN JAMES R JORDAN,    0293978, CE
        CAPTAIN SAM P DAUGHERTY,   0375437, CE
        CAPTAIN JOHN N DAVIS,      0260333, Inf
        Wong, Hoy W Pfc            32820162
```

    2. Individual equipment and personal baggage not to exceed one hundred and twenty pounds (120) per individual will be taken. One (1) field desk and one (1) field safe not to exceed one hundred sixty pounds (160) are authorized to be taken with this movement.

    3. All personnel will continue to have mail addressed as at present pending receipt of further instructions. Attention is directed to paragraph 18, WDPOM dated 1 Aug 1943.

    4. TC will furnish necessary rail transportation.

    5. IGF. TC will furnish necessary meal tickets to one (1) EM.

    6. PCS. TDN. 501-31 P 431-02-03-04-05-07-08 A 212/50425
(Authority: WD Ltr. WD 370.5 (18 Dec 44) OB-S-E-SPMOT-M) dated 19 Dec 44, subj: "Movement Orders, Shipment 4441" as amended; TWX CG, NSC, dtd 27 Jan 45.)

BY COMMAND OF MAJOR GENERAL PATCH

OFFICIAL: FRANK ROYSE
                                                   Col GSC
                                                   Chief of Staff

    JAMES E BURNETT
    Capt AGD
    Adjutant General

DISTRIBUTION:
TAG -5	Transp Off -5
CG, ASF -5	Audits & Budget Br -2
CG, NSC -2	CO, Hamilton Fld -5
CO, Shipment 4441-A -15	TMO -10
Each Off & EM (10 ea) -80	Post Rec -1

AIR TRANSPORT COMMAND
PACIFIC DIVISION, WEST COAST WING
1504TH AAF BASE UNIT
Fairfield-Suisun AAB, California

7 February 1945

SPECIAL ORDERS)
)
NUMBER   38)

Auth: CG, Pacific Div, ATC
Initials: *RBC*
Date: 7 February 1945

E X T R A C T

*   *   *   *

7. The following named pers (WOS, NCO and Comp - Unknown) (2d Adv Det Hq & Hq Co, 1st Engr Spec Brig) having reported to this Port of Aerial Embarkation in compliance with par 8, S 34, ATC, Pacific Div, West Coast Wg, 1503d AAFBU, Hamilton Fld, Calif, will proceed without delay by first available mil, naval, or commercial acft (Auth: par 3b (2) AR 55-120 as amended) (AIR # UST-2-2343-AGF) to Hawaii, reporting upon arrival thereat to the CG, Pacific Ocean Areas for asgmt. Travel by air is directed and is necessary to accomplish an emergency war mission. This is a permanent change of station to an overseas destination. EDCMR 11 February 1945.

Clothing and equipment are prescribed in accordance with T/E 21, 1 Jun 44, as modified. Clothing and equipment to be transported by air will be limited to sixty-five (65) lbs of personal baggage per individual.

Personnel will use APO # 18336-AI, c/o Postmaster, San Francisco, Calif.

SHIPMENT NO. ****-AI

Rank	Name	ASN	Br	Race
LT COL	DODSON O GIVENS	0282912	CE	(W)
LT COL	EARL W HOUSTON	0907654	CE	(W)
LT COL	FRANK L BRICK	0250777	CE	(W)
MAJ	ROBERT F HUNTER	0923505	CE	(W)
CAPT	JAMES R JORDAN	0293978	CE	(W)
CAPT	SAM L DAUGHERTY	0375437	CE	(W)
CAPT	JOHN N DAVIS	0260333	INF	(W)
Pfc	Hoy W Wong	32820162	Engr	(C)

Section II, WD Cir #356, dated 2 Sept 44, applies.

PCS TDN 501-31 P 431-02-03 212/50425.

(Auth: Ltr, Hq West Coast Wg, Pacific Div, ATC, 1502d AAFBU, Hamilton Fld, Calif dated 15 Nov 44, Subj: Auth to Issue Tvl Orders, and Confidential Ltr, WD, Wash, DC dated 19 Dec 44, File AG 370.5 (18 Dec 44) OB-S-E-SPMOT-M, Subj: Movement Orders, Shipment **** amended.)

APPENDIX F

THE BUNKER HILL STORY

(An example of what the fleet faced from the Japanese Kamikazes)

THE WARTIME STORY OF A FIGHTING FLAT-TOP
and HER *UNFORGETTABLE FIGHTING MEN*

Stettinius Quits Cabinet WAR EXTRA

Los Angeles Examiner

MITSCHER'S CARRIER BLASTED; 392 LOST

Stettinius Appointed Aide to World Group

Truman to Pick New State Bureau Head Next Week

By Robert G. Nixon

Hard Fighting on New Isle

Japs Fear Landing Is Step to China

By John B. Henry

Blazing Flat-Top Starts Daring Maneuver That Saved Her Life

WOUNDED BY SUICIDE PLANES

Flagship Survives Nip Suicide Attack

Gallant Craft to Fight Again
Casualties Total 656

Nip-and-Tuck Battle

Carrier to Fight Again

1-Page Color Map Story of War Coming in Examiner

Flames and smoke from seering gasoline flames and exploding ammunition shoot into the air from the USS BUNKER HILL after being hit by two kamikazes.
(U. S. Navy Photo)

The BUNKER HILL, decks aflame, swings into the wind.
(U. S. Navy Photo)

BUNKER HILL fights to bring fires under control. (U. S. Navy Photo)

Wrecked planes on the end of the flight deck. (U. S. Navy Photo)

USS WILKES-BARRE suffered damage while assisting the stricken BUNKER HILL (U. S. Navy Photo)

Squad ready room aboard the BUNKER HILL where a bomb exploded killing several of the ship's pilots. (U. S. Navy Photo)

Looking out through a gaping hole of number two elevator bombed by a kamikaze before crashing into the island itself. (U. S. Navy Photo)

Crewmen of the BUNKER HILL fight courageously to bring the gasoline inflamed flight deck under control. (U. S. Navy Photo)

APPENDIX G

PEE WEE DAVIS AND SHUG JORDAN

Many Memories Recalled For
J.N. "PeeWee" Davis Of Leesville

A letter, a Christmas card and an old snapshot recalled many memories for J.N. "PeeWee" Davis of Leesville. The letter was from his good friend, Ralph Jordan, Head Football Coach of Auburn University. The card was from another friend, Sam Daugherty of Chicago. The snapshot of "PeeWee" and Ralph, known as "Shug", was taken aboard the S.S. Warwick Castle, an English troop ship during World War II.

In the letter from Jordan was enclosed the Christmas card and picture sent him by Sam Daugherty, another wartime friend. While visiting Thanksgiving at his mother's home, Sam found the old snapshot of Davis and Jordan. He had not seen it for thirty years. He sent the picture in a Christmas card to "Shug", who sent both to "PeeWee".

During World War II, Davis was Commanding Officer of Company G, 531st Engineer Shore Regiment. Jordan was his executive officer. They were on the Warwick Castle, enroute to Africa to participate in the North African Invasion, when the snapshot was made. The first big invasion of the war, it was successful.

Unbeknowing to Davis, in the landing of the First Infantry Division was a Batesburg native, the late Banny Jones. The first man on shore in the First Division would plant a small American Ensign Flag. In Africa, Davis failed to get the flag but succeeded in the Sicilian battle.

When Mr. and Mrs. Davis later moved to Batesburg, they became friends with Banny. Conversation about their war years revealed that Banny had been in the same African invasion as Davis. The flag which "PeeWee" had saved, he gave to Banny.

Through the years, the Davis and Jordan families have stayed in touch via letter and football games. Jordan retires this year as head coach of Auburn University. He is the only active football coach who has a college stadium named after him and has the distinction of serving as trustee of Auburn.

A letter, a Christmas card and a snapshot turned the clock back thirty years for "PeeWee".

J.N. "PeeWee" Davis, on the left, and Ralph "Shug" Jordan standing on the deck of the S.S. Warwick Castle. Time is World War II.

191

Sam Daugherty

Shug Jordan: In Many Ways, He Was Auburn

AUBURN, Ala. (AP) — At Auburn, the Shug Jordan Era never really ended.

When he retired in 1975, and most poignantly following his death Thursday, Ralph "Shug" Jordan remained a triumphal figure — a man whose zest for competition and whose warm, generous character left an indelible imprint on Auburn.

"In many ways, he was Auburn," said Athletic Director Lee Hayley.

"His achievements as athlete and coach at Auburn University have forever enshrined his name in the proud athletic tradition and history of that institution and of the Southeastern Conference," said SEC Commissioner Boyd McWhorter.

"His traits of being a warm and gentle man and loyal friend," said McWhorter, "have left a lasting impression on all who were fortunate enough to know him."

For many years, a large part of the state felt it knew him. Those were the years when Jordan gave a football-happy state the delirium of a national championship and the every-Saturday sight of blue-and-orange Tigers running to his command, usually running toward victories.

It almost became something out of the richest Southern literature when Shug was joined by Bear — the growling Paul Bryant of Alabama. The two, on Saturdays and then again on Sunday afternoons when they aired their television replays, captivated the state's football imagination.

Following Jordan's death, Bryant said: "I am very saddened by the news. He meant a lot to football and to the state of Alabama. His loss is certainly a great one. I will miss him personally. I was very fond of him, despite the fact we worked against each other" during football seasons.

When he retired, the university's Jordan-Hare Stadium already bore his name — an honor recognizing the impact of his personality on Auburn as well as his achievements: A 175-83-7 record, 12 bowl trips, one national championship.

"He was like a second father to me," said Morris Savage of Jasper, a former player who later joined Jordan on Auburn's board of trustees.

"I was not a good football player," said Savage, "but he cared about me and enabled me to get an education. His compassion for the people who played for him was the singular most outstanding thing about him."

A former star halfback for Jordan, Alabama Gov. Fob James, said Jordan was "a great teacher and I consulted him on many things over the years. I spent an hour with him last week. His mind was as sharp as ever.

"I feel a sense of great personal loss. He meant an awful lot to thousands of people."

Heisman Trophy winner Pat Sullivan said of Jordan: "We were very close. I just thought the world of the man. Besides being a coach, he was a friend."

192

James Ralph Jordan
HEAD FOOTBALL COACH
AUBURN UNIVERSITY

January 8, 1976

P.O. Box 351
AUBURN, ALABAMA 36830

Mr. S. P. Daugherty
425 W. Aldine Avenue
Chicago, Illinois 60657

Dear Sam:

God bless you and I have wondered about you all these years.
Let me hear from you again and tell me all about the family.

I retired at the first of this year and Evelyn and I will
continue to live in Auburn. All three of our children have
left Auburn.

With your permission I am sending the snapshot on to Pee Wee
Davis. I am sure that he will be able to recall a few years
ago.

Thanks for the Christmas card and it was good to hear from
you.

Sincerely,

Shug

Ralph Jordan

RJ:ef

JAMES RALPH JORDAN
HEAD FOOTBALL COACH
AUBURN UNIVERSITY

P.O. Box 351
AUBURN, ALABAMA 36830

6/23/76

Dear Sam.

Sent the picture on to John Davis (Reuben) as the enclosed clipping will indicate.

We (Evelyn) are leaving on July 4th for a trip to the Pacific Northwest. San Francisco, Seattle, Victoria Vancouver, Lake Louise, Banff Calgary ect.

Our children are grown married w/ grandchildren. Why not write me a letter telling all about

JAMES RALPH JORDAN
HEAD FOOTBALL COACH
AUBURN UNIVERSITY

P.O. Box 351
AUBURN, ALABAMA 36830

yourself — family, children Dot — the works. Also McGraw.

Was always extremely fond of Sam Daugherty and would love for you to fill in the gaps.

Your friend

Shug.

APPENDIX H

MISCELLANY
APPENDIX H—TABLE OF CONTENTS

H1 Why I didn't go to war .

WAR DEPARTMENT
THE ADJUTANT GENERAL'S OFFICE
WASHINGTON

EOH-ap-4606

IN REPLY REFER TO AG 201 Daugherty, Sam Pershing, (0-375437)
(7-29-41)RH

August 4, 1941

SUBJECT: Status.

THROUGH: C.G., 3rd C.A.

TO:

    Second Lieutenant Sam Pershing Daugherty, Engr-Res.,
    229 North Dithridge Street,
    Pittsburg, Pennsylvania.

    1. It has been determined that, in view of your civilian position, you will not be immediately available, in emergency, for mobilization assignment under your Reserve commission.

    2. You, therefore, are transferred to the War Department Reserve Pool without eligibility for assignment or promotion, and with eligibility for active duty only when authorized by the Secretary of War.

    3. If you become available for mobilization assignment by reason of change in occupational status consideration will be given to the question of your transfer out of the War Department Reserve Pool.

    By order of the Secretary of War:

Copy to: Chief of Engineers

Adjutant General.

196

H2 Liaison Officers for Invasion of Sicily

S E C R E T

HEADQUARTERS I ARMORED CORPS, REINFORCED
A. P. O. # 758

SECRET
Auth: CG, IAC REINF
Initial:
Date: 15 June 1943
::::::::::::::::::::

210.31   AG   15 June 1943

REF. NO. Q-608

SUBJECT: Orders for Liaison Officers.

TO   : CG, 1st Engr Special Brigade.

1. You will issue the necessary orders attaching the following named Officers to Sub-Task Forces to act as liaison officers with respective G-4 Sections and to observe beach operations and supply procedures:

Atchd to 3d Div	– IST LT SAM P. DOUGHERTY	0375437
Atchd to II Corps	– CAPT JOHN J. MC GRANN	0393887

2. These officers will be returned to your Headquarters upon call, after arrival in HORRIFIED.

3. Movement by air is authorized.

By Command of LIEUTENANT GENERAL PATTON:

/s/ EDWARD FOX.
/t/ EDWARD FOX,
Major, AGD,
Asst Adj General

1 cc: CG II CORPS
1 cc: CG 3rd Div

A CERTIFIED TRUE DOPY:

Charles W. Sullivan

CHARLES W. SULLIVAN,
1st Lieut, C. E.
Adjutant (Acting.)

S E C R E T

197

H3 Patton's Letter to 7th Army Pre-Sicily

HEADQUARTERS SEVENTH UNITED STATES ARMY
A.P.O. No. 758, U.S. Army

At sea.

Soldiers of the 7th American Army:

We are indeed honored in having been selected by General
Eisenhower as the American component of this new and greater
attack against the Axis. We are teamed with the justly famous
British 8th Army, which attacks on our right, and we have for
the Army Group Commander that veteran and distinguished soldier,
Sir Harold Alexander.

In addition to the two armies, our attack will be supported
by the annihilating might of the Allied Navies and Air Forces.

Owing to the necessity for secrecy, I am unable to put
in writing the location of our impending battle. However, I
hereby direct the officers who will read you this after you
are at sea to tell you where you are going and why.

When we land we will meet German and Italian soldiers
whom it is our honor and privilege to attack and destroy.

Many of you have in your veins German and Italian blood,
but remember that these ancestors of yours so loved freedom
that they gave up home and country to cross the ocean in search
of liberty. The ancestors of the people we shall kill lacked
the courage to make such a sacrifice and remained as slaves.

During the last year we Americans have met and defeated
the best troops Germany, Italy and Japan possess. Many of us
have shared in these glorious victories. Those of you who have
not been so fortunate, now have your opportunity to gain equal
fame.

In landing operations, retreat is impossible. To surrender
is as ignoble as it is foolish. Due to our Air Force and our
Navy the enemy is unable to evacuate prisoners. Therefore, our
soldiers who are taken prisoner, will remain to starve and run
the added risk of being bombed or shelled by their own comrades
who will be unable to tell prisoners from the enemy.

Above all else remember that we as the attackers have the
initiative. We know exactly what we are going to do, while the
enemy is ignorant of our intentions and can only parry our blows.
We must retain this tremendous advantage by always attacking;
rapidly, ruthlessly, viciously, and without rest. However tired
and hungry you may be, the enemy will be more tired and more
hungry--Keep punching! No man is beaten until he thinks he is.
Our enemy knows that his cause is hopeless.

The fact that we are operating in enemy country does not
permit us to forget our American tradition of respect for private property, non-combatants, and women. Civilians who have
the stupidity to fight us we will kill. Those who remain
passive will not be harmed but will be required to rigidly con-
form to such rules as we shall publish for their control and
guidance.

The glory of American arms, the honor of our country, the
future of the whole world rests in your individual hands. See
to it that you are worthy of this great trust.

God is with us. We shall win.

(Signed)
G. S. PATTON, Jr.,
Lieut. General, U. S. Army
Commanding.

H4 Orders to 5th Army for Salerno Landings

S E C R E T

HEADQUARTERS 1ST ENGINEER SPECIAL BRIGADE
A.P.O. 758, U.S.ARMY

210.432/220.432   26 August 1943.

SUBJECT: Travel Orders.

TO   : All Personnel Listed Below.

    The following named officers and enlisted men, Hq & Hq Co, 1st Engr Spec Brig are placed on TD and will proceed immediately to Mostaganem, Algeria, reporting upon arrival to the Commanding General, Fifth Army. Travel will be by military aircraft:

GRADE	NAME	A.S.N.
Colonel	EUGENE M. CAFFEY	09329
Captain	JOHN J. MCGRANN	0393887
Captain	HARRY E. JACOBSEN	0306231
1st Lt	SAM P. DAUGHERTY	0375437
1st Lt	LILA H. PAUL, JR.	0422330
T/4	Devanney, John J.	32315615
T/5	Harvey, Andrew L.	34026105
T/5	Stewart, Robert E.	37140208
Pfc	Karlsruher, Ernst	32320276
Pfc	Singer, Carl H.	33265031
Pfc	Sonnier, Leonce	34074595
Pvt	Pacheco, Antonio S.	11018457
Pvt	Lesh, Robert J.	35153965

By order of Colonel CAFFEY:

Charles W. Sullivan

CHARLES W. SULLIVAN,
1st Lieut., C. E.,
Adjutant.

DISTR:
One each O concerned-5
CC, HqCo, 1st ESB----1
File----------------1

S E C R E T

H5 General Eisenhower's Great Crusade Speech.

SUPREME HEADQUARTERS
ALLIED EXPEDITIONARY FORCE

Soldiers, Sailors and Airmen of the Allied Expeditionary Force!

You are about to embark upon the Great Crusade, toward which we have striven these many months. The eyes of the world are upon you. The hopes and prayers of liberty-loving people everywhere march with you. In company with our brave Allies and brothers-in-arms on other Fronts, you will bring about the destruction of the German war machine, the elimination of Nazi tyranny over the oppressed peoples of Europe, and security for ourselves in a free world.

Your task will not be an easy one. Your enemy is well trained, well equipped and battle-hardened. He will fight savagely.

But this is the year 1944! Much has happened since the Nazi triumphs of 1940-41. The United Nations have inflicted upon the Germans great defeats, in open battle, man-to-man. Our air offensive has seriously reduced their strength in the air and their capacity to wage war on the ground. Our Home Fronts have given us an overwhelming superiority in weapons and munitions of war, and placed at our disposal great reserves of trained fighting men. The tide has turned! The free men of the world are marching together to Victory!

I have full confidence in your courage, devotion to duty and skill in battle. We will accept nothing less than full Victory!

Good Luck! And let us all beseech the blessing of Almighty God upon this great and noble undertaking.

Dwight D Eisenhower

H6 My Bronze Star Medal.

HEADQUARTERS
FIRST UNITED STATES ARMY
APO 230

AL ORDERS)
:
44)   8 August 1944

E X T R A C T

SECTION

1 of Bronze Star Medal--- II

II--AWARD OF BRONZE STAR MEDAL-- Under the provisions of AR 600-45, 22
mber 1943, and pursuant to authority contained in paragraph 3c, Section
ircular No. 32, Hq ETOUSA, 20 March 1944, as amended, the Bronze Star
is awarded to the following officers and enlisted men:

Lieutenant Colonel Ernest C. Adams, 020933, Corps of Engineers,
ed States Army, for meritorious service in connection with military
ations against the enemy, as Operations Executive, 1st Engineer Special
, in England and in France, from 22 November 1943 to 24 June 1944.
red military service from Illinois.

Lieutenant Colonel Stephen L. Force, 0365895, 531st Engineer
Regiment, United States Army, for heroic achievement in connection
military operations against the enemy, in France, on 6 June 1944.
ed military service from Colorado.

Major Earl C. Paules, 021447, Corps of Engineers, United States
, for meritorious service in connection with military operations against
enemy, as Beach Operations Officer, 1st Engineer Special Brigade, in
e, from 7 June 1944 to 18 June 1944. Entered military service from Ohio.

Captain Sam P. Daugherty, 0375437, Corps of Engineers, United
es Army, for meritorious service in connection with military operations
nst the enemy, as Assistant Beach Operations Officer, 1st Engineer
ial Brigade, in France, from 6 June 1944, to 25 June 1944. Entered
tary service from Ohio.

Captain Joseph L. Raub, 0422546, 1st Engineer Special Brigade,
ed States Army, for meritorious service in connection with military
ations against the enemy, in England and in France, from 9 February
to 24 June 1944. Entered military service from Connecticut.

Captain Henry J. Robinson, 0471774, 261st Medical Battalion,

H7 Orders Ft. Dix to Ft. Lewis with 30 days Delay en Route.

R E S T R I C T E D

Army Service Forces
Second Service Command
RECEPTION STATION NO 2
1245th SCSU Personnel Center
Fort Dix, New Jersey   /bap

SPECIAL ORDERS)
                :   31 Dec 44
NUMBER   118)   E X T R A C T

*   *   *

16.   Fol Off of the Hq & Hq Co, 1st Engr Special Brigade are reld fr
atchd this RS and WP therefrom to pt designated. Upon arrival at pt designated
Off are granted twenty-seven (27) days for recuperation, rehabilitation, and
recovery upon exp of which they WP Fort Lewis Wash RUAT CO Hq & Hq Co, 1st Engr
Special Brigade reporting no later than 1 Feb 45 for duty. Auth, Ltr WD TAGO
AG 370.5 (19 Dec 44) OB-S-E-SPMOT-M dtd 21 Dec 44, Subj: PRI M/O 1st Engr
Special Brigade and Component Units. The provisions of WD Cir 260, cs, apply
for period of travel only between Ft Dix NJ and Fort Lewis Wash.

NAME	A. S. N.	ARM/SERV	POINT FOR RECUPERATION
Lt Col FRANK P BROCK	0250777	CE	601 W Mill St Carbondale Ill
*Maj THEODORE P KOSZALKA	01689673	MC	8908 Woodhaven Blvd Woodhaven LIN
Maj FOSTER A DUNLAP	0370190	IGD	1553 W Seltzer St Phila Pa
*Maj ROBERT F HUNTER	0923505	CE	1516 S 16th St Birmingham Ala
Maj HORACE N ELKINS JR	0483742	FD	254 Kelly St Statesville NC
*Maj AMBROSE A McAVOY	0498615	ChC	3026 Waterloo Court Chicago Ill
*Capt JAMES R JORDAN	0293978	CE	Keysville Ga
*Capt SAM P DAUGHERTY	0375437	CE	146 Tibet Road Columbus Ohio
*Capt JOHN N DAVIS	0260333	Inf	Saluda SC
Capt FRANK H WALK	0431995	CE	2010 Myrtle Ave Baton Rouge La
Capt ROGER R MONTGOMERY	01108868	CE	3670 E 1st St Long Beach Calif
Capt CHARLES W SULLIVAN	0304759	Inf	Shannon Miss
*Capt THOMAS G WHITFORD	0354328	CMP	219 Mt Zoar St Elmira NY
Capt DANIEL J McSTAR	0450315	CWS	1840 Wynhurst St Pittsburgh Pa
Capt WILLIAM S EASMAN	0910592	CE	436 S.E 17th Ave Ft Lauderdale Fl
1st Lt FLOYD P LACY JR	0383349	CE	428 W 15th St Hopkinsville KY
*1st Lt JAMES J CLARK	01100914	CE	1328 E Blvd Charlotte NC
1st Lt MARION F GRACE	01112730	CE	N Church St Huntsville Ala
CWO WALTER E RODDA	W2115544	USA	RFD Jacksonville Fla
*Capt THOMAS H LOGAN JR	01573370	CE	60 Atlantic Rd Swanpscott Mass

Off entitled to food rat for 27 days at address indicated.

TPA for Off indicated by asterisk (*).

Such additional travel between Ft Dix, NJ; NYPE; and Boston PE, as
may be necessary to carry out the orders of the CO 1st Engr Special Brigade is
directed for Capt THOMAS H LOGAN JR 01573370 CE. Auth: VOCG ASF 30 Dec 44.
FSA 501-5 P 432-02 212/50425.
      TNT   TDN   FSA 501-31 P 431-02-03 212/50425

H8 French President DeGaulle cites Engineer Brigades.

D E C I S I O N No 758

-:-:-:-:-:-:-:-

LE PRESIDENT DU GOUVERNEMENT PROVISOIRE DE LA
REPUBLICQUE FRANCAISE, Chef des Armees.

CITE A L'ORDRE DE L'ARMEE

"Pour services exceptionels de Guerre rendus au
cours des Operations de Liberation de la FRANCE"

La Iere Engineer Special Brigade, comprenant toutes
les Unites affectees a cette Brigade ou y etant de-
tachees, qui ont fait partie de la Force d'Assaut
"U" et ont ete engagees dans l'assaut des plages
Normandes.

Cette citation comporte l'attribution de la
Croix de Guerre avec Palme

PARIS, le 25 Mai 1945

signed::Charles DE GAULLE

Le General d'Armee JUIN
Chef d'Etat-Major General de la
Defense Nationale

CERTIFIED TRUE COPY:

s/ Eugene M. Caffey
Colonel, CE

A CERTIFIED TRUE COPY:

DRURY M. NIXON,
Major, A. G. D.
Adjutant
Hq 1st Engr Sp Brig

H9 Colonel Caffey's Speech at The Monument 6-6-45

On The First Anniversary of D-Day in Normandy, Charles DeGaulle the President of France, announced the awarding of the French Croix de Guerre with Palm to The First Engineer Brigade for the part we played in the Normandy Invasion. At that time, Colonel Eugene M. Caffey, long-time commander of the Brigade, addressed an assemblage at the Monument on Utah Beach. (Ironically the Headquarters of the Brigade was at that moment thousands of miles away on the Island of Okinawa, supporting one of the biggest battles of the Pacific war in WWII).

Colonel Caffey's Speech on that First Anniversary of D-Day follows:

Mr. Minister, distinguished guests, my friends:

Last summer over eight hundred thousand American soldiers crossed this strip of sand to engage in battle with the enemy. Uncounted airmen thronged these skies. Unnumbered sailors for the British and American navies and merchant fleets came to this coast. The great military, naval, and civil leaders of our time have visited this place. It is of none of these that I wish to speak: their fame needs no words from me.

All but hidden in the events that took place here are the officers and men of the 1st Engineer Brigade. As their long-time commander in Africa, in Sicily, in Italy, in Normandy, it is my desire and it is my duty to them to mention them to you.

It was the task of the 1st Brigade to land promptly on this beach and to assist in every way possible the debarking of the American forces. Its work began with the destruction of the obstacles that had been placed along the water's edge and in the water to wreck our craft and drown our soldiers. Its work continued with the breaching of the sea wall with charges of explosives so that tanks and cannon could get off the beach and at the enemy. It neutralized the flame throwers along the sea-wall; removed the mine fields which lay back of the dunes, even on the spot where we are now standing; assaulted enemy points of resistance; and dragged the dead and wounded from the surf. Inland it opened up routes of advance and speeded the army's forward movement. For over five months it labored here without rest until the storms of winter made it impossible to continue. During this period it landed about half the American forces which came to Normandy; over two hundred thousand guns and vehicles; seven hundred thousand tons of supplies and equipment; evacuated forty thousand wounded and sixty thousand prisoners-of-war; and shipped out two divisions. Had Brigade failed or faltered, history might have been very different.

The 1st Brigade did not come here to fail. It came here to do all that men could do. It did much more than that. The condition of the newly-won port of Cherbourg was such that much of the load intended for that port was laid on the shoulders of the Brigade. For months the success of the American forces depended on the successful operation of the beach, Utah, and of Omaha, just around yonder point.

The 1st Brigade did not come here with any illusions as to what lay before it. It had been to the wars before. It came here with the fixed purpose of overcoming all obstacles or of leaving its bones in the sands. No matter what happened; no matter how badly the day went; no matter what others might do; the orders to the 1st Brigade were to hold fast as long as the breath of life remained. I am very certain that the Brigade would have obeyed.

To the members of Brigade who have gone from this world, but whose spirits are here today, your old commander says, "Well done". Wherever you rest, in Algeria, in Tunisia, in Sicily, in Italy, in England, in the waters of the Channel, in Normandy, we remember you always. May the Almighty God, Who loves brave soldiers, grant you a place of refreshment, peace and light.

Especially do I commend to Him my orderly and my friend, Private 1st Class Leonce Sonnier, who died here that first D-Day morning.

To you others, you men of the Brigade who are here today. I remember how, in spite of wounds and death and destruction, you went calmly about your appointed tasks. Not only our country, but the whole world of freedom owes you admiration and homage. To you I say, too, "Well done". Remember your dead; remember your duty; and surround with your hopes and your prayers those others of the Brigade who have gone ahead of us to the Pacific. At this moment they are locked with the enemy in the far reaches of Western Ocean. To them I say, "Hold fast. We are coming".

H10 Award of Bronze Arrowhead for Normandy Assault .

R E S T R I C T E D

HEADQUARTERS 1ST ENGINEER SPECIAL BRIGADE

GENERAL ORDERS)
NUMBER   9)

A.P.O. 357, U.S. ARMY
12 June 1945

AWARD OF THE BRONZE SERVICE ARROWHEAD

1. Under authority of letter, Headquarters, European Theater of Operations, United States Army, dated 9 May 1945, file 200.6, CFGA, subject: "Individual Service Award of the Bronze Service Arrowhead", the following officers and enlisted men, who at the time of the invasion of France were either assigned or attached to Headquarters and Headquarters Company, 1st Engineer Special Brigade, are awarded the Bronze Service Arrowhead to be worn on the European-African-Middle Eastern Theater Service Ribbon for participation in the assault which secured the initial Normandy Beachhead in France on 6 June 1944:

Rank	Name	Number
Colonel	Ernest C. Adams	020933
Colonel	Eugene M. Caffey	09329
Colonel	Harry E. Meyer	014663
Lt Col	Rand S. Bailey	0908635
Lt Col	Samuel W. Forgy	0442949
Lt Col	Robert L. Humphreys	0235384
Lt Col	Elzie K. Moore	0223985
Lt Col	John B. Shinberger	019396
Major	Joseph P. Crowley	0277297
Major	Edward C. Heuss	0339845
Major	Harry E. Jacobsen	0306281
Major	John S. Kellog	0361623
Major	Thomas R.M. Lindsey	0365616
Major	Ambrose A. McAvoy	0498615
Major	John J. McGrann	0393887
Major	Daniel J. McStay	0430315
Major	Pierson E. Miller	0295782
Major	Earl C. Paules	021447
Major	Charles W. Sullivan	0304759
Major	Thomas G. Whitford	0354328
Captain	Charles E. Doyle	01101748
Captain	Virgil A. Busch	0466745
Captain	Sam P. Daugherty	0375437
Captain	Arthur Gervais	0471740
Captain	Malcolm Hawkins	0413711
Captain	James R. Jordan	0293978
Captain	Harry K. McHarg	0336595
Captain	Roger R. Montgomery	01106868
Captain	George W. Rice Jr.	0453201
Captain	James F. Rushing	0388431
Captain	Thomas J. Sammons	0373005
Captain	John H. Sanders	0384914
Captain	Robert W.M. Weir	0985843
1st Lt	Robert J. Elias	01106114
1st Lt	William H. Fishback	01633210
1st Lt	Marion F. Grace	01112730
1st Lt	Charles J. Kobs	0383466
1st Lt	William J. Moore	01106971
1st Lt	Lila H. Paul	0422330
1st Lt	Thomas I. Pearsall	0364363
1st Lt	Leon T. Struble	01557916
1st Lt	Peter Thomas	01796378
1st Lt	John E. Wagenhals	01582239
1st Lt	Robert H. Wheeler	01587723

H11 Personal Commendation for my part in Okinawa.

HEADQUARTERS 1ST ENGINEER SPECIAL BRIGADE
APO 357,   U.S. ARMY

26 June 1945

SUBJECT: Commendation.

TO   : Captain Sam P Daugherty, 0-375437, Corps of Engineers.

1. As Assistant S-3, 1st Engineer Special Brigade, during the period 9 April 1945 to 31 May 1945, your thorough knowledge, skillful analysis and diligent supervision of matters pertaining to the control of shipping and craft contributed greatly to the effective regulation and thorough coordination of ships discharge during the Okinawa campaign.

2. It is my desire to commend you for efficient performance of this important task.

B. B. TALLEY
Colonel, Corps of Engineers
Commanding

1 Incl - Ltr Subject, "Commendation", 25 June 1945, Hq ISCOM, APO 331.

'Vast U.S. armada' impressive to soldier

By STEPHEN PRUDHOMME
Staff Writer

Sam Daugherty remembers being in awe of the number of ships, planes and men that took part in D-Day nearly 50 years ago.

Right then and there, Daugherty knew the invasion would be a success.

Sam Daugherty

Daugherty is a 76-year-old Columbus, Ohio, native who now makes his home on Hilton Head Island. He moved to the Island with his wife in 1986 after retiring from IBM two years earlier.

On the morning of June 6, 1944, Daugherty, a 26-year-old captain in the First Engineer Special Brigade who had participated in the invasions of North Africa, Sicily and Italy, was in an LCM (landing craft-mechanized) headed for Utah Beach.

Daugherty was one of two officers in a group of 10 men assigned to set up temporary headquarters for their brigade. They landed on the beach at about 9:30 a.m., some three-and-a-half hours after the first troops had gone ashore.

"We could see gunfire," Daugherty recalls. "Plumes of sand would go up around us. We got hit with the sand. The fighting we could see wasn't that intense. I didn't even fire my pistol. I was more curious than scared."

That quickly changed.

As the men began moving northward along the beach, they were suddenly hit by enemy artillery fire.

One of the enlisted men, Leonce Sonnier, was never found and was presumed dead. Wounded was Capt. Ralph Jordan, who had been shot in the arm. He was treated for the wound and left at an aid station by the seawall. Following the war, "Shug" Jordan displayed his leadership skills in a more peaceful venue, serving as the football coach and athletic director at Auburn.

Daugherty and the remaining men made their way inland and set up temporary headquarters. Later that day, Gen. Omar Bradley, commander of all U.S. ground forces, visited the new command post, and reinforcing paratroopers and gliders from

Sam Daugherty

the 82nd and 101st Airborne divisions dropped in just west of the site.

Daugherty will return to Normandy this year to commemorate the 50th anniversary of the D-Day Invasion. A half century after a young officer landed on French soil, Daugherty's most vivid memory is that of America's display of military might.

"If you looked at the vast armada, you couldn't help but think we'd succeed," Daugherty said. "I was impressed with the might of the United States. We knew we had to do the same thing we did in North Africa, Sicily and Italy. We absolutely knew it was a historic occasion."

It was also an occasion which caused men to ponder their futures, wondering if they'd be among the lucky ones to return from the French shores. Yet, along with trepidation there was a feeling of pride at taking part in such a momentous undertaking, with the peace and freedom of the world at stake, Daugherty said.

"Even if you were scared, which most of us were, you were pleased to participate in it," Daugherty said. "I wasn't a hero; I wasn't a coward. I was just one of thousands who were very proud to be there."

208

APPENDIX I
ACKNOWLEDGMENTS

1. The work of Mr. Irv. Udoff who prepared the brochure entitled

THE BUNKER HILL STORY excerpted herein as Appendix **F.**

2. The Associated Press for Use of the Article **"Shug Jordan: In Many Ways, He Was Auburn".** (/Mr. Norman Goldstein, 3-13-02) Appendix **G.**

3. The Twin Cities News for use of the article **"Many Memories Recalled for J.N. "Pee Wee" Davis of Leesville"** (Editor Sarah B. 3-15-02) Appendix **G.**

4. The Savannah Morning News for the use of the article **"Vast U.S. Armada impressive to soldier"**(Managing Ed. by 'phone 3-13-02.)

Sam Daugherty

INDEX (SORT OF)

Index, by chapter numbers, of some names, places and things mentioned in this book. Items marked ** are common throughout the story.

Vallery, Harry, Lt.	XII
Wakefield, USS	III, XI
Wales, United Kingdom	III
Welch, Junior, Lt.JG	XIV
Willis, Jim, Lt.	I
Wolfe, Col.	**

Sam Daugherty

ABOUT THE AUTHOR

Born in Columbus, Ohio, Sam Daugherty, eighty-five, has had at least four careers: steel mill management, for twenty years; "temporarily" interrupted for a four-year second career with the Army. Sam resigned from Steel in 1961 to work for IBM and to escape from nineteenth century into the twenty-first. For IBM he worked with the steel industry in systems development, and marketing. In 1984 at age 67 he embarked upon his fourth career, Retirement. As age and health inevitably displaced golf, Sam, at 83 unearthed one-liners he hoarded since 1945 and wrote *On Hostile Shores*. He and wife, Peggy, moved to Hilton Head in 1986. His son, Greg Daugherty, lives with wife, Sheila, and two children in Mamaroneck, New York.

NOTE:

Sam completed the manuscript in August 2000. After he had proof read the first galley proof, a stroke and other complications severely limited further effort. Sam passed away on December 11, 2002, just months before publication.

The completion of this book would not have been possible without the generous help of Wes Taylor, friend, technical and editorial consultant.

Printed in the United States
966400005B